NORFOLK AND SUFFOLK SURNAMES IN THE MIDDLE AGES

ENGLISH SURNAMES SERIES

Edited by R. A. McKinley

Department of English Local History
University of Leicester

II
Norfolk and Suffolk Surnames in the Middle Ages

by

Richard McKinley

With a Foreword by
Professor Alan Everitt
Hatton Professor of Local History
University of Leicester

PHILLIMORE

1975
Published by
PHILLIMORE & CO. LTD.,
London and Chichester
Head Office: Shopwyke Hall,
Chichester, Sussex, England

© Richard McKinley, 1975

ISBN 0 85033 196 X

*This is the second volume in the
English Surnames Series
which is published for
The Marc Fitch Fund*

Text set in Baskerville 169
and printed on Clan Volumetric 90 G/m²
by Eyre & Spottiswoode Ltd,
Her Majesty's Printers
Grosvenor Press, Portsmouth, Hants.

Contents

Abbreviations

P.R.O.

Public Record Office.

R.O.

Record Office.

Rye, *Cal. Norf. Fines*, vol. i

W. Rye, ed., *Short Calendar of the Feet of Fines for Norfolk, for the Reigns of Richard I, John, Henry III, and Edward I* (1885).

Rye, *Cal Norf Fines*, vol ii

W. Rye, ed., *Short Calendar of the Feet of Fines for Norfolk*, Part ii (1886).

Rye, *Cal. Suff. Fines*

W. Rye, ed., *Calendar of the Feet of Fines for Suffolk* (1900).

Foreword

By Alan Everitt

Over the last generation the study of local history has opened up a new world for many English people and extended the horizons of historiography in numerous unsuspected directions. Antiquarian research into local records is of course no new development; it goes back at least as far as the reign of Queen Elizabeth I. What is new about much of the current study of local history is its basic aim, that is to say the scientific reconstruction of those countless social microcosms that make up the community of the realm. Quite as important as the difference of aim, however, has been the growing realisation in recent years that, in addition to a vastly increased corpus of documentary resources, whole tracts of historical evidence of quite another kind lie ready to hand: for example, the evidence of place-names, of local maps and surveys, of aerial photography, of vernacular buildings, of regional dialects, of industrial archaeology, and of the landscape itself.

Yet strangely enough the massive body of material available to local and national historians in the form of English surnames has been relatively little explored. Much has been written on the meaning and philology of surnames; but until the English Surnames Survey was established by the Marc Fitch Fund in the English Local History Department at Leicester in 1965, there was little scholarly work in progress on the historical origins and geographical distribution of surnames. The present monograph by Mr. R. A. McKinley, following his earlier study of *Norfolk Surnames in the Sixteenth Century*, and based as it is on an exhaustive analysis of many thousands of names in medieval East Anglia, marks an important advance in the subject. A microscopic yet encyclopaedic study of this kind is essential to place the subject on a precise and scientific basis. Its conclusions, modestly advanced but pregnant with historical suggestion, confirm my own belief that ultimately the study of surnames will be found as fruitful a field of enquiry as the study of place-names. Just as the latter has been found to unlock many secrets in the settlement history of this country, so the former, I believe, will be found to illuminate many unexplored areas of its economic and social development.

At the time when surnames developed, in the centuries following the Conquest, East Anglia was the wealthiest and most populous region in the country. In Domesday Book there were more churches recorded for Suffolk and Norfolk than for any other part of England —nearly 500 for Suffolk alone. With so advanced an economy, it is not surprising that surnames should be adopted by most classes in East Anglia at a relatively early date, notably earlier than in the north, for example, and in some cases within a generation or two of the Conquest. Although the process was a very gradual one and was not fully completed for another four centuries—as long a span of time as separates us from the reign of Queen Elizabeth—the most formative period, in this as in so many developments of English history, seems to have been the two centuries or so preceding the Black Death. It was this same period that also saw the creation of most of our English towns, and the coincidence between urban development and the adoption of surnames was probably not entirely fortuitous. As Mr. McKinley shews, geographical mobility was an important factor in the adoption of surnames, and in the high degree of mobility that evidently obtained in East Anglia, urban development played a major part. Its influence is evident, for example, in the fact that many more occupational surnames derived from urban trades, particularly from the cloth industry, than from rural occupations. It is also evident in the very high proportion of 14th-century townsmen whose surnames derived from the names of other places, whence they or their forebears must have migrated. In early 14th-century Norwich, for example, nearly half the freemen had locative surnames derived from other places, and in Lynn the proportion was nearly two-thirds.

The extent of geographical mobility is further indicated in Mr. McKinley's study by the fact that, whereas in the 13th and early 14th centuries more than half the people in the area with locative surnames were living within ten miles of the places from which their names derived, by the early 16th century their descendants had dispersed over much greater distances. In the period covered by the present paper, the author points out that the general pattern of migration suggests a population given to fairly frequent moves over comparatively limited distances. In the long run, however, by the Tudor period, these local movements had amounted to a general migration of population of quite massive proportions.

Quite as significant as the degree of geographical mobility indicated by Mr. McKinley's monograph is the extent of social mobility in East Anglia. In the early medieval period, for instance, it appears that a much higher proportion of aristocratic and wealthy families derived their surnames from place-names than did families of peasant stock. In a list of tithingmen and fugitives of Richard I's reign, barely a tenth of those recorded had locative surnames, whereas more than half the owners of knights' fees recorded in the 'Cartae' of 1166 had names of this character. In the subsidies of the 14th century the distinction was still a striking one, and the surnames of the wealthier taxpayers were much more frequently derived from place-names than were those of the poorer classes. By the 16th century, however, this distinction had almost completely disappeared and a high proportion of locative surnames was no longer characteristic of the wealthier sections of society. There had evidently been a dramatic shift of wealth between the two periods, and a great deal of movement both up and down the social scale.

Mobility is not the only feature of medieval society in East Anglia to be illuminated by Mr. McKinley's study. No less interesting to the present writer is the suggestion that many surnames in the region probably originated with a single family. This is perhaps especially true (though by no means exclusively so) of locative surnames derived from small settlements or single farms. In the late 13th century, for example, as Mr. McKinley shews, the locality of Larwood in Horstead parish, north-east of Norwich, gave rise to the distinctive Norfolk surname of Larwood. By the early 16th century there were at least 16 persons in the county bearing this name, most of them still living within a few miles of Horstead. Four branches of the family, however, had by this date spread further afield: one was found at Fakenham in north-west Norfolk and one at Carlton Rode in the south-east of the county, whilst two had crossed the county boundary into Suffolk. One would like to know more of the subsequent history of a family like the Larwoods; for nowadays their surname is no longer confined to East Anglia but is also found in Leicestershire and Kent, and no doubt other counties as well.

Mr. McKinley's conclusion 'that many names, more perhaps than has usually been allowed, go back to a single origin' seems to me one of the most suggestive to emerge from his study. Working in different areas and in more limited fields, I have found the same conclusion borne in upon me. The family of the Hanoverian historian of Kent, Edward Hasted, to cite a case in point, was one branch of an extensive local connexion originally of small yeomen and husbandmen in Kent who must have derived from a common ancestor. By the 16th century the family name had come to be spelt in a bewildering variety of ways—Hasted, Haisted, Heighsted, Heghsted, Heysted, Haysted, Hoysted, Hysted, Highsted, and Histed—but these varied forms related to the same dynasty and indeed sometimes occurred together in the same will. Although the early relationships of the family cannot be established with certainty, and the historian's own ancestry cannot definitely be traced beyond his great grandfather, Moses Hasted of Canterbury (fl. 1650), the early distribution of the surname in a group of eight or nine parishes between Faversham, Sittingbourne, Hollingbourne, and Lenham suggests that it originated at a farm-settlement in this area called Highsted. The fact that Highsted appears in early medieval records in such forms as *Heystede* and *Heghsted*, as well as *Highsted*, further supports this view. There is strong presumptive evidence, in fact, that all those bearing the surname of Highsted or Hasted and its many variant forms derived from a single common ancestor of the name who held Highsted at the end of the 12th century. In this case the family has remained throughout its history almost entirely confined to a single county. There are now 24 branches of it represented in the current telephone directories for the Canterbury and Tunbridge Wells areas, which between them cover Kent and East Sussex, whilst beyond this area the name is still very rarely met with.

I have mentioned the case of the Hasted family not because they were exceptional but because they were typical of hundreds of other families of medieval origin in Kent, and because, as Mr. McKinley shews, the same pattern obtained in East Anglia. Everyone recognises that the various branches of important county families, like the Courtenays and Aclands in Devon or the Sackvilles and Twysdens in Kent, must have stemmed from a common ancestor. The lineage of such dynasties is naturally easier to establish than that of more ordinary mortals and has of course received much more attention from genealogists. What Mr. McKinley's findings suggest, however, is that this kind of ancestral pattern was by no means confined to county dynasties but was also characteristic of many Norfolk and Suffolk families with no pretensions to gentility. And certainly, in my own experience, the pattern he describes was equally true of Kentish families, whether they were of mixed social status like the Hasteds—husbandmen, tradesmen, merchants, and small squires—or whether they remained throughout their history obscure village gentry, like the Blaxlands of Blaxland, or never rose above the standing of yeomen and labourers, like the Wickendens of Wickenden.

It is one of the many interesting puzzles brought to light by the present study that, whereas certain families of this kind (like the Larwoods) ramified at quite an early date and have since extended themselves into many parts of the kingdom, others (like the Hasteds in Kent) have remained throughout their history extraordinarily localised. On this question, as on so many of the topics discussed in the present volume, many further local studies need to be undertaken

Foreword

before we can arrive at very definite or general conclusions. But it is the hallmark of all truly creative historical research that it poses as many questions as it answers, and in this respect Mr. McKinley's monograph will, I believe, prove a seminal one. It is indeed rich with suggestive lines of enquiry for the economic and social history of England and the family texture of the local community.

Regional studies, like the present one, are an essential foundation for research into the history of surnames. Yet there are many questions that can only be answered by an investigation on a national scale, which ought eventually to be undertaken. The ultimate aim of the Surnames Survey is to produce a national dictionary of surnames on genealogical principles. Such a dictionary would not be concerned primarily with the etymology or the linguistic aspect of surnames, though such matters could not be ignored, and it would be essential to draw on the valuable work already done in those fields by various scholars. It would be concerned chiefly with the distribution over the whole country of individual surnames, and the changes that the distribution underwent at different periods; with the extent to which the bearers of a given surname share a common ancestry; with the way in which some surnames become more numerous and widespread, while others fail to increase, and always remain scarce; with the implications that such evidence has for both geographical and social mobility; and more generally with the social, economic, and perhaps genetic factors that lie at the root of all these subjects for investigation. Such a dictionary would be immensely valuable to genealogists, to social and economic historians, and to students of English dialects. The task of compiling it will obviously be correspondingly onerous. Before such a work can be planned it is essential for the subject to be explored in local studies such as the present one. Only when a succession of local studies has been completed will there be sufficient understanding of the subject for the planning, and eventually the compilation, of a national dictionary of surnames to be put in hand.

Introduction

The present work is an attempt to investigate the history of surnames in certain of its aspects by examining the surnames of one particular region. Despite much valuable work on English surnames, mostly directed towards research into origins from the linguistic point of view, and despite much genealogical research into the pedigrees and histories of individual families, much still remains to be elucidated about the development of surnames in England. The chronology of the rise of stable hereditary surnames, in the different regions of the country, and in the different social classes, has not been satisfactorily described in detail though some rather general statements have been made by the late Dr. Reaney and others. The extent to which each region had its own distinctive set of surnames, and the degree of geographical mobility of surnames at various periods, are also questions that have largely remained unanswered. Indeed, little has been done to examine such topics since Guppy's vigorous but not altogether successful attempt, 80 years ago, to discover the 'homes' of British family names.[1] Little or nothing has been done, either, to discover if there were in origin, any differences in the types of surnames adopted by the various social classes, or to examine the regional distribution of surnames derived from occupation or office. Such issues are not only of interest to the genealogist and the student of surnames. They have a bearing on the nature of regional dialects at various periods, and in particular they are closely related to certain basic topics of social and economic history. We cannot hope to understand the fundamental characteristics of any society without understanding such factors as the degree of social and geographical mobility, the rigidity, or otherwise, of the divisions between classes, and the extent to which the members of any community were bound to one another by ties of consanguinity and intermarriage. The investigation of such matters is often difficult, and research into the history of surnames is one approach that can produce useful evidence.

To attempt a detailed examination of these issues over the whole of England would be an operation on an impossibly large scale, and one obvious method of reducing the task to manageable size is to deal with one region only. The present work is concerned with the surnames of Norfolk and Suffolk, two counties that form a region not geographically isolated, yet sufficiently distinct in character from the rest of the country to form a suitable unit for an investigation of the nature here undertaken. Where the history of surnames is concerned, of course no region is a water-tight compartment, nor was East Anglia such a compartment at any period since hereditary surnames first began to appear. As this study, it is hoped, shows, East Anglian surnames appear early in other regions, notably in London itself, and surnames from outside the region can be found, too, at an early period in East Anglia. The region must therefore be thought of as an area into which there was a continuous, though perhaps limited, infiltration of surnames from outside, while similarly surnames originating in Norfolk and Suffolk migrated to other regions, in some cases to survive there while becoming extinct in their native counties. This situation complicates the task of dealing with the history of surnames regionally, but at the same time an inquiry into surname migrations can be illuminating. It is hoped that the result shows that useful results can be obtained from a regional study of surname history.

I have to acknowledge the valuable help I have received from Sir Anthony Wagner, Dr. Marc Fitch, and Professor A. M. Everitt, all of whom have, in spite of their many other commitments, found the time to read the draft of this study, and to make comments and criticisms that have led to many improvements and corrections being made in the text. For any errors that have escaped scrutiny the responsibility is of course mine. I also have to acknowledge the generosity of the trustees of the Marc Fitch Fund, without which this work, like so much else, could not have been written.

Reference
[1]H. B. Guppy, *Homes of Family Names in Great Britain* (1890, reprinted 1968)

CHAPTER 1

THE RISE OF HEREDITARY SURNAMES

No clear cases of hereditary surnames existing in East Anglia have been found before 1066. There are of course instances of individuals having bye-names or designations of one sort or another, such as the pre-Conquest holders of land who appear in Domesday with designations derived from localities in which they had holdings, but none of these can be considered as stable hereditary surnames.[1] Judging by the names of pre-Conquest holders of land as given in Domesday, however, bye-names of any kind were rather exceptional immediately before the Conquest. Amongst the 'vavassors' holding in Suffolk, for instance, none of those holding either under King Edward or under King William is given any bye-name at all.[2] Bye-names derived from place names were in use in England long before 1066, and there are examples of such bye-names being used in East Anglia,[3] but so far as can be seen such names did not become hereditary before the Conquest, though later they were to form one of the main categories of hereditary surnames. Both before and after the Conquest, bye-names consisting of a personal name with the addition of the suffix 'suna' occur in England.[4] These were in use during the late 11th century and the first half of the 12th in East Anglia, though after the mid-12th century they seem to have gone out of use, or at least to disappear from the sources.[5] Such names were of course hereditary in the sense that the bearers derived them from parents, but there is no evidence that bye-names of this type were passed on by their original bearers to later generations.

It is not until after 1066 that any East Anglian surnames can be clearly shown to have become hereditary. The surnames of some East Anglian tenants-in-chief listed in Domesday certainly survived as the hereditary surnames of their descendants. The surname of Roger Bigot, a great landholder in Norfolk and Suffolk in Domesday, was transmitted to his direct descendants, later the Earls of Norfolk, and was borne by them throughout the 12th and 13th centuries, though the senior branch of the family became extinct in the male line in the 14th.[6] Another Domesday tenant-in-chief whose surname long survived in East Anglia was Ralph Bainard, an important holder of land in Norfolk, Suffolk, and elsewhere, in 1086.[7] Ralph had a brother, Geoffrey Bainard,[8] and from the two brothers

3

having the same surname it may be deduced that they had inherited it. It has in fact been suggested that their surname was
derived from their father's personal name.[9] Ralph Bainard's lands
were forfeited by his grandson, William Bainard, under Henry I,[10]
but Geoffrey's descendants long continued to hold lands in Norfolk.
Geoffrey himself was succeeded by his son, Roger Bainard, and
Roger in turn by his son, Fulk Bainard. All three used the surname
Bainard.[11] The later history of the family does not concern us here,
but it is evident that Bainard was already an established hereditary
surname in the 12th century, and was probably already so when
the first members of the family settled in England. The surnames
of some other Domesday tenants-in-chief in East Anglia could be
shown to have survived and become hereditary.[12] A family of
rather less standing than those just mentioned was that descended
from William Pecche, a Domesday under-tenant in Essex, Suffolk,
and Norfolk. His descendants continued to be fairly important
landowners in East Anglia all through the 12th and 13th centuries,
and they continued to bear the name of Pecche. The name still
survived in Norfolk in the 16th century.[13] Other examples could be
given of Domesday under-tenants in Norfolk and Suffolk whose
surnames were hereditary in the sense that they continued to be
borne by the under-tenants' descendants for several generations.[14]

It would, however, doubtless be a mistake to suppose that most
Domesday under-tenants had surnames which were passed on to
their descendants. Many minor sub-tenants holding in East Anglia
in 1086 are not given surnames at all in Domesday, and even well
into the 12th century some men of knightly rank do not seem to
have had surnames at all. The 'cartae' sent in 1166 to Henry II,
listing the knights enfeoffed by tenants-in-chief, include a number
of under-tenants holding by knight service in Norfolk and Suffolk
who are not noted as having bye-names of any kind.[15] Many
though not all of these are listed as the holders of only fractions of
a knight's fee; such, for instance, were Wibert, who held one
quarter of a knight's fee from the Abbey of Bury, Eustache, who
held a quarter of a fee from the Earl of Norfolk, Robert, Hamo,
Jordan, and a second Robert, who between them held two knight's
fees from the same Earl, Bertram, who held half a knight's fee from
the honour of Clare, or Avenel who held half a fee from the Countess
of Hertford.[16] It is reasonable to deduce that they were fairly small
tenants, though holding by knight service. Similarly towards the
end of the 12th century there were knights on the Suffolk lands of
Bury Abbey who do not seem to have had any bye-names.[17] Such
evidence suggests that for some time after the Conquest, and up
to the end of the 12th century at least, some knightly families did

not have hereditary surnames, and that some members of the knightly class had no settled bye-names at all.

During the 12th century, however, hereditary surnames came to be possessed by many East Anglian landed families, some of them of only very moderate wealth and standing. In some cases it is possible to establish which generation first bore the surname which was to become hereditary. Thomas Noel, who was holding land in Thingoe Hundred, Suffolk, about 1186-88, was the son of Robert Noel, whose own father was William son of Albold. This family had held land from Bury Abbey for at least three generations by the late 12th century, and William son of Albold seems to have been living about 1135-45. In this case Robert Noel seems to have been the first to bear the surname, having presumably been born at Christmas time.[18] A family that held a knight's fee at Worstead, Norfolk, during the 12th century is a parallel case. Early in the century the head of the family was Robert, usually called Robert *Arbalistarius*. It has been suggested that this Robert was the same person as the Robert *Balistarius* who was holding the same lands in 1086, but this seems rather unlikely. A Robert *Balistarius* and his son, Odo, are witnesses to a charter of Anselm, abbot of St. Benet's of Holme, and he did not become abbot until 1134, 48 years after Domesday.[19] It is more probable that there were two Roberts, who may well have been father and son, though this cannot be proved. The Robert *Balistarius* who was holding the family lands at Worstead in the first half of the 12th century certainly had a son called Odo, who is referred to in documents as Odo *Arbalistarius* or Odo of Worstead, and who was in possession of the family lands by about 1140.[20] Odo was succeeded by his son Richard, who is usually described in the documents as Richard of Worstead, and who was in possession of the family lands by 1166.[21] Richard in turn was succeeded by his son Robert of Worstead.[22] In the case of both these families the surname evidently became settled about the middle of the 12th century. In the case of many other landed families in Norfolk and Suffolk a hereditary surname seems to have become established during the middle or late 12th century. The de Bedon family, whose name is attached at the present day to two Norfolk villages, Stow Bedon and Kirby Bedon, can be traced back to a Hadenald de Bedon, sometimes referred to alternatively as Hadenald de Holcham, who was certainly in possession of the family's lands in 1166. His descendants seem to have borne consistently the surname of de Bedon.[23] Another landed family with lands in Norfolk, the Kerdestones, certainly possessed a hereditary surname from the end of the 12th century. The earliest member of the family who can be traced with certainty is

Roger de Kerdestone, who was in possession of the family lands by 1199.[24] Roger had a brother, Hugh de Kerdeston,[25] and the fact that both brothers had the same surname may indicate that it was already hereditary. A William de Kerdiston, who was living about 1180, may have been their father.[26] Roger died about 1206, leaving an heir under age, and by 1222 his lands were being held by William de Kerdeston, who was probably his son.[27] William in turn was succeeded by Fulk de Kerdestone.[28] It is not necessary to pursue any further the history of the family, which was prominent in 14th-century Norfolk,[29] but in this case too the surname was apparently hereditary by at any rate the end of the 12th century. Other examples could be given of landed families in East Anglia whose surnames had been hereditary since the middle or late 12th century.[30]

The families discussed so far were all of knightly or even baronial rank, but there is some evidence that during the 12th century the growth of hereditary surnames extended rather further, to tenants in sergeantry, some of them people of only very moderate standing. In 1212, for instance, William May was the tenant of 20 *solidatae* of land at Cawston in Norfolk, held of the king by sergeantry. William's father was Robert May, and in 1212 it was said that the land had been given by Henry I to an earlier William May. The William May of 1212 held a carucate at Stanhoe, Norfolk, besides his land at Cawston, but his landholdings were obviously fairly modest.[31] Another family of similar status bore the distinctive name of Corndebof, or Cordebof. In 1198-99 John Corndebof was the tenant of land at Banningham, Norfolk, which he held from the king in sergeantry by service as a crossbowman in time of war.[32] John was succeeded by his son, Hubert Cordebof or Corndebof in 1205, and Hubert, at his death in or before 1235, was succeeded by another John Cordebof, who was probably his son. William Cordeboef, who occurs in Suffolk in the early 13th century, probably belonged to the same family, though his relationship has not been discovered. The second John Cordebof died about 1250, and was succeeded by his son Thomas.[33] The family held some land in Suffolk in sergeantry by arbalast service besides their Norfolk fief, but never seem to have been landowners on any great scale. In 1212 Hubert Cornedebof's Norfolk lands were said to have been granted to his predecessors by William I, or according to another statement made at the same date, by Henry I, but there is no evidence that the family surname goes back beyond the late 12th century, and there is no evidence that they were descended from any of the Norfolk crossbowmen listed in Domesday.[34] Similarly it was said in 1212 that Aviz Tursard was then holding

land at Banningham, Norfolk, in sergeantry, that had been given
to Walter Tursard by Henry I. Aviz was the daughter of Hamo
Tusard.[35]

It is much more difficult to be certain what the position about
hereditary surnames was in the 11th and 12th centuries amongst
the East Anglian peasantry, free and unfree, or amongst the
inhabitants of the region's towns. Such evidence as there is for the
surnames of the peasant population would suggest that before 1200
hereditary surnames were rare amongst them. An account of the
tenants on the Suffolk lands of Bury Abbey, drawn up towards the
end of the 11th century, lists many small free tenants without any
bye-names at all. On the abbey's lands at Troston, for example,
34 tenants were listed, and out of these, 27 had no bye-names; at
Honington, out of 11 tenants, 10 had no bye-names at all, and the
11th was a priest; at Walsham, out of 15 tenants listed, only two
had bye-names of any kind.[36] If the Bury Abbey estates were at all
typical, it seems that the East Anglian peasant population in general
did not have bye-names in the late 11th century, and probably
very few if any of them had hereditary surnames. A century later,
the position on the same estates was not very different. A survey of
the same abbey's holdings at Troston, made about 1186-88, lists
14 small free tenants, and of these three have no bye-names at
all, and a further eight are only described as the sons of some
person, in the common formula 'Johannes filius Hugonis'. Similarly
at Honington at about the same date out of 12 tenants named, five
are given no bye-names at all, and two others are only described as
the sons of some person, although at Walsham out of nine tenants,
only one has no bye-name at all, and only one is described merely
as the son of some person.[37] The general impression derived from
the names of small free tenants on the Bury Abbey lands in
Suffolk, as set out in the late 12th-century surveys made for Abbot
Sampson, is that few can have had hereditary surnames.[38] There
are a few cases where there are some grounds for suspecting continuity in the surnames of the smaller free tenants between the late
11th century and the late 12th century; for example, a Goduy ad
Westmere is mentioned at Rougham, Suffolk, in 1087-98, and an
Aluricus de Westmere occurs there in *c.* 1186-88;[39] Aelward
pellicarius and Stannard *pellicarius* occur at Fornham St. Genevieve,
Suffolk, in 1087-98, and Willelmus tanner occurs there *c.* 1186-88;[40]
Lemmer Croperer occurs at Rougham in 1087-98, and Ailric
Croppars is mentioned in *c.* 1186-88 as a former holder of land at
the same place.[41] In none of these cases, however, can the hereditary
descent of a surname be proved, and where it does seem reasonably
likely that descendants of one of the late 11th-century tenants can

be traced in the late 12th century, there is no continuity of sur-name.[42] The position on the Norfolk estates of Ramsey Abbey (Huntingdonshire) during the 12th century seems to have been very similar. There are extents of about 1160 for the abbey's lands at Brancaster, Burnham, Ringstead, Holme by the Sea, Wimbots-ham, Downham Market, and Hilgay, with some rather later extents, under Richard I and John, for Walsoken and Wells.[43] The great majority of tenants, free and customary, in these extents are not given bye-names of any kind, and it seems clear that most cannot have had hereditary surnames. There are, however, indi-cations that hereditary surnames were not unknown among the Ramsey tenants in the 12th century; a William Curtais, an abbey tenant at Walsoken under John, had a grandfather called Elfem Curtais; this same William, and two other persons called Curtais or le Curteis, occur as abbey tenants at Wells at the same date, which suggests that the surname was already beginning to ramify on the abbey's estates; similarly on the abbey's lands at Ringstead and Holme, a tenant with the rare personal name of Marlesuein was holding land under Henry I, and a Guibertus Marlswein, who occurs on the same lands under Henry II, may well have been a descendant, though that cannot be proved.[44] Though the frag-mentary nature of the evidence makes it impossible to be dogmatic on the point, it seems likely that up to 1200 at least hereditary surnames were rare amongst the peasant population, though not unknown.

It is one degree more difficult to discover what the position was amongst the unfree population between the Conquest and the early 13th century than it is to discover the position among the free peasantry, but such evidence as there is suggests that the difference between the free and the unfree peasants was small. If we consider the names of serfs listed in a series of fines levied under Richard I and John, and involving lands in Norfolk and Suffolk, then out of 63 serfs mentioned, eight are given no bye-names at all, 19 are described only as the sons, or daughters, of some person, while the remaining 36 have bye-names.[45] Where the same serfs are mentioned twice, as in the case with two fines which mention serfs at Tudden-ham, Suffolk, their bye-names are not given consistently, which suggests that their bye-names were not stable, and probably not hereditary.[46] It seems unlikely that many bondmen had hereditary surnames before the 13th century.

After 1200, evidence about the surnames of all classes becomes much more copious. It is clear from the inquisitions *post mortem* and from much other evidence that a great many knightly families in East Anglia had hereditary surnames during the 13th century.

Occasionally it is possible to trace such surnames back to their origins. Early in the 13th century Charles of Yarmouth held land at Loddon, Norfolk, and was a person of sufficient consequence to have a private chapel there. He was also the holder of land in Lothingland Hundred, Suffolk.[47] Charles of Yarmouth was succeeded by his son, William Charles, and then by his grandson, Edward Charles, who was in possession of the family's Suffolk lands in 1275.[48] William, son of Charles of Yarmouth, was sometimes referred to as William Charles, sometimes as William 'filius Karoli', so that the family surname was not altogether settled in his day, but under Edward Charles and his son, Edmund Charles, the name seems to have been stable.[49] The Hacon family of Snettisham, who appear to have been descended from a Richard son of Hacon, alive in 1158, were perhaps a similar case.[50] In such cases it is possible to determine the generation in which the family name originated, because the surname is derived from a personal name, and it is possible to discover the individual who bore the personal name in the first instance.

Many landed families in the 13th century, however, have surnames derived from place names, and in such cases it is very difficult to be sure when the surname originated. There is usually no certainty that the individual who first appears bearing the name was in fact the earliest to do so, or whether he had predecessors who have left no trace in the surviving records. Many East Anglian landed families can be shown to have had hereditary locative surnames during the 13th century. To give a few examples, the surnames de Ingelose,[51] de Hautbois,[52] de Ingham,[53] de Hastings,[54] and de Ingoldisthorpe[55] were all in use by landed families in East Anglia during the 13th century as hereditary names, and many other examples could be given.[56] Were there more evidence available for the 12th century, it might well be possible to show that many landed families had hereditary surnames from about 1150 onwards.[57]

Although it is clear that hereditary surnames were common among baronial and knightly families during the 13th century, there remained some which had no settled surnames for most of that period. One of the wealthiest landowning families in East Anglia, the baronial line which was later named FitzWalter, only developed a stable surname in the early 14th century. The Walter from whom the family name was derived was Walter son of Robert, who died in 1258.[58] His son, Robert, was known as Robert 'filius Walteri', Robert fitz Wauter, or Robt le Fyuz Water, and it is doubtful if in his case it can really be said that he bore the name Fitzwalter as a surname. It is significant that in the chronicle of a religious house closely connected with the family not only is he himself described as Robert 'filius Walteri', but his sons are referred to as Walter 'filius Roberti' and Robert 'filius Roberti'.[59] Robert son of Walter died in 1326, and it is only with his son and heir, Robert who was known as Robert 'le Fitz Wautier', 'le FuitzWater', or 'le Fitzwater', that it is possible to be certain that an hereditary surname has been developed.[60] In this case an important landed family cannot be said to have had an hereditary surname until the 14th century. Other landed families of rather less importance similarly lacked stable surnames during the 13th century. In the late 12th century, for instance, one Osbert son of Hervey was the holder of lands at Tibbenham, Norfolk, and elsewhere.[61] His son and successor was known as Roger son of Osbert, and Roger's sons were known as Peter son of Roger son of Osbert, and Simon son of Roger son of Osbert. Peter in turn had a son who was known sometimes as Roger son of Peter son of Roger son of Osbert, sometimes as Roger son of Osbert, and who died in 1306.[62] In this case too the family does not seem to have had an hereditary surname during the 13th century. Another similar case was that of a family who were lords of an estate at Horsford, Norfolk, during the 13th century. Early in the century the head of the family was one Robert son of Roger. He was succeeded by his son, Roger, and then by his grandson Robert, who at his death in 1310 was succeeded by his son, John of Clavering. John died without male issue, and this landed family too seems to have existed throughout the 13th century without an hereditary surname.[63] Some other examples could be given of East Anglian landed families which had no settled surnames in the 13th century, though for families of such status this was probably rather exceptional.

For smaller freeholders, too, there is evidence that some were acquiring hereditary surnames in the 13th century. Some deductions on this subject can be made from the facts reported in the Hundred Rolls of Edward I's reign about socage tenants in the Suffolk Hundred of Lothingland. Some of these were people who held considerable lands elsewhere, like the Charles family who have already been mentioned,[64] but most appear to have been small socage tenants, often with holdings of 12 acres. The return in the Hundred Rolls is valuable because it gives the names of previous tenants of many holdings, back to the reign of Henry II in some cases, and because it sometimes tells if the tenant holding under Edward I, in 1275, had inherited his land, or purchased it.[65] In many cases it can be seen that the 1275 tenants have surnames derived from the personal names of previous holders of their lands; for instance, Robert Mannekin was holding in 1275 land at Boyton formerly (*quondam*) held by Mannekinus de Boyton, William Randolf held land in 1275 held under Henry III by Ranulf Cristan, Gerald Gunwine in 1275 held land at Coston held under John by Gundewynus de Nethergate, Stephen Godric held in 1275, as one of two parceners, land at Herringfleet held under King Henry 'senior' (either Henry I or Henry II) by Godric of Herringfleet, and Thomas Benne and John his brother held land in 1275 at Newton, held under Henry III by Benedict de Neuton.[66] In all these cases, and some others given in the same source, the tenant in 1275 has a surname derived from his predecessor's personal name. In some instances the 1275 tenant was probably the son of the predecessor from whom he took his name, but it seems unlikely that a man living in 1275 was the son of a tenant who lived under Henry II, or even under John.

Besides these cases, the same source furnishes some examples where the 1275 tenant had the same surname as a predecessor. For example, land at Somerleyton, held under John by Edric Quintyn, was held in 1275 by Richard Quintin, Henry Quintin, and their sub-tenants; land at Bradwell, held by Robert Seman under Henry III, was held in 1275 by Ralf Seman, and land in Lothingland manor, held in 1275 by William Reynald, had formerly been held by his father, Henry Reynald.[67] These surnames are derived from personal names, but the same source provides similar instances of locative surnames surviving; land at Boyton, held under Henry II by Ranulf de Lund,[68] was held in 1275 by Robert de Lund; land in Herringfleet, held by William de Akethorp under Richard I, was held by Robert de Akethorp in 1275; land at Ness, held in 1275 by William de Nes, had formerly been held by his father, Gilbert de Nes; and other examples could be given.[69] Some surnames of other categories also seem to have been hereditary among these socage tenants; land at Somerleyton held by Thomas le Bercher under Henry III was held in 1275 by John le Bercher and Robert le Hirde; land in Herringfleet, held under John by Nicolas Sket, was held in 1275 by Alexander Sket, and another socage holding, held under Richard I by Alexander Sket the elder, was held in 1275 partly by Alan Sket, and partly by the Prior of Herringfleet; and John del Childrehous under Richard I held land at Herringfleet that was held in 1275 by Nicolas del Child'hus.[70]

In the whole body of socage tenants listed in the Hundred Rolls for Lothingland Hundred, there are 26 socage tenants for whom no predecessors are named; there are 61 cases where the tenant occupying a holding (or part of it) in 1275 had either the same surname as a predecessor listed in the Hundred Rolls, or a surname derived from his predecessor's personal name, and in addition there are two further cases where the continuity between the tenant's surname and that of his predecessor must be considered dubious;[71] there are 30 cases where the 1275 tenant has a name not connected with that of a named predecessor, but where the sources provide some reason for the lack of connection, such as the purchase of the property by the 1275 tenant or by his father, or the descent of the property to female heirs; and there are 43 cases where tenants have names quite unconnected with their predecessors' names, without any obvious reason for such a lack of connection.[72] There must be some uncertainty about how far the continuity of names that can be found in this instance necessarily implies the existence of hereditary surnames, and to lay too much stress on such figures might be unjustified, but they give some indication of how common hereditary surnames were among the free peasantry in East Anglia by the late 13th century. It may be added that there was an active land market for socage land in Lothingland Hundred, as the frequent references to the purchase of holdings in the Hundred Rolls show,[73] and that the holding in numerous cases of tenements by groups of *participes* suggests that partible inheritance prevailed.

It is unlikely that Lothingland Hundred was exceptional, and in fact many instances can be found elsewhere in East Anglia of hereditary surnames in use among those below the knightly class in status during the 13th century. A few examples will illustrate this. A certain Herman of Breckles, apparently living in the early 13th century, is known to have had two sons, one a cleric, known as Richard the chaplain or Richard the son of Herman, who became vicar of Narford, Norfolk, the other known as Luke Herman; Luke Herman had a son, Richard Herman, also a cleric, who was alive in 1306, and with this younger Richard the name has clearly become hereditary.[74] Simon de Wighton appears to have lived towards the end of the 12th century, and in 1206 his son Alan de Wighton, was in possession of some land at Holkham, Norfolk; Alan in turn had a son, Hubert de Wighton, living about the middle of the 13th century, and Hubert in turn had a son, Ralf de Wighton, and Ralf himself a son called Hubert. This family were the holders of land at Wighton and Holkham, but not landowners of any great wealth.[75] A John Payn, who was holding land at South Creake, Norfolk, in the mid-13th century, or rather earlier, was the son of William Payn; John was apparently dead by about 1260, and his son was another William Payn, who was holding land at South Creake about 1280-85. This family were freeholders at South Creake.[76] Presumably their surname was derived from the personal name of an ancestor, Payn, who can hardly have lived later than the late 12th century. Many similar instances of hereditary surnames amongst small free tenants could be given, and there are also a few cases where a surname can be shown to have descended to females during the 13th century. A family called Fleggard, holding land at Heacham, Norfolk, is a case in point. Walter Fleggard of Heacham had two daughters, Christiana Fleggard and Miracula Fleggard. Miracula had a son, Andrew, who was referred to as Andrew, son of Miracula Fleggard, rather suggesting that his mother's surname was descending to him.[77] Such descents of surnames to females were probably rare, though cases of surnames derived from feminine personal names were fairly numerous in 13th-century Norfolk and Suffolk.[78]

The origin of surnames derived from female personal names has been discussed at length by various writers, notably the late Dr. P. H. Reaney, but without any conclusive result. In some cases such surnames may have been borne originally by illegitimate children, but it cannot be assumed that this was true in all instances. The reasons why any individual acquired one surname rather than another, why for instance one man had an occupational surname rather than a patronymic or topographical one, are very obscure. There are several possible reasons why a man might have acquired a metronymic surname; he might be a posthumous child, his mother might have been an heiress, or simply of higher social standing, or more forceful character, than his father.

Apart from instances where a family name can be traced through several generations, there are very many cases during the 13th century in which sons can be shown to have borne the same surnames as their fathers. Such cases occur both in the towns and in the countryside, and many of those concerned were certainly persons of no great wealth or standing. In these instances, however, it is not always certain that the surname has become a stable, hereditary one, and to catalogue numerous examples would prove nothing about the proportion of the whole population that had acquired hereditary surnames by, say, 1300. There are also very many cases where the frequent occurrence of a surname, perhaps a rather uncommon one, in a single village leaves little doubt that a surname has become hereditary, and is ramifying locally. In the village of South Creake, in north-west Norfolk, for example, the surname Siger occurs early in the 13th century, and persists well into the 14th. The bearers of the name cannot be shown to be all related, but there can be little doubt that in fact they were. They may have been descended from Sigar of South Creake, who held land in the village, apparently during the 12th century.[79] Over about the same period the surname Helle was in use at South Creake, and though the relationships cannot be traced, there can be little doubt that here too the surname had become hereditary, and was well established in the village.[80]

Late 13th- and early 14th-century subsidy rolls, too, provide many instances of a single surname being borne by a group of individuals in one township, and in such cases it is likely that the group is composed of relatives. The Norfolk subsidy for 1329-30, for example, lists six taxpayers called Nodel at Weasenham, seven called Frost at Upwell and Outwell, six called Gloz at Wiveton, six surnamed Attechildrus and 10 surnamed Godwine at Mattishall, six called Ribald and five called Akeman at Tilney.[81] None of these names are particularly common. The assessment for this subsidy lists very many similar groups. A Suffolk subsidy roll for 1283 lists four persons called Threm at Ashfield Parva, three persons with the surname *Henricus* at Barnham, four persons called Keneman at Euston, and three called Honge at Barningham.[82]

All this evidence reinforces the impression that by the late 13th century stable hereditary surnames were becoming common, even for families of no particular rank or wealth, but it stops a long way short of revealing the precise proportion of families that had hereditary names by about 1300. During the late 13th and early 14th centuries there were still many people without hereditary surnames, and some examples have already been given of baronial and knightly families that were without hereditary surnames during the 13th century. Many similar examples can be found, both among the smaller free tenants in the East Anglian countryside, and amongst townsmen in the region, during the 13th and early 14th centuries. It was pointed out many years ago by William Hudson that many inhabitants of Norwich did not have stable surnames at the end of the 13th century, so that a single individual was variously known by several different surnames, and he illustrated his statement with some instances, drawn from the proceedings of the Norwich court leet.[83] Apart from these instances, many examples can be found in the deeds enrolled in the Norwich city records in the late 13th and early 14th centuries of cases where sons did not have the same surnames as their fathers; for instance, in 1287, Roger del Sartryn of Norwich had a son called Richard de Lingwood, though the name del Sartryn seems to have been hereditary then, or a little later, at Norwich;[84] in 1294, William de Atteburgh of Norwich was described as the son of Roger Curwen, in 1298 John Petyt of Norwich was described as the son of Henry de Thorp, in the same year William Pryce was described as the son of Clement Nayn, in 1287 the father of John de Stonhus was described as Adam le Clerk of Norwich, in 1305 he was described as Adam de Stirston.[85] There are similar cases in Norwich deeds of persons whose surnames were clearly not fixed.[86] Other examples can be found outside Norwich. Towards the end of the 13th century, it was felt necessary to enter in the register of St. Benet's of Holme the names of the descendants of Richard, son of Bond, a free tenant of land in Thwaite and Thurgarton, Norfolk. The names of Richard's descendants, recorded for five generations, show no hereditary surname.[87]

Pedigree of the descendants of Richard, son of Bond.

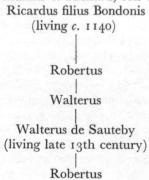

Ricardus filius Bondonis
(living *c.* 1140)

Robertus

Walterus

Walterus de Sauteby
(living late 13th century)

Robertus

An account of the successive holders of some land at Shropham, Norfolk, as set out under Edward I, gives no hereditary surname, though the land descended in the same family for several generations.[88] In this case too the holders appear to have been small free tenants, and other examples could be given. There are also many cases to be found outside Norwich and the other East Anglian towns during the 13th and early 14th centuries where sons are not bearing the same surnames as their fathers.[89] Cases where individuals plainly had no fixed surnames but were known by several designations, are also fairly common in East Anglia during the 13th and early 14th centuries.[90] Though it would be possible to cite very many examples of families that had hereditary surnames between about 1200 and 1350, and though it would also be possible to instance many individuals whose surnames were clearly not stable, or who did not use the same surnames as their immediate ancestor or to note families at various social levels who had no hereditary surnames during the same period, such evidence fails to reveal with any great accuracy what proportion of the population, or of any one social class, acquired hereditary surnames during the period. It does, however, leave little doubt that hereditary surnames were already widespread by about 1300, though by no means universal.

An examination of occupational surnames tends to the same conclusion. Between about 1250 and 1350 there are some women to be found bearing surnames derived from offices that were not occupied by them[91] and many women with surnames derived from trades that were not normally exercised by females.[92] There are also numerous and widespread cases during the same period of men with occupational surnames that differed from the trades they were practising. The names of Suffolk incumbents in the first half of the 14th century, for example, included Peter le Mareschal, William Mareschall, John le Mustardor, Richard Pottere, William le Smyth, John Warde, and Roger le Barkere, and a clerk in major orders could hardly have followed any of the occupations denoted by those names.[93] Parallel cases of clergy with occupational surnames can be found in Norfolk.[94] Cases of laymen with occupational surnames that do not correspond with the trades they in fact practised are numerous in East Anglia about 1250-1350.[95] This evidence suggests that many occupational surnames were already hereditary by the early 14th century, but against it must be set numerous instances that show that about the same period many men were still acquiring surnames from the occupations they in fact followed. A great many instances can be adduced where the bearer of an occupational surname had a different surname from his father,[96] and there are other instances where a father's occupational surname was not inherited by his son.[97] There are indications that men were still acquiring surnames from the trades they exercised at Norwich until the end of the 14th century, or even in the 15th century. In 1350, for example, David Fishmonger was a dealer in freshwater fish at Norwich, in 1390-91 Robert Cook was said to be a common cooker of victuals in the city, and about the same date it was said that Walter Goldsmith was exercising his craft as a goldsmith in the city although he was not a citizen.[98] As late as 1479-80 Robert Brasier, then admitted as a freeman of Norwich, was a brasier by trade, and a former apprentice of Richard Brasier.[99] This looks very much as if Robert had acquired his surname, either from his occupation, or just possibly from his master. Evidence from the late 14th-century poll tax returns, discussed below, indicates that occupational surnames were being formed at that period elsewhere in East Anglia.

The evidence from occupational surnames shows that hereditary surnames were common by the early 14th century, but that there were still many persons whose surnames were not fixed, and new ones were still arising. Some light can be thrown on the general position by examining East Anglian subsidy rolls. In the subsidy roll for the Suffolk hundred of Blackbourne in 1283, about 17 per cent of those listed are described only as the sons of some other person, in the usual formula 'Eadmund filius Walteri',[100] and besides these there are a very few persons, mostly women, who do not have any surnames or bye-names at all.[101] In the Suffolk subsidy roll for 1327, less than two per cent of the taxpayers are described merely as the sons of some person,[102] and in the Norfolk subsidy roll for 1329-30, the proportion is much the same.[103] It is possible that some of the persons listed in subsidy rolls under the formula 'Willelmus filius Johannis' and so forth, were in fact already the possessors of surnames with a filial desinence ('Johnson', and so forth) and that the Latin formula in the subsidy rolls and other documents is merely a translation, but for reasons discussed elsewhere it is unlikely that this can be true in any great number of cases.[104] It therefore seems reasonable to deduce that most persons described in subsidy rolls and similar documents merely as the son of some person had no stable surnames, hereditary or otherwise. On the other hand it is obviously not possible to argue that all those who appear with surnames in for example 14th century subsidy rolls possessed surnames that were by then hereditary. What does seem clear from the subsidy rolls is that in the early years of Edward III's reign those of sufficient means to be assessed for subsidies still included a small proportion who had no established surnames.

Evidence from the subsidy rolls fails to give any accurate guide to the proportion of people who had hereditary surnames, even for the classes that possessed sufficient wealth to be assessed for taxation, and it still leaves unresolved the issue of what the incidence of hereditary surnames was amongst those too poor to be assessed, including the unfree peasantry. Manorial records provide some evidence on this. In the court rolls for South Elmham, a large Suffolk manor, 198 different surnames were found in the court rolls for 1278-9, and of these, 114 can be found in the court rolls up to 1337, 73 up to 1348, and 26 up to 1400.[105] Possibly in a few cases a surname may have died out in the manor, and later have been re-introduced by immigrants, but this seems unlikely to have happened frequently because some surnames involved are uncommon, and in many cases there are fairly continuous occurrences of given surnames in the court rolls over a period. For instance, between 1278 and 1400 at least 14 individuals surnamed Peeke occur in the South Elmham manor court records, including some who were clearly villeins;[106] at least nine individuals with the name Brithwald or Brickald occur during the same period, five persons with the unusual name of Clinkbelle, nine called Kidewyne, another villein family, and 13 called Elmy, also a family of villeins.[107] Many other surnames could be instanced, some of them borne by villein families. It must be remembered that the names of a manor's tenants only occur rather spasmodically on its court rolls, and that complete lists of any township's inhabitants cannot usually be complied from manorial records, least of all in East Anglia where manors are often geographically fragmented. There is consequently no assurance that

even if a surname survives in a township over a long period, it will
appear more or less continuously in manorial records over that time.
If these considerations are borne in mind, it is clear that hereditary
surnames were already fairly common among the South Elmham
tenants, free and unfree, by about 1300. On the other hand it is
equally clear that there were still many who had no hereditary
surnames. All through the 14th century tenants occur who are
described only as the son of some person, although as the century
goes on such descriptions become fewer, and are rare by 1400.[108]
It is also clear that even where a surname was well established in the
manor, and had apparently become hereditary, it was not necessarily inherited by all members of the family. At South Elmham,
for example, a tenant, John Sparhauk at his death in 1348 was
found to have as heir William Newman, son of John's brother
Robert Sparhauk.[109] Robert Sparhauk had evidently not transmitted his surname to his son, although the name Sparhauk survived in the manor all through the 14th century.[110]

The situation at South Elmham seems to be paralleled elsewhere.
In the large Norfolk manor of Forncett, instances can be found
where surnames borne in some cases by free tenants, in others by
bondmen, survived from the early 14th century, or in some cases
even from the 13th, until the 16th century.[111] In Fareswell manor
at Fincham, Norfolk, out of 44 surnames that occur in the manor
court rolls in 1341-43, 18 occur in manorial documents relating to
Fincham during the 15th century, and 12 still occur in manorial
documents concerning Fincham during the 16th.[112] This suggests
that many surnames in use at Fincham in the first half of the 14th
century were hereditary, especially since the manor in question only
comprised part of Fincham township, and it must have been easy
for tenants to move into and out of the manor.

The study of the surnames occurring in the records of a single
manor has the disadvantage that it was easy for persons to move out
of, or into, a particular manor, often without leaving one township,
and in East Anglia this factor is made more serious by the region's
manorial structure, with many manors possessed of outlying portions
in several townships, and with many townships divided between
several manors. An examination of the surnames in a larger unit.
the hundred of Blackbourne in north Suffolk, may furnish more
useful evidence on the hereditary nature of 13th- and 14th-century
surnames. A list has been complied from several sources of surnames
to be found in the hundred in 1275-1300,[113] and the list so formed
has been compared with the surnames occurring in returns for the
poll tax of 1381 for the hundred.[114] Out of 162 different surnames
that occur in the extant returns for the hundred in 1381, 84 occur

in the late 13th century list just described, and a further 16 occur in the 1327 subsidy roll for the hundred.[115] Only 62 do not occur within the hundred either in the late 13th-century sources, or in the 1327 subsidy return. It is perhaps not surprising that common patronymic or occupational surnames should occur both in the late 13th century, and in the late 14th, and by itself such a persistence of common surnames might not imply that the names were hereditary. The survival of much less common surnames, such as Blaunch-payn,[116] Bossard,[117] Cokewald,[118] Grenegres,[119] Toffay,[120] Wolf-uard,[121] and many others that could be cited, indicates more convincingly that many surnames in use during the late 13th or early 14th centuries in Blackbourne Hundred were inherited by future generations. Since the surviving returns for the hundred in 1381 are not complete, it is not feasible to calculate how many of the surnames occurring in the late 13th century sources were not listed in the 1381 poll tax returns. However, it would seem from this evidence that perhaps about half the surnames in use in Blackbourne Hundred in 1381 had been inherited from ancestors who bore the names in question in the late 13th century, and it may reasonably be supposed that the surnames which were hereditary formed a larger proportion by the late 14th century.

The poll tax returns of Richard II's reign give fuller lists of the population than do subsidy rolls, and include labourers and *servientes*. Some deductions on the inheritance of surnames can be made from the returns. There were in 1381 still people who did not have any surnames, or at least are not listed in the returns as having any, in both Norfolk and Suffolk. Persons lacking surnames are nearly all categorised as *servientes* in the poll tax returns.[122] It is difficult to be certain that persons who appear in the poll tax lists under such descriptions as *Walterus serviens Henrici Blauncpayn* were in fact without surnames, and were not merely described in this fashion because it appeared a convenient means of identification, but in any case the large numbers of persons with surnames listed in the poll tax returns as *artifices, laboratores,* and *servientes*[123] make it clear that the great majority, even of manual workers, possessed surnames by the late 14th century, and the evidence about Black-bourne Hundred already cited strongly suggests that most surnames were already hereditary. On the other hand, there are suspiciously numerous cases in the Suffolk returns for the 1381 poll tax of men whose stated occupations coincide with their surnames, and it seems likely that new surnames were still being derived from a man's occupation in the late 14th century. The occupations of artificers are only given spasmodically in the extant Suffolk poll tax returns for 1381, but where they are given 41 persons have surnames that coincide with their occupations, while only 25 have occupational surnames that are different from their stated occupations.[124] Besides these 25, there are a few cases of persons listed as *servientes*, or *laboratores*, who have names hardly consistent with such descriptions. Persons with the surnames Millere, Clerk, Skynner, and Smyth are listed as *laboratores*, for example.[125]

One other characteristic of the late 14th-century poll tax returns, and especially of the returns for some Suffolk townships in 1381, is the existence of groups of persons bearing the same surname in a single township, or in several neighbouring townships. At Euston in Suffolk, for example, the 1381 poll tax list contains four persons named Jade, three persons called atte Chirche, and three called Leveday; 53 persons, including 13 married couples, have 23 surnames between them.[126] At Wetherden in Suffolk in 1381 the poll tax returns list (counting married couples as one) three persons called Motonn, three called Bauleie, three called Wodecok, three called Westbron or Westbroun, three called Densi, three called Ros, and three called Bonde, out of 66 persons in all listed.[127] Similar cases can be found in Norfolk; a poll tax assessment for Gooderstone lists five persons called Cowhirde, a rather uncommon occupational name; an assessment for Southacre and Newton lists three called Personesman, and three called Cok; an assessment for Swaffham lists three called Lord, and three called Wyne or Wynne.[128] None of the names given in these examples is at all common in East Anglia, and it is reasonable to deduce that where surnames are grouped in this fashion, families with hereditary surnames exist.

The cumulative effect of the evidence put forward above is that by the end of the 14th century, a majority of persons, perhaps the great majority, in East Anglia, appear to have had hereditary surnames, and this seems to be true of all social classes.

Evidence for the 15th century is unfortunately very incomplete. It is not difficult to find cases of landed families which had hereditary surnames during the century, or to discover many instances where amongst persons of lesser status sons succeeded to their father's surnames, but since it is clear that many families already had hereditary surnames by about 1400, such instances however numerous prove very little. Manorial records suggest that most inhabitants of East Anglia had hereditary surnames during the 15th century. The records of Forncett manor in Norfolk show that many surnames survived in the manor through the century, despite considerable movement by both the free and the unfree population.[129] The position at Fincham in Norfolk seems to have been much the same. Out of 48 tenants whose names occur at a court leet for Fincham in 1467, for example, 30 have names that occur in Fincham manorial records during 1350-1450. In many cases the frequent occurrence of the surnames in question during the 14th and 15th centuries makes it clear that the names were borne hereditarily by families long resident at Fincham.[130] Similarly of 66 persons listed at Fincham in a 1525 subsidy roll, 40 had surnames that occur in Fincham manorial records during the 15th century.[131] The Fincham documents leave the general impression that during the 15th century the position there was much the same as at Forncett, with a certain number of families, resident for long periods during the 15th and 16th centuries, so that some surnames persist from the end of the 14th century into the 16th, while there are also a larger number of surnames that appear only for quite short periods, often as the name of a single individual only, and which were probably held by individuals or families that did not strike any deep roots. The 15th-century records of a manor at Hacheston in Suffolk show that tenants there were regularly succeeded by their sons bearing the same surnames, and these records too leave the impression that most if not all of the manor's inhabitants had hereditary surnames in the 15th century.[132]

There are, however, during the 15th and early 16th centuries still occasional mentions of people who do not appear to have surnames at all. In 1467, for example, one John, servant of John Talyour, occurs at Fincham.[133] In 1522 Isaak, a servant, occurs at Yarmouth.[134] In 1524 Richard and William, both without surnames, occur at Castle Acre,[135] John, servant of Thomas Newman, and another John, servant of Henry Thool, occur at Hillingdon, near King's Lynn,[136] another Richard occurs at West Walton in Norfolk,[137] and another William at Cromer.[138] Similar examples can be found in Suffolk.[139] These all may be instances of men who were still without surnames at a relatively late date, though it is quite possible that they may have had surnames that were simply omitted in the sources.

To summarise the conclusions of this chapter, it seems that before 1200 hereditary surnames were very largely confined to aristocratic and knightly families, though tending to spread to landholders of rather lesser standing, and that even among families of some rank hereditary surnames were not universal. During the 13th century hereditary surnames became much more widespread, and by about 1300 possibly as many as half the families in East Anglia may have had hereditary surnames. During the 14th century the proportion of families with hereditary surnames further increased, and by the middle of the century such surnames were possessed by many free tenants, by many bondmen, and by many inhabitants of Norwich, and probably by many inhabitants of the region's other towns, so that by about 1350 probably a large majority of the region's population had hereditary surnames. By 1400 it was becoming exceptional for families not to have hereditary surnames, though even as late as the early 16th century there seem to have been cases of persons still without any surnames. In the nature of the case evidence about the proportion of persons having hereditary surnames at any one date is hard to find. Nevertheless the general trend of developments seems clear.

One fact that emerges from the foregoing discussion is that there was no uniformity about the period when the members of any one social class acquired hereditary surnames. Members of aristocratic or gentry families tended, on the whole, to acquire stable surnames at a rather earlier time than members of less exalted social classes, but there are instances of important families not having surnames until a relatively late date. It must be concluded that during the 13th and 14th centuries there was little or no prestige attaching to the possession of a hereditary surname. A surname was not a status symbol.

References

[1]E.g. Edric Grim *Domesday Book, seu Liber Censualis* (1783), vol. ii, f. 293, Edric of Laxfield (*ibid.*, vol. ii, ff. 306, 309, 310), Turmod of Parham (*ibid.*, vol. ii, f. 286), Ansgar Stalre (*ibid.*, vol. ii, f. 149), Leofric of Thorndon (*ibid.*, vol. ii, f. 293)

[2]*Ibid.*, vol. ii, f. 446

[3]G. Tengvik, *Old English Bynames* (1938), pp. 30, 31, 54-57; C. R. Hart, *Early Charters of Eastern England* (1965), pp. 66, 68

[4]Tengvik, *op. cit.*, pp. 147-148

[5]Tengvik, *op. cit.*, pp. 148-164; D. C. Douglas, *Feudal Documents from the Abbey of Bury St. Edmunds* (1932), pp. 26-9, 33, 36-7, 42, 116; C. Johnson and H. A. Cronne, *Regesta Regum Anglo-Normannorum, 1066-1154*, vol. ii, p. 334; D. Whitelock, *Anglo-Saxon Wills* (1930), p. 78; *Domesday Book*, vol. ii, f. 337

[6]H. A. Doubleday and Lord Howard de Walden, eds., *Complete Peerage* (1936) vol. ix, pp. 575-96

[7]*Domesday Book*, vol. ii, ff. 247. 413

[8]J. H. Round, ed., *Calendar of Documents Preserved in France, 918-1206* (1899), p. 512

[9]J. H. Round, *Feudal England* (1909), p. 461

[10]H. R. Luard, ed., *Annales Monastici* (1865), vol. ii, p. 214

[11]J. H. Bullock, ed., *The Norfolk Portion of the Chartulary of the Priory of St. Pancras, Lewes* (Norfolk Record Society, vol. xii) (1939), pp. 38, 78; B. Dodwell, ed., *Feet of Fines for the County of Norfolk, 1198-1202* (Pipe Roll Society, New Series, vol. xxvii) (1950), p. 106

[12]*See*, e.g., on the de Reymes family, J. H. Round, *Geoffrey de Mandeville* (1892), pp. 399-404, and A. L. Raimes, 'The Family of Raymes of Wherstead in Suffolk', *Proceedings of the Suffolk Institute of Archaeology and Natural History* (1937-9), vol. xxiii, pp. 89 ff. On the Muntchesney family, *see* J. H. Round, ed., *Rotuli de Dominabus et Pueris et Puellis* (Pipe Roll Society, vol. xxxv) (1913), pp. xliv-xlv

[13]H. A. Doubleday, G. H. White and Lord Howard de Walden, eds., *Complete Peerage* (1945), vol. x, pp. 331-8; P.R.O., E101/61/16; E179/150/247

[14]*See* e.g. the account of the de Chesney family in W. Farrer, *Honors and Knights' Fees* (1925), vol. iii, pp. 313-18

[15]H. Hall, ed., *Red Book of the Exchequer* (1896), part i, pp. 391-412

[16]*Ibid.*, part i, pp. 393, 396, 404, 407

[17]R. H. C. Davis, ed., *Kalendar of Abbot Samson* (Camden Society, 3rd Series, vol. lxxiv) (1954), pp. 9, 21, 25, 26, 31, 36, 40, 41, 47, 48, 52

[18]R. H. C. Davis, *op. cit.*, pp. 29, 30, 31, 100, 116-7; D. C. Douglas, *Feudal Documents from the Abbey of Bury St. Edmunds* (1932), pp. 180-85

[19]J. R. West, ed., *St. Benet of Holme, 1020-1210* (Norfolk Record Society) (1932), vol. i, pp. 69, 76; vol. ii, pp. 212, 213, 234-5; *Domesday Book*, vol. ii, f. 269

[20]West, *op. cit.*, vol. i, pp. 34, 69, 74, 76, 80, 81, 87, 88, 91, 94, 96

[21]West, *op. cit.*, vol. i, pp. 91, 96, 114, 117, 118; H. Hall, ed., *Red Book of the Exchequer*, part i, p. 394

[22]West, *op. cit.*, vol. i, p. 172; vol. ii, p. 247; *Book of Fees* (1920), part i, pp. 128, 281, 346, 403

[23]J. H. Round, ed., *Rotuli de Dominabus et Pueris et Puellis*, pp. xli-xliii; W. Farrer, *Honors and Knights' Fees*, vol. i. pp. 1-4

[24]D. M. Stenton, ed., *Great Roll of the Pipe for the 2nd Year of John* (Pipe Roll Society, New Series, vol. xii) (1934), p. 148; B. Dodwell, ed., *Feet of Fines for the County of Norfolk, 1198-1202*, pp. 110, 115-16; *Curia Regis Rolls* (1922). vol. i, pp. 162, 207; *Book of Fees*, vol. ii, p. 1327

[25]*Curia Regis Rolls, 11-14 John* (1932), pp. 17, 79

[26]J. R. West, ed., *St. Benet of Holme, 1020-1210*, vol. i, p. 123

[27]W. Rye, ed., *Cal. Norf. Fines*, vol. i, p. 38; C. Robinson, ed., *Great Roll of the Pipe for the 14th year of Henry III* (Pipe Roll Society, New Series, vol. iv) (1927), p. 157; J. H. Bullock, ed., *The Norfolk Portion of the Chartulary of the Priory of St. Pancras, Lewes*, p. 24

[28]W. Rye, *op. cit.*, vol. i, p. 97; *Book of Fees*, vol. ii, p. 903

[29]There is an account, needing revision, of the family in W. Rye, *Norfolk Families* (1913), pp. 432-3; see also H. A. Doubleday and Lord Howard de Walden, eds., *Complete Peerage* (1929), vol. vii, pp. 190-9

[30]*See* e.g., for an account of the de Reedham family, whose name was hereditary from *c.* 1140 at least, J. R. West, ed., *St. Benet of Holme, 1020-1210*, vol. ii, pp. 235-6; for an account of the de Ingelose family, whose name seems to have been hereditary from the late 12th century, see W. Farrer, *Honors and Knights' Fees*, vol. iii, p. 116

[31]*Book of Fees*, vol. i, pp. 127, 137

[32]*Ibid.*, vol. ii, p. 1326

[33]*Ibid.*, vol. i, pp. 127, 138, 280, 282, 593; vol. ii, 916; *Calendar of Inquisitions Post Mortem* (1904), vol. i, p. 49; C. Roberts, ed., *Excerpta E Rotulis Finium* (1836), vol. ii, p. 79; S. Smith, ed., *Great Roll of the Pipe for the Seventh Year of John* (Pipe Roll Society, New Series, vol. xix) (1941), p. 235; *Curia Regis Rolls, 3-4 Henry III* (1938), pp. 63, 166, 257

[34]*Book of Fees*, vol. i, pp. 127, 138

[35]*Ibid.*, vol. i, p. 127; *Feet of Fines for the Reign of Henry II and the First Seven Years of Richard I* (Pipe Roll Society, vol. xvii) (1894), pp. 66-7

[36]D. C. Douglas, ed., *Feudal Documents from the Abbey of Bury St. Edmunds*, pp. 37-9

[37]R. H. C. Davis, ed., *Kalendar of Abbot Samson* (Camden Society, 3rd Series, vol. lxxxiv) (1954), pp. 43-6, 49-50

[38]Davis, *op. cit.*, *passim*

[39]Davis, *Kalendar of Abbot Samson*, p. 18; Douglas, *Feudal Documents from the Abbey of Bury St. Edmunds*, p. 28

[40]Davis, *op. cit.*, p. 7; Douglas, *op. cit.*, p. 36

[41]Douglas, *op. cit.*, p. 28; Davis, *op. cit.*, p. 18

[42]*See* the remarks on the descendants of Rerus, Davis, *op. cit.*, pp. 4, 13

[43]W. H. Hart and P. A. Lyons, eds., *Cartularium Monasterium de Ramseia* (Rolls Series) (1893), vol. iii, pp. 261-98. On the dates of these extents, *see* J. A. Raftis, *The Estates of Ramsey Abbey* (1957), pp. 305-8

[44]*Cartularium Monasterium de Ramseia*, vol. iii, pp. 268-9, 295-6, 298

[45]B. Dodwell, ed., *Feet of Fines for the County of Norfolk, 1201-1215, and for the County of Suffolk, 1199-1214*, pp. 125, 144, 146-7, 213, 215, 259; B. Dodwell, ed., *Feet of Fines for the County of Norfolk, 1198-1202*, pp. 76, 164

[46]B. Dodwell, ed., *Feet of Fines for the County of Norfolk, 1201-1215, and for the County of Suffolk, 1199-1214*, p. 259. On serfs' names generally, *see* below, pp. 144-46

[47]W. Farrer, *Honors and Knights Fees*, vol. iii, p. 116; *Rotuli Hundredorum* (1818), vol. ii, p. 161

[48]*Rotuli Hundredorum*, vol. ii, p. 161; Farrer, *op. cit.*, vol. iii, pp. 116-17; *Calendar of Charter Rolls, 1257-1300* (1906), p. 49

[49]Farrer, *op. cit.*, vol. iii, pp. 116-17; *Calendar of Charter Rolls, 1257-1300*, pp. 49, 53; W. Rye, ed., *Cal. Norf. Fines*, vol. i, pp. 68, 141; *Rotuli Hundredorum*, vol. ii, p. 161; *Calendar of Inquisitions Post Mortem* (1909), vol. vii, p. 159

[50]Farrer, *op. cit.*, vol. iii, pp. 138-9

[51]Farrer, *op. cit.*, vol. iii, p. 116

[52]Farrer, *op. cit.*, vol. iii, pp. 431-2

[53]*Calendar of Inquisitions Post Mortem* (1906), vol. ii, p. 240; C. Roberts, ed., *Excerpta E Rotulis Finium*, vol. ii. p. 169

[54]*Calendar of Close Rolls, 1254-6* (1931), p. 303; F. Hervey, ed., *Pinchbeck Register* (1925), vol. i, pp. 272-3; *Calendar of Inquisitions Post Mortem* (1904), vol. i, p. 228; *Calendar of Close Rolls, 1247-51* (1922), pp. 311, 316

[55]Farrer, *op. cit.*, vol. iii, pp. 425-7

[56]For other examples, *see* Farrer, *op. cit.*, *passim*. Many other examples occur in W. Rye, *Norfolk Families* (1913), but this work lacks references to original sources. Some other examples can be traced in the Hundred Rolls; *see* e.g., on the Mundy family of Norfolk, *Rotuli Hundredorum* (1812), vol. i, p. 483

[57]On the high proportion of locative surnames amongst the more important landed families, *see* below, pp. 141-43

[58]*Calendar of Patent Rolls, 1258-66* (1910), p. 13; V. Gibbs and H. A. Doubleday, *Complete Peerage* (1926), vol. v, p. 472. On the family's importance, *see* J. H. Round, 'King John and Robert Fitzwalter', *English Historical Review* (1904), vol. xix, pp. 709-10

[59]W. Dugdale, *Monasticon Anglicanum* (ed. Caley, Ellis, and Bandinell) (1830), vol. vi, p. 148; *Calendar of Inquisitions Post Mortem* (1910), vol. vi, p. 445; *Calendar of Patent Rolls, 1272-81* (1901), p. 98

[60]*Calendar of Inquisitions Post Mortem* (1909), vol. vii, p. 126

[61]J. R. West, ed., *St. Benet of Holme, 1020-1210*, vol. i, p. 140; J. H. Round, ed., *Ancient Charters Prior to A.D. 1200* (Pipe Roll Society, vol. x) (1888), p. 107

[62]*Calendar of Charter Rolls* (1906), vol. ii, p. 145; W. Farrer, *Honors and Knights' Fees*, vol. iii, p. 429; *Calendar of Patent Rolls, 1247-58* (1908), p. 112; *Calendar of Fine Rolls* (1911), vol. i, p. 257; *Book of Fees*, vol. ii, pp. 577, 592; *Calendar of Close Rolls, 1302-7*, p. 462; *Calendar of Inquisitions Post Mortem* (1912), vol. iii, pp. 368, 478; *Feudal Aids* (1904), vol. iii, pp. 403, 412, 421, 428 and *passim*

[63]W. Farrer, *op. cit.*, vol. iii, p. 321; W. Rye, *Cal. Norf. Fines*, vol. i, p. 259. For other cases of a 13th-century landed family without a hereditary surname, *see* the names of the descendants of John son of Hugh, in *Rotuli Hundredorum*, vol. ii, p. 509, and the descendants of Gilbert of Ilketshall, Farrer, *op. cit.*, vol. ii,, pp. 230-31

[64]*See* above, p. 9

[65]*Rotuli Hundredorum*, vol. ii, pp. 161-7. There are some references to persons holding land under King Henry 'senior'. It is not clear if this means Henry I or, more probably, Henry II

[66]*Ibid.*, vol. ii, pp. 162, 163, 164, 166

[67]*Ibid.*, vol. ii, pp. 161, 162, 163

[68]Probably Lound near Lowestoft

[69]*Rotuli Hundredorum*, vol. ii, pp. 163, 165

[70]*Ibid.*, vol. ii, pp. 163, 164, 165

[71]These two cases are (a) Land held under John by Ranulf del Childerhous, and held in part by Henry Child in 1275; (b) land held in 1275 by John le Hoppere, held formerly (*quondam*) by Gerald Roppere, or Gerald le Hoppere, *ibid.*, vol. ii, pp. 163, 167, 185

[72]*Ibid.*, vol. ii, pp. 161-7

[73]*Ibid.*

[74] W. Rye, *Calendar of Deeds relating to Norwich, 1285-1306*, pp. 109-110

[75]A. L. Bedingfeld, ed., *Cartulary of Creake Abbey* (Norfolk Record Society, vol. xxxv) (1966), pp. 100, 104, 105; B. Dodwell, ed., *Feet of Fines for the County of Norfolk, 1198-1202*, p. 127; B. Dodwell, ed., *Feet of Fines for the County of Norfolk, 1201-15, and for the County of Suffolk, 1199-1214*, pp. 2, 46

[76]Bedingfeld, ed., *Cartulary of Creake Abbey*, pp. 31, 35, 55

[77]J. H. Bullock, ed., *The Norfolk Portion of the Chartulary of the Priory of St. Pancras of Lewes*, pp. 8, 26, 27, 28. Miracula is possibly a translation into Latin of Mirabelle

[78]On surnames derived from personal names, *see* below, pp. 127-38

[79]Bedingfeld, ed., *Cartulary of Creake Abbey*, pp. 10. 38, 40, 41, 46, 60, 68, 116; B. Dodwell, *Feet of Fines for the County of Norfolk, 1198-1202*, p. 25

[80]Bedingfeld, *op. cit.*, pp. 46, 57, 66, 67

[81]P.R.O., E179/149/7, mm. 32, 33, 42, 51, 59, 69

⁸²E. Powell, ed., *A Suffolk Hundred in 1283* (1910), tables 2, 5, 6, 9

⁸³W. Hudson, ed., *Leet Jurisdiction in the City of Norwich* (Selden Society) (1892), pp. xci, xcii

⁸⁴W. Rye, *Calendar of Deeds Relating to Norwich, 1285-1306*, p. 18

⁸⁵Rye, *op. cit.*, pp. 12, 52, 65, 69, 70, 108

⁸⁶*See*, e.g. *ibid.*, p. 26 (Seman Grym of Heigham, otherwise Semann de Higham), pp. 7, 25 (Wido le Chapeler, otherwise Gwydo de Norwich)

⁸⁷J. R. West, ed., *St. Benet of Holme, 1020-1210*, vol. i, p. 76

⁸⁸*Placita de Quo Warranto* (Record Commission) (1818), p. 489

⁸⁹*See*, e.g., W. Rye, *Calendar of Norwich Deeds, 1307-41* (1915), p. 58 (Thos. de Horstede, son of John de Larwode), p. 68 (Roger de Dilham, son of Henry atte Medewe); Bullock, ed., *The Norfolk Portion of the Chartulary of the Priory of St. Pancras of Lewes*, p. 28 (William de London, son of Reginald de Staninges)

⁹⁰*See*, e.g., Rye, *Calendar of Deeds relating to Norwich, 1286-1306*, p. 59 (Geoffrey attehil, merchant, also referred to as Geoffrey of Fundenhall, merchant 1296); *ibid.*, p. 20 (Jn. le Cartere, also referred to as John de Gissing, 1287); *ibid.*, pp. 6, 25 (Richard Skilman, otherwise referred to as Richard son of Simon Skilman, or Richard of Hethersett); Rye, *Calendar of Norwich Deeds, 1307-41*, p. 31 (William de Dicelburgh, called Sallman, 1311)

⁹¹*See*, e.g., *Rotuli Hundredorum*, vol. ii, pp. 142-3 (Eva la Justice); E. Powell, *A Suffolk Hundred in the Year 1283*, table 14 (Matilda *Prepositus* and Basilia *Prepositus*)

⁹²*See*, e.g., P.R.O., E179/149/7 m. 28, Matilda Faber at West Beckham; m. 29, Agnes Mareschal at Alby; m. 34, Alice Hirynmongar; m. 58, Margery le Mazoun at Terrington (all in Norfolk, 1329-30); W. Rye, *Calendar of Deeds relating to Norwich, 1285-1306*, pp. 11-12, Cecilia le Skirmescher of Forncett, 1287; E. Powell, *op. cit.*, table 5, Margaret Sumener at Barnham; *ibid.*, table 31, Matilda le Mayster, at Ixworth Thorpe; *ibid.*, pp. 15, 89, Katerina le Heyward at Stow Langtoft, Clare le Heyward at Rickinghall Inferior (all Suffolk, 1280-1283); Anon., *Suffolk in 1327* (Suffolk Green Books, no. IX) (1906), p. 191, Alice le Talyour at Bardwell (1327); Ipswich and East Suffolk Record Office, H.A/12/C2/1, m. 2, Agnes Faber at South Elmham, 1278; H.A/12/C2/11, m. 3, Christiana Smith at South Elmham, 1349 ; W. Hudson, *Leet Jurisdiction in the City of Norwich*, p. 5, Matilda le ledbettere at Norwich, 1287/88; *ibid.*, p. 42, Olyva le Orfevre at Norwich, 1292-93

⁹³C. Morley, 'Catalogue of the Beneficed Clergy of Suffolk, 1086-1530', *Proceedings of Suffolk Institute of Archaeology and Natural History* (1936), vol. xxii, pp. 64, 66, 70, 75, 82; *Suffolk in 1327*, p. 80

[94]*See*, e.g., Rye, *Calendar of Deeds relating to Norwich, 1285-1306*, pp. 45, 71, Thomas le Warenner of Congham, *capellanus*, 1293; P.R.O., E179/149/7, m. 33, Simon Kegel, *capellanus*, at Mileham, 1329-30; Hudson, *Leet Jurisdiction in the City of Norwich*, p. 15, John le Mercer, Dean of Norwich

[95]*See*, e.g. *Rotuli Hundredorum* (Record Commission), vol. ii, p. 152, Hugh le Taylur (1274-5), farmer of Kedington, Suffolk; W. Rye, *Calendar of Deeds relating to Norwich, 1285-1306*, p. 71, John Wodeman, *pheliparius*, 1298, at Norwich; *ibid.*, p. 44, Adam le Chapeleyn, fishmonger, 1292, at Norwich; P.R.O. E179/149/7, m. 68, Jn. Catour, *faber*, at Horning, 1329-30; W. Rye, *Calendar of Norwich Deeds, 1307-41*, p. 108, John Sopere the Hattere, 1322, at Norwich, and *see* G. Fransson, *Middle English Surnames of Occupation* (1935), p. 38

[96]*See*, e.g. Rye, *Calendar of Deeds relating to Norwich, 1285-1306*, p. 8 (Peter le Chaucer, son of John le Tundur, 1286-7); p. 17 (Nicholas le Chaucer, son of Master Simon de Coselayne, 1287); p. 38 (Robert le Taylur, son of Adam Wace of Hoxne, 1291); p. 54 (Geoffrey le Belgmakere, son of Hugh de Denton, 1294); and *passim*; A. L. Bedingfeld, ed., *Cartulary of Creake Abbey*, p. 124 (Simon le Mason, son of Bonet de Harple, 1246-62); Rye, *Calendar of Norwich Deeds, 1307-41*, p. 99 (Robert le Taillur, son of Simon Carpenter, 1321)

[97]*See*, e.g. Rye, *Calendar of Deeds relating to Norwich, 1285-1306*, p. 7 (William de Pulham, son of Sarlo Chaumpeleyn, 1286-7); p. 10 (William de Horsted, son of Geoffrey le Chapman, 1287); p. 56 (Simon le Feliper, son of Ranulph le Furmager, 1295); p. 70 (William le Sauser, son of Henry Aurifaber, 1298); p. 106 (Alfreda, widow of John le Luminur, and Robert le Peyntur her son, 1305)

[98]Hudson, *Leet Jurisdiction in Norwich*, pp. 71, 72, 80

[99]J. L'Estrange, ed. *Calendar of the Freemen of Norwich, 1317-1603* (1888), p. 20

[100]E. Powell, *A Suffolk Hundred in 1283*, tables 1-37

[101]E.g. 'Alicia ancilla W. prepositi', *ibid.*, table 3

[102]*Suffolk in 1327*, *passim*

[103]P.R.O. E179/149/7

[104]*See* p. 130

[105]Ipswich and East Suffolk R.O. HA/12/C2/1, HA/12/C2/2, HA/12/C2/7, HA/12/C2/11, HA/12/C2/14, HA/12/C2/20

[106]Ipswich and East Suffolk R.O., HA/12/C2/1, m. 4 (Simon Pekk); HA/12/C2/2, m. 1 (John Pecke, a fugitive serf); HA/12/C2/7, m. 1 (William Pecke, deceased, and his son John), m. 5 (Henry Pekke, and his brothers, Bartholomew and Richard), m. 10

(John Pekke, Richard Pekke, Juliana Pekke), m. 11 (Roger Peeke, deceased and his son Simon), m. 12 (Stephen Pecke); HA/12/C2/11, m. 1 (William Pecke, Simon Pecke, and Richard Pekke, who seeks a licence to marry), m. 4 (Walter Pecke); HA/12/C2/20, m. 2 (Stephen Pecke)

[107]Ipswich and East Suffolk R.O., HA/12/C2/1, mm. 2, 3, 4; HA/12/C2/2, mm. 1, 2, 9; HA/12/C2/7, mm. 1, 2, 3, 5, 8, 9, 10, 14; HA/12/C2/11, mm. 1, 2, 3, 4; HA/12/C2/14, m. 2; HA/12/C2/20, m. 2

[108]*See* references cited in n. 105 above

[109]Ipswich and East Suffolk R.O., HA/12/C2/2, mm. 1, 2; HA/12/C2/11, m. 1

[110]*Ibid.*, HA/12/C2/11, m. 4; HA/12/C2/14, m. 2; HA/12/C2/20, m. 2

[111]R. A. McKinley, *Norfolk Surnames in the Sixteenth Century* (1969), pp. 47-8

[112]P.R.O., S.C.2/192/75, S.C.2/192/76, S.C.2/192/80, C135/12/7; Norfolk and Norwich R.O., MSS. 7237, 7238

[113]The sources are: an assessment of Blackbourne Hundred to a thirtieth, 1283 (Printed in E. Powell, *A Suffolk Hundred in 1283* (1910), tables 1-37); a return as to land tenure in the hundred, *c.* 1280 (Printed *ibid.*, pp. 5-75); references to persons living in the hundred in the Hundred Rolls (Printed *Rotuli Hundredorum*, vol. ii, pp. 142-200); an extent of the manor of Wykes, in Bardwell, Suff., late 13th century (Printed in W. Hudson, 'Three Manorial Extents of the Thirteenth Century', *Norfolk Archaeology* (1910), vol. xiv, pp. 42-53); and extents of the manors of Ixworth and Ashfield, 1299 (P.R.O., C133/89/8)

[114]E. Powell, *The Rising in East Anglia in 1381* (1896), pp. 102-111

[115]Anon., *Suffolk in 1327* (Suffolk Green Books, no. ix) (1906), pp. 180-95

[116]*Suffolk in 1327*, p. 195; Powell, *The Rising in East Anglia in 1381*, pp. 103-4

[117]Powell, *A Suffolk Hundred in 1283*, p. 94, and tables 5, 37; *Suffolk in 1327*, p. 193; Powell, *The Rising in East Anglia in 1381*, p. 111

[118]Powell, *A Suffolk Hundred in 1283*, table 12; Powell, *The Rising in East Anglia in 1381*, p. 106.

[119]Powell, *A Suffolk Hundred in 1283*, table 10; *Suffolk in 1327*, p. 185; Powell, *The Rising in East Anglia in 1381*, p. 102

[120]*Suffolk in 1327*, p. 193; Powell, *The Rising in East Anglia in 1381*, p. 107

[121]Powell, *A Suffolk Hundred in 1283*, pp. 30, 64, and table 37; *Suffolk in 1327*, p. 194; Powell, *The Rising in East Anglia in 1381*, p. 111

[122]*See*, e.g. P.R.O. E179/238/112, m. 1, assessments for Horsford and Catton; P.R.O. E179/149/53, m. 11, assessment for Southacre and Newton, and for West Bradenham; E. Powell, *The Rising in East Anglia in 1381*, pp. 78, 86, 87, 90, 91, 97, 103, 108, 117

[123]Powell, *The Rising in East Anglia in 1381*, pp. 68-119

[124]*Ibid.*

[125]*Ibid.*, pp. 87, 93, 103

[126]*Ibid.*, pp. 103-4. Married couples are not counted as one

[127]*Ibid.*, pp. 95-6. The total has been arrived at by counting married couples as one person

[128]P.R.O. E179/149/53, m. 11

[129]McKinley, *Norfolk Surnames in the Sixteenth Century*, pp. 47-53

[130]P.R.O. S.C.2/192/75; Norfolk and Norwich R.O., MS. 7237

[131]P.R.O. E/179/150/227; S.C.2/192/75; S.C.2/192/76; S.C.2/192/80; Norfolk and Norwich R.O., MS. 7237

[132]Sybil Andrews and Lilian J. Redstone, 'Suffolk Courts in English', *Proceedings of the Suffolk Institute of Archaeology and Natural History* (1930), vol. xx, pp. 201-13

[133]P.R.O. S.C.2/192/75

[134]P.R.O. E36/25

[135]P.R.O. E179/150/247

[136]*Ibid.*

[137]P.R.O. E179/150/239

[138]P.R.O. E179/150/222

[139]Anon., *Suffolk in 1524* (1910), pp. 341, 380

CHAPTER 2

SURNAMES DERIVED FROM OCCUPATION, STATUS, OR OFFICE

In many works on surnames a distinction is made between names derived from occupations, and those derived from office, rank or status. While such a division is no doubt clear in theory, in practice there are surnames that do not fall neatly into any of the above categories. There is a group of surnames that are derived from lay and ecclesiastical offices, but appear to have been bestowed as nicknames, rather than to be derived from actual holding of the offices concerned, a group including such surnames as King, Bishop, Sheriff, Abbot, and so forth. There is also a further group of surnames about which it is difficult to decide if they should be classified as derived from office or from occupation. Such names as Reeve, Bailly, Sergeant, for example, were derived from offices, but also must often represent an individual's main occupation, and any classification is bound to be rather arbitrary. These considerations make it seem advisable to deal with the surnames derived from occupation, status, or office in a single chapter.

Occupational surnames occur amongst the East Anglian peasantry in the late 11th century, although such names seem to have been rather rare, and being frequently given in Latin are not easy to connect with the surnames that occur later. In a late 11th-century document concerning some Suffolk estates belonging to Bury Abbey the surnames *Faber* (Smith), Horsthein, *Prepositus* (Reeve), *Molendinarius* (Miller), *Mercator* (Merchant), Haiuuard (Hayward), Croperer, *Aurifaber* (Goldsmith), *Sutor* (Cobbler), *Bercarius* (Shepherd), Hueluurihte (Wheelwright), and Blodletere are amongst the surnames borne by peasants, but such names are not frequent.[1] At the village of Troston, for example, only one man out of 34 is given a surname from occupation or office; at Langham, two men out of nine; at Rougham, 11 persons out of 91. On some manors no tenants with occupational names are listed.[2] In a late 12th-century survey of the Bury Abbey estates in Suffolk, which lists many tenants, only seven per cent of those mentioned have surnames derived from occupation or office.[3] Some 12th-century extents of Ramsey Abbey's Norfolk lands, too, give occupational surnames to only a very few tenants, either free or unfree.[4] A list of 150 inhabitants of Kings Lynn, drawn up in 1166, includes only 23 with occupational surnames, including some doubtful cases, though townsmen might be expected to have occupational surnames rather more frequently than other sections of the population.[5] At Lynn, only seven per cent of the freemen admitted before 1300 had occupational surnames, compared with nine per cent in the years 1301-50, 13 per cent in 1351-1400, and 18 per cent in 1401-50. The register of Norwich freemen does not begin until 1317, but of the freemen admitted up to 1350, 11 per cent had occupational surnames; for 1351-1400 the figure was 13 per cent, and for 1401-50, 15 per cent. These figures may be compared with the 19 per cent of occupational surnames found amongst a large number of names in early 16th-century Norfolk.[6]

Discussion of occupational surnames for any period before the late 13th century is made difficult by the lack of sources that list a substantial proportion of the population, and because a majority of occupational surnames occur in the source material in Latin, while it is often difficult to be sure precisely what vernacular word the Latin term represents. These factors make it difficult to discuss the distribution or relative frequency of occupational surnames in the early Middle Ages with any certainty. It seems clear, however, that those occupational names which were later most common were already in widespread use during the 12th century, and perhaps earlier. Hayward, for example, later a very common surname in East Anglia, occurs frequently in the vernacular form from the late 11th century onwards,[7] while the very frequent occurrences of the Latin *Faber* as a surname must in most cases be translations of the ubiquitous Smith, though other surnames such as Marshall may be involved.[8] Other occupational surnames that are common from the late 13th century onwards, such as Baker,[9] Carpenter,[10] and Tanner,[11] also occur fairly widely in the 12th and early 13th centuries, either in the vernacular, or in their Latin equivalents. In some cases it is possible to be reasonably certain what surname is being translated by a given Latin word, and obtain corroboration from fairly numerous occurrences of the surname in the vernacular form. There are, however, many cases in which this is not true. The Latin *Fullo*, for example, may be a translation for either Fuller, Walker, Bleykester, or Tucker, while it is difficult to say what vernacular surname is represented by the Latin *Rusticus* that occurs occasionally in 12th-century East Anglia.[12] Because of these difficulties it seems best to proceed by discussing occupational surnames in Norfolk and Suffolk as they are found in approximately 1250-1350, and to consider the earlier evidence in the light of the position existing at that period, when sources are more adequate, and when surnames occur more frequently in their vernacular forms.

When the occupational surnames of East Anglia are considered, as they appear *c.* 1250-1350, one obvious characteristic is the relative scarcity of surnames derived from either agricultural occupations, or from the social classes to be found amongst the free and unfree cultivators. The most common names connected with agriculture are those derived from offices, such as Reeve and Hayward. Reeve occurs 15 times as a surname in the Norfolk subsidy for 1329-30,[13] and 36 times in the Suffolk subsidy for 1327.[14] The Latin word *Prepositus*, which is found as a surname in East Anglia from the late 12th century onwards, is probably in most cases a translation of the English Reeve,[15] and so too is the French word *Provost* or *Prevost* in its rare occurrences as an East Anglian surname.[16] Hayward occurs 28 times in the Norfolk subsidy for 1329-30,[17] and 33 times in the Suffolk subsidy for 1327.[18] The Latin term *Messor*, found fairly frequently as a surname during the 13th and 14th centuries, is probably a translation of the English Hayward.[19] Unlike some Latin occupational terms, *Messor* does not seem to have survived at all as a surname. Other fairly common surnames derived from manorial or estate offices are Parker,[20] Warner,[21] and Forester.[22] The only other surname connected with agriculture comparable in commonness with these names derived from offices is Shepherd, which in East Anglia is much the most common surname of those derived from actual agricultural occupations.[23] Several Latin words are used to translate the English Shepherd; one of these, certainly, is *Pastor*, which occurs with moderate frequency;[24] another is *Bercator*, which is also fairly common.[25] The Latin *Bercarius* and the French *le Bercher* also occur commonly as surnames,[26] but unfortunately it is usually difficult to be certain with both these words whether they are the equivalent of the English Shepherd, or whether they are equivalent to the English Barker, so that it is difficult to draw any firm conclusions from the frequency of either name. Were similar figures available for other English regions, it would probably be found that Shepherd was one of the more common surnames derived from agricultural occupations over the whole country, and not only in East Anglia.[27] Of the other surnames derived from occupations connected with herding livestock, none is at all common, and the only two that are other than rare are Bullman[28] and Woodherd.[29] It has been suggested that the surname Woodruff, widespread in East Anglia, is a corruption of the occupational term 'Woodreeve', but no forms have been found to support this view, and Woodruff seems to have a different origin.[30] Other surnames that occur connected with the herding of animals are

Herd,[31] Stedeman,[32] Wulward, probably an alternative term for a shepherd,[33] Shepdrivere,[34] Wetherhird, which has only been found at one place, in West Norfolk,[35] Cowherd,[36] Vacher,[37] Neathird, which has been found only at Norwich,[38] Bover,[39] Swineherd,[40] Porcher,[41] Boreward,[42] Gotegrom,[43] Foder,[44] Hirdegrom,[45] Stoteherd,[46] Palfrey,[47] Palfreyman,[48] and Palefreur.[49] In addition to these surnames, it has been suggested that the rare name le Barwere, found in both Norfolk and Suffolk, may mean a pig-keeper, though other explanations are possible.[50] Several surnames which have been held to derive from occupation concerned with herding stock in fact have other origins. Hirdman, which occurs in East Anglia from the 12th century onwards, is in many cases to be derived from a personal name.[51] Goter, which occurs in 15th-century Norfolk, has been taken to mean a goatherd, and may do so in some cases, but in 1327 the surname occurs as atte Goter in Suffolk, so that it probably has a topographical origin.[52] And Neathird may in some cases be derived from the Norfolk village of Neatishead.[53] Many of these surnames derived from tending livestock were always rare, and some perhaps never became hereditary. If a search is made in the Suffolk returns for the subsidy granted in 1523, the Norfolk returns for the same subsidy and the Norfolk returns for the 'Military Survey' of 1522,[54] then the surnames Shepdrivere, Wetherhird, Vacher, Neathird, Bover, Swineherd, Porcher, Boreward, Gotegrom, Hirdegrom, Stoteherd, Palfrey, and Palefreur are not to be found, nor are any surnames that may be corruptions of these, while Stedeman, Cowherd, Foder and Palfreyman remain rare. Even Woodherd, relatively common in 14th-century East Anglia, has disappeared, unless the surname Woodhard, which occurs in Suffolk, is a corruption of it.[55] Woodherd as a surname seems to have been one of the few occupational names peculiar to East Anglia during the Middle Ages.[56] Herd is not so rare in the 16th century sources as the other surnames just mentioned, and Shepherd, Bulman, and Wulward remain relatively common. This seems a meagre band of survivors out of the surnames derived from the care of livestock.

Surnames derived from occupations connected with tillage are less common still. Ploughman and Tillman each occur only once as a surname in the Norfolk subsidy for 1329-30 and neither occur in the Suffolk subsidy for 1327,[57] though the Suffolk returns include Tiller. Harwer, a name meaning 'harrower', occurs once in the Suffolk subsidy for 1327, but is absent from the Norfolk subsidy for 1329-30, though the name occurs in Norfolk under Edward I and Edward II.[58] Thresher occurs once in the Norfolk subsidy for 1329-30, but not in the Suffolk 1327 subsidy[59]. Reaper occurs once as a surname in the Norfolk 1329-30 subsidy, and twice in the Suffolk subsidy for 1327.[60] Croperer occurs as a bye-name in the late 11th century in Suffolk, but has not been found there, or in Norfolk, at any later period.[61] The surname Fanner, probably derived from the operation of winnowing, occurs in the Suffolk 1327 subsidy, but not in the Norfolk subsidy for 1329-30, though it occurs in both counties at later dates.[62] These surnames together only amount to a very few names drawn from the operations of arable farming, despite the great economic importance of that activity. All the names given in this paragraph are quite rare. Only Ploughman, Tillman, and Fanner occur in the early 16th-century returns for Norfolk and Suffolk mentioned in the preceding paragraph, and even these three occur in but a few instances. The persons named Fanner who occur in the 16th-century sources all resided in two parishes close together in north Suffolk, and were very probably all related.[63]

Occupational surnames linked with haymaking are equally sparse. The surname Mower does not occur in either the Norfolk 1329-30 subsidy returns, or the Suffolk subsidy returns for 1327. There are however several medieval instances of its occurrence,[64] and it is a fairly common name in both counties in the early 16th century.[65] Cocker, a name probably derived from the work of heaping up hay in cocks, is absent from both the Norfolk 1329-30 and the Suffolk 1327 subsidies, though there are occurrences in East Anglia during the Middle Ages, and Tassemakere, a name meaning a stacker of hay or peat, has been found only once in all.[66] Only one person named Cocker occurs in the early 16th-century sources (already mentioned) for both counties. The origin of the surname is however uncertain.[67] Le Stackere occurs in Suffolk in 1327, but has not been found in Norfolk during the Middle Ages.[68]

Other surnames from predial occupations are not numerous, nor are any of them particularly common besides those already mentioned. Granger is found as a surname in East Anglia from the 12th century onwards, but it is always rare, and in the early 16th-century returns for Norfolk and Suffolk mentioned above it occurs only in two neighbouring parishes in West Norfolk, so that all the bearers of the name probably belonged to the same family.[69] Surnames derived from the office of bailiff are rather more common; in the Norfolk 1329-30 subsidy rolls the name Baillie occurs four times, and the form le Bailiff occurs twice, while in the Suffolk subsidy for 1327 Bailie occurs once, and Bayllif twice.[70] In the early 16th-century returns for both counties Bailie is a moderately common surname in each, but Baillif is not found.[71] Greve occurs as a surname only twice in the Norfolk 1329-30 subsidy rolls, and it is absent from the Suffolk 1327 subsidy through it did exist in Suffolk about that date.[72] By the early 16th century it seems to have become proportionately more common in Norfolk, for 16 persons of the name appear in the sources for that time. Four persons of the name occur in the Suffolk sources at the same period.[73] Neither Baillie nor Greve, however, is nearly so common as Reeve. The name Punder, which occurs rather rarely in Norfolk, probably derives from the official whose function it was to impound stray animals, though other origins are possible.[74] Pinder has not been found in East Anglia during the Middle Ages. Two persons with the surname Bernegreyve or Bernereve occur at Framlingham in Suffolk during the first half of the 14th century, but no other occurrences of the name have been found, and it does not seem to have survived.[75]

As for other surnames from agricultural occupations, a few from beekeeping occur, such as Hiver, probably derived from the tending of bee-hives,[76] and Bikere, meaning a beekeeper,[77] and there are two names Wykeman and Wichur, both occurring in a few instances in medieval Suffolk and Norfolk, that may be derived from dairy-farming, but which may both have other origins.[78]

The paucity of surnames drawn from farming occupations no doubt arises from the extreme commonness of such tasks. In the average medieval village so high a proportion of the inhabitants would be engaged at one time or another in the main farming operations that a surname so derived would be insufficiently distinctive. It is however surprising that a manorial office such as hayward should have given rise to a common surname. On many East Anglian manors the hayward (or haywards, for there were sometimes more than one for a manor) was elected yearly, and in some places the office passed round amongst the holders of certain tenements according to a rough system of rotation. There are other offices normally held annually, such as that of constable, that have also given rise to fairly common surnames. Possibly these surnames may have arisen in places where, rather exceptionally, the offices in question were held more or less permanently by an individual, instead of being held annually, but surnames in this category seem too numerous and widespread for all of them to have so originated, and it is probably true that frequently such surnames were derived from offices held only for brief periods.

Surnames derived from the social classes of the countryside are also relatively scarce. None of the surnames derived from the unfree classes are at all common, despite the large numbers of bondmen who existed in East Anglia during the earlier Middle Ages. A few instances of the surname Vilein have been found in Suffolk during the 13th and 14th centuries, but the name has not been found in Norfolk, and seems to have disappeared by the 16th century.[79] Coterel (meaning cottager or cottar) occurs as a surname in Suffolk about 1200, but it has not been found in the county later, nor has it been found in Norfolk during the Middle Ages.[80] The name occurs in both counties in the early 16th century, but is rare at that period.[81] Coteman occurs in Norfolk and Suffolk as a surname in the 13th and 14th centuries, but seems to have disappeared subsequently.[82] The surname Cotmay, which occurs at Norwich about 1438, may be a feminine form of the same word.[83] Coter occurs in Suffolk in the 14th century, and is still found there in the 16th, but it has not been found in Norfolk. Coterer has been found once as a surname in Norfolk,[84] but the name Border has not been found in East Anglia. All these names are rare.

The surname Bonde is common in medieval East Anglia, but it is very doubtful if it is in this region derived from the servile status. Only one instance has been found in East Anglia of this surname in a form that indicates that the name is so derived, although such forms have been found in other regions,[85] and it is likely that the surname when it occurs in East Anglia is derived from the Scandinavian personal name Bonde, which was particularly common in Norfolk during the early Middle Ages.[86] However, there are some surnames occurring in East Anglia that are clearly compounds formed with the word 'bond' in its significance as a bondman or peasant. The rare surname Newbond occurs in Norfolk in the 13th century.[87] The surname Husbond occurs in both Norfolk and Suffolk during the 13th and 14th centuries, though it is not common[88], and only a single example of the name occurs in the early 16th-century sources, mentioned above, which include a large number of names for both counties.[89] In the Suffolk subsidy for 1327 the compound surnames le Yonggehosebond and le Newehosebonde each occur once, and Younghusbande has been found once in Norfolk, but no other East Anglian example of either surname has been noted during the Middle Ages.[90] The surname Heybonde occurs once in the Norfolk subsidy for 1329-30, but has not been found elsewhere.[91]

Surnames derived from the classes of cultivators who were personally free are also relatively scarce. Though sokemen were numerous in East Anglia, Sokeman as a surname is rare. It occurs twice in the Suffolk 1327 subsidy roll, but not at all in the Norfolk subsidy for 1329-30.[92] There are a few occurrences of the name in Suffolk during the 13th and 14th centuries, but it only occurs once in the early 16th-century sources for the two counties.[93] The surname Akerman (husbandman) occurs once in the Norfolk subsidy rolls for 1329-30, but not in the Suffolk subsidy for 1327, and though there are occasional instances in the 14th and 15th centuries, it does not appear in the early 16th-century sources for the two counties.[94] There are only a very few examples of the surnames Holde or Holder in East Anglia during the Middle Ages; in the early 16th-century sources there are two occurrences of Holder, both in a single Suffolk hundred.[95] Surnames derived from the word 'theyn' occur in Norfolk and Suffolk during the Middle Ages, but they are rare, and only a single person with such a surname occurs in the early 16th-century sources for both counties.[96] The surname Franklin is very rare in any of the medieval sources searched for Norfolk and Suffolk, though the term franklin is occasionally used when status is being noted.[97] The name is however present in early 16th-century Norfolk, though uncommon.[98] The surname Farmer or Fermour, a word probably signifying a lease-hold tenant, occurs once in the Suffolk 1327 subsidy, but not at all in the Norfolk subsidy rolls for 1329-30. The name is also found in a few instances in medieval Suffolk, but it is uncommon there.[99] In the early 16th century it occurs, though rarely, in each of the two counties.[100] Tenant has not been found in any of the medieval sources that have been searched for this paper, in either Norfolk or Suffolk. In the early 16th-century sources the name is borne by one person in Suffolk, and four in Norfolk, but the Norfolk cases were all in one small area, and probably involve only one family.[101]

When it is considered how numerous free tenants were in medieval East Anglia, and the importance that must have attached to a man's status in the rural community, the fewness of the surnames derived from the various classes of freeholder is surprising. To some extent this situation may be explained by the relatively large number of surnames derived from the mere condition of being a free man. Of such names, Freeman is by far the most common; it occurs 11 times in the Norfolk subsidy rolls for 1329-30, and seven times in the Suffolk 1327 subsidy, and is fairly common in both counties in the late 16th century.[102] Other names that occur occasionally in East Anglia during the Middle Ages are Freblod,[103] Frebody,[104] and Freborn.[105] The name Franchome, which occurs at Lynn early in the 14th century, is probably a translation into French of the English Freeman, for most occupational names are given in French in the Lynn records at that period.[106] Apart from Freeman, all these names are rare.

There are certain surnames, such as Squire, Knight, Lord, and so forth, which are drawn from the higher social classes, but which are often, perhaps usually, nicknames in origin, rather than names derived from actual rank or status, and which are therefore left to be dealt with later in this chapter. There are also a variety of surnames with the general meaning of servant or employee. The names Hine, Hewe, Joman or Yeoman, and Knave all appear, though rarely, in East Anglia during the 13th and 14th centuries.[107] The surname Swain or Sweyn, though probably derived in many cases from a Scandinavian personal name, is clearly sometimes derived from the occupation of servant.[108] The surnames Boy, Ladde, and Arlot, which despite their literal meanings probably signify servant in most instances, are also very uncommon in Norfolk and Suffolk during the Middle Ages.[109] A much commoner surname in East Anglia is Dey or Day, derived from a word the original meaning of which seems to have been a kneader or baker of bread, but which was later used more generally in the sense of servant. This surname occurs in Suffolk in the late 11th century, and was later widespread in East Anglia.[110] Fifteen persons of the name are listed in the Norfolk subsidy for 1329-30 and 12 in the Suffolk subsidy for 1327.[111] In the early 16th-century returns mentioned above the name is very common in both counties, with 69 persons bearing the name listed in Norfolk, and 62 in Suffolk.[112] This surname seems to have been much more common in East Anglia than elsewhere. The figures just given for Norfolk and Suffolk may be compared with the seven persons of the name in the Buckinghamshire rolls for the subsidy granted in 1523, the two listed in the Sussex rolls for the same subsidy, or the 10 listed in the returns for that subsidy for Essex.[113] These figures are of course not directly comparable; there are about 17,000 entries in the Suffolk returns for the subsidy granted in 1523, compared to about 8,000 in the Buckinghamshire returns, and about 12,000 in the Sussex ones, but allowing for this it is clear that the name was particularly common in Norfolk and Suffolk, although it was not derived from a specifically regional occupation.

The numbers of persons bearing surnames derived from farming occupations, or from the classes of rural society, must, as already remarked, be considered surprisingly small, and this despite the commonness of a few individual surnames in the category, such as Reeve, Hayward, or Day. This is in contrast to the great number and variety of occupational surnames connected with textile manufactures. Of the basic processes, spinning has given rise to very few surnames. The surname le Spinner occurs once in the Suffolk subsidy of 1327, but no name derived from spinning occurs in the Norfolk 1329-30 subsidy, and by the early 16th century the surname Spinner seems to have disappeared from both counties.[114] The rareness of the name was probably due to spinning being largely a female occupation. The surname Thrower, perhaps derived from the production of silk thread, is rather more common. There are a moderate number of instances of the name in Norfolk and Suffolk in the period *c.* 1250-1350, and the Latin *iaculator*, which appears as a bye-name in Suffolk early in the 12th century, may be a translation of Thrower.[115] If this surname is connected with such a specialised, and luxury, trade as the production of silk thread, it is surprising to find that those bearing the name are dispersed in rural areas, and that they are concentrated neither in major towns, such as Norwich, nor in any rural area where it might be supposed such a trade had become specialised. Wool-combing, another operation in the early stages of textile production, has given rise to the surnames Comber, Combester or Comester, and Kempster, none of which are at all common. The French form Peyneresse, which occurs once, is probably a translation of one of them. Most of the instances found of all these names are at Norwich.[116] Combester seems to have disappeared by the early 16th century, and of the other two names, Comber (or Comer) is much the most common in Norfolk, Kempster in Suffolk. However, most of those called Kempster in Suffolk are concentrated in a fairly small area in the two adjoining hundreds of Bosmere and Claydon, and Carlford, while of those called Comber (or Comer) in Norfolk, more than half are in one area in northwest Norfolk, in Gallow and Brothercross hundreds.[117] It is reasonable to see in this distribution the ramification of a single family called Kempster in Suffolk, and of another called Comber in Norfolk. The distribution of these surnames in the early 16th century bears no resemblance to the way occurrences of the surnames concerned are distributed *c.* 1250-1360, nor does it seem possible that it is linked with the distribution of wool-combing as an occupation at any period.

It is, however, the later stages of textile production, weaving, fulling, dyeing, and tailoring, that have given rise to the greatest number of surnames. In medieval East Anglia the most common surname derived from weaving was Webster, which occurs five times in the Norfolk subsidy for 1329-30, and five times also in the Suffolk subsidy for 1327.[118] Occurrences of the name in other sources are fairly numerous.[119] In the Suffolk subsidy for 1327 le Webbere occurs three times, and le Webbe occurs seven times, but neither name occurs in the Norfolk subsidy for 1329-30.[120] These three names seem originally to have had a marked local distribution in East Anglia. The name Webster occurs in Norfolk in a moderate number of instances before 1329-30,[121] and the occurrences of the name in Suffolk in 1327 are all in north Suffolk, all save one in places closely adjoining the Norfolk boundary, though widely separated.[122] The surname occurs in the same part of Suffolk in

the 13th century.[123] The name Webbe does not appear in the
Norfolk 1329-30 subsidy, though it can be found, exceptionally, in
the county during the 13th and 14th centuries,[124] and the examples
of the name in the Suffolk 1327 subsidy are all in one area in
south-west Suffolk, around Lavenham and Kersey.[125] The few
Suffolk references to the name Webber in 1327 are rather dispersed.[126] This distribution seems to persist into the late 14th and
early 15th centuries; in the Suffolk feet of fines, for example, for
that period, the name Webster occurs only in north Suffolk, while
Webbe occurs only in the south of the county, and the occurrences
of Webber remain dispersed.[127] If Norfolk and Suffolk are considered together, the three surnames under discussion seem too
widely dispersed to have been all produced by the ramification of
three individual families, all the more because by *c.* 1300 such
surnames, if hereditary at all, cannot have been so for many
generations. It has been suggested that Webbe, for long a common
surname in Essex, is a 'Saxon' surname, while Webster is an
'Anglian' one, but it would seem that the geographical division
between the two lay across the middle of Suffolk, which should
presumably be classified as an 'Anglian' county.[128] The distribution
of the three names survives in large part in some early 16th-century
sources. In Suffolk, the few instances of the name Webber are
scattered, while the name Webbe is still largely concentrated in the
southwest of the county. Of the seven occurrences of the name
Webster in the county, five are in the northeast, close to the Norfolk
border. In Norfolk, in the sources for the same period, the name
Webbe occurs only twice, while the name Webster occurs 35 times,
and is widely dispersed throughout the county. In the equivalent
sources for Essex, Webbe occurs 46 times, and Webster only twice.[129]
Weaver does occur as a surname in Norfolk during the Middle Ages,
but it is very rare.[130]

Several Latin words were used in East Anglia as translations of
the various occupational surnames derived from weaving. The
words *Telarius, Telegator, Telator, Tixtor, Textor,* and *Textrix* are
all found, but it is impossible to say what English surname these
words may represent in any instance.[131] The French terms le Tistur
and le Teler also occur.[132]

Much the most common surname derived from the operation of
cleaning cloth is Fuller, which occurs 31 times in the Norfolk
subsidy for 1329-30, and 27 times in the Suffolk subsidy for 1327.[133]
This is indeed one of the most common and most widespread occupational surnames. No certain examples of the surname Tucker
have been found in East Anglia during the Middle Ages.[134] In the
early 16th century Walker was fairly common in Norfolk, and some

instances were to be found in Suffolk, but it has not been found earlier.[135] In view of the presence in East Anglia during the Middle Ages of locative surnames from Yorkshire and Lincolnshire, where the name Walker was common, the absence of the name during the Middle Ages is surprising. The name Walkestr', which appears in 14th-century Norfolk, may perhaps have been formed from Walker on the analogy of other occupational names with the suffix -ester.[136] Of other names derived from bleaching, Battere (Beater) occurs a few times in Norfolk, and le Wllebetere (Wool Beater) occurs in one instance.[137] Blekester or Bleykester (Bleacher) also occurs in a few cases.[138]

A number of surnames are derived from cloth dyeing, but none are at all common. Lister occurs twice in the Norfolk subsidy rolls for 1329-30, and seven times in the Suffolk 1327 subsidy, and there are a moderate number of examples for both counties in other sources.[139] Litester occurs only once in the Norfolk 1329-30 subsidy, and not at all in the Suffolk 1327 subsidy returns, but there are some other occurrences in both counties.[140] These two names were presumably derived from the words normally used in medieval Norfolk for dyers. The name Dyer has been found in Norfolk during the 13th century, but it has not been noticed in the 14th and 15th centuries. It occurs twice in Suffolk in the 1327 subsidy returns.[141]

Unlike the names just discussed, Dexter (meaning 'dyer') is mainly a Suffolk name. In the form le Dykestere the name appears at Hadleigh, in Suffolk, in 1306.[142] The name was not common, and only appears once in the Suffolk 1327 subsidy, at Creeting, and once in the surviving returns for the 1381 poll tax, when it is again found at Hadleigh.[143] Other appearances of the name in Suffolk during the 14th and 15th centuries are scanty.[144] The name has not been found in Norfolk during the Middle Ages, and so far as East Anglia is concerned it seems to have been confined to a limited part of south Suffolk around Hadleigh and Ipswich. It is, however, not true that there are no early occurrences of the name outside Suffolk.[145] Early in the 16th century, however, the name appears in south Norfolk.[146] A French word meaning 'dyer', Teynturer, occurs as an East Anglian surname in the 13th and 14th centuries, but does not seem to have survived.[147]

There is a group of surnames connected with two substances used in dyeing, woad and madder. In the 13th and 14th centuries five persons with the surname Wayder or Wader have been noted in Norfolk, and there are instances of the word being used as an occupational term.[148] The name probably means either a dealer in woad, or someone who used woad for dyeing. The name seems to have disappeared in Norfolk by the 16th century, possibly having been assimilated to the much more common Wade. Wayder has not been found in Suffolk, but there another name with the same significance, Wodebetere, occurs there during the 13th and 14th centuries.[149] This name has not been found in Norfolk, and it too seems to have been lost by the 16th century. Wayder and Wodebetere were clearly always uncommon surnames, derived from a specialised occupation, but the existence of distinct surnames, derived from one trade, in two counties so closely connected as Norfolk and Suffolk indicates how local some occupational surnames were, and presumably this was also true of some occupational terms.

Similar to Wayder is the surname Mader or Madour, derived from dealing in, or dyeing with, madder. This surname appears in Norfolk from the early 13th century onwards, and there are five persons of the name in the Norfolk 1329-30 subsidy.[150] The name has not been found in Suffolk before the 16th century.[151] Some related surnames, such as Maderman, Madster, and Madermanger, which appear in other counties have not been found in either Norfolk or Suffolk, but the surname Mader appears in Lincolnshire.[152] This appears to be another example of an occupational surname with a restricted distribution.

Another stage of textile manufacture that gave rise to occupational surnames was shearing. In the 13th and early 14th centuries the most common name in Norfolk and Suffolk derived from cloth-shearing seems to have been Tunder or Thunder, which occurs in both counties, particularly at Norwich.[153] At the end of the 13th century the name Sherman appears, in Norfolk, and it is subsequently found in both counties, appearing four times in the Norfolk 1329-30 subsidy, though it is lacking from the Suffolk subsidy for 1327.[154] In the 16th-century sources Sherman is much the most common of the two names, though it is noticeable that the incidence of the name is concentrated on two areas, one in west Suffolk, the other in west Norfolk. In the same sources Thunder is only found in one area near Norwich.[155]

Many other occupational terms derived from the process of textile manufacture appear as bye-names or surnames in medieval East Anglia. There are only a few rare instances of surnames or bye-names connected with flax-dressing. Flaxman occurs twice in the Norfolk 1329-30 subsidy, but it has not been found in the Suffolk subsidy for 1327, and other occurrences of the name are few.[156] Flaxere has been found as a name once, in Norfolk, but not at all in Suffolk.[157] Linter, which probably means a flax-dresser, occurs at Norwich in the 15th century, and le Rybbere, probably derived from the process of scraping flax, occurs in Suffolk in the 14th.[158] Of these names only Flaxman appears to have survived into the 16th century, and it is unlikely that the others were ever stable hereditary surnames.[159] The name Lindraper, meaning either a maker or dealer in linen cloth, was rather more common, though so far as East Anglia is concerned the bearers of the name all seem to have been connected with Norwich.[160] This name too seems to have disappeared from East Anglia by the 16th century.

There are a number of names derived from textile processes, or from the manufacture of finished articles from textiles, that occur only once or twice in East Anglia, and many of these should probably be regarded as bye-names used occasionally, rather than as having ever been stable surnames. Names in this category were Brayd (probably a maker of braids or cords, though other origins are possible), Calour (maker of caps or coifs), Capman (cap-maker), Caperun (maker of hoods), Cardemaker (probably derived from the production of cards for wool-combing), Ceynturer (belt-maker), Clother, Felter (felt-maker), Gerdlere (girdle-maker), Gerthmakere, Kellerer (maker of cauls or caps), Lacebreyder (cord-maker), Lavender (washer of wool, flax, etc.), Mitenmaker, Packer (i.e., of wool), Quylter, Sayer (possibly a maker of serge or silk), Sekker (maker of sacks), Sheppestr' (dressmaker), Sorter (probably a sorter of wool), Sowestre (sewer), and possibly Winder.[161] Out of all these names, only Lavender and Sekker survive to appear in the early 16th-century sources in Norfolk and Suffolk[162]. Sayer survives, but has more than one possible origin.

There is a further group of occupational surnames connected with textile manufactures, rather more common than those just listed. Surnames in this category are Cappe (a metonymic for Capper), Challoner, Chapeler, Dubber, Hatter, Hood (for a maker of hoods), Hosier, Sloper, Sower, and Upholder. These surnames occur in Norfolk and Suffolk during the Middle Ages in limited numbers.[163] Of these, only Cappe, Hatter, Hood, and Sower, appear in the early 16th-century sources, and the occurrences of Hatter and Sower there appear to represent single families only.[164]

Much the most common surname derived from the production of articles out of cloth is Tailor, a name very common and widespread in East Anglia at all periods from the 13th century onwards. Another name derived from the same occupation, Parmenter, though it occurs much less frequently than Tailor, is still a common surname, and has been from the late 12th century onwards.[165] Both surnames are of course very common in England generally during the Middle Ages.[166]

Of the occupational surnames derived from the leather trades, the most numerous is Barker, in both Norfolk and Suffolk much more common than Tanner, the other name derived from the same occupation. In the Norfolk subsidy for 1329-30, Barker appears as a surname 27 times, and there are some further occurrences where it is uncertain if the surname involved is a form of Barker, or a contraction of one of the medieval Latin words meaning shepherd.[167] In the Suffolk 1327 subsidy the same surname occurs 29 times, mostly in central Suffolk.[168] The corresponding figures for Tanner are five in Norfolk and two in Suffolk.[169] The Latin *Tannator*, which occurs in both the Norfolk and Suffolk subsidies, may be a translation of either name.[170] If the distribution of the surnames Tanner and Barker in Norfolk in 1329-30 is examined, it is clear that the great majority of the occurrences of Barker are in east Norfolk, and especially in the northeast of the county, while Tanner occurs only in west Norfolk, and the Latin *Tannator*, which only appears in a few hundreds and is apparently there a translation of Tanner, is very largely confined to west Norfolk too. The surnames involved here seem to be too numerous and widespread to represent merely the ramification of a few families, especially at such an early date as 1329, and it is probable that different terms were in use for those engaged in tanning in different parts of Norfolk. It is perhaps significant that in the list of Norwich freemen Tanner does not occur as a surname until Elizabeth I's reign, whereas Barker occurs quite frequently from the mid-14th century onwards.[171] In Suffolk, Barker appears to have been much the most common name. However, it seems likely that in the 13th century the surnames Tanner and Barker were at times interchanged; for example, the Walter Barkere who appears at South Creake, Norfolk, *c.* 1260-80, is almost certainly the same person as Walter Tannur, who occurs at South Creake during the same period.[172] In the early 16th-century sources, Barker is quite a common name in Norfolk and Suffolk, while Tanner is rare in Norfolk, and has not been found in Suffolk.[173]

The only other surname derived from the leather trades that was at all common in medieval East Anglia was Sutor, or Souter, which occurs 42 times in the Norfolk 1329-30 subsidy, and 26 times in the Suffolk 1327 subsidy, and is also common in other medieval sources for both counties[174]. By the early 16th century this name had become for some reason much less common, and in the sources for that period it occurs much less frequently in both counties than it does in the 14th century. Moreover the Norfolk examples of the name in the early 16th-century sources are nearly all concentrated in the north east of the county, and it may be suspected that they represent the ramification of a single family only.[175] The surnames

Cobler and Cluter, both derived from shoe repairing, were always rare, but do occur in both Norfolk and Suffolk during the Middle Ages.[176] Both are absent from the early 16th-century sources for the two counties. Other surnames derived from related occupations have similarly declined or disappeared in East Anglia. Cordwainer occurs as a surname three times in the Norfolk 1329-30 subsidy, and three times in the Suffolk subsidy for 1327, but in the early 16th-century sources (which contain many more names than the 14th-century ones) there is only one occurrence of Cordwayner, and one further occurrence of Cordner.[177] Corviser occurs as a surname or bye-name in 13th-century Norfolk but subsequently disappears.[178] The extinction of a few rare surnames is not surprising, but the sharp decline of a very common name like Souter is difficult to explain. It can hardly have been due to a fall in shoemaking, and does not seem to have been caused by the rise of any new occupational surname. Shoemaker appears in Norfolk as a surname in the early 16th century, but it remained rare.[179]

One other surname connected with shoemaking is worth mentioning. Clouting, a name derived from the cobbling of shoes, occurs in Hoxne hundred, Suffolk, in 1327, and also later in the 14th century in the same part of the county. In the 16th century the name is still to be found in the same hundred.[180] The surname has not been found elsewhere in Suffolk, or in Norfolk, and this does seem to be an instance of a rare occupational surname remaining confined to a limited district for more than two centuries.

There are numerous surnames derived from metal-working, but for the most part these are not peculiar to East Anglia, and do not merit detailed discussion here.[181] Smith, and its Latin translation *Faber*, if taken together were already much the most common occupational surname in the 14th century, and Marshall, which in most cases should probably be taken to mean a blacksmith, though much less numerous than Smith is one of the more common surnames at the same period. A third surname derived from the smith's occupation Ferrour, is much less common than either Smith or Marshall, but it is nevertheless widely dispersed throughout Norfolk and Suffolk from the 13th century onward.[182] The French *le Fevere* occurs during the 13th century and the first half of the 14th, but it is noticeably confined to a few sources, such as final concords and some of the Norwich city records, and it seems likely that it is a translation of the vernacular Smith.[183] The Latin *Faber*, which is very common in certain sources, is no doubt also usually a translation of Smith. Neither *Faber* nor Fever occur as surnames in the early 16th-century sources for Norfolk and Suffolk.[184]

When the surnames derived from the rarer and more specialised metal trades are examined, it can be seen that the distribution of some is surprisingly scattered. It might be expected that goldsmiths would only be found in the larger towns, such as Norwich, Lynn, Ipswich, and Bury St. Edmunds, and that early examples of surnames derived from their trade would be found in such places; though this would obviously cease to apply as surnames became hereditary, and gradually became dispersed from the localities where they originated. However, if the persons in East Anglia bearing bye-names or surnames derived from goldsmithing (Goldsmith, Gelder, Goldbeater, with the Latin *Aurifaber* and the French *Orfevre*) listed in a wide selection of sources for the period 1100-1400 are considered, it can be seen that while they occur at Norwich, Bury, and Lynn, they also occur in many small villages.[185] The same is true of the various surnames derived from working with lead (Leadsmith, Leadbeater, Plummer, and Plumbe), and also of some other surnames derived from the metal trades, such as Tinker and Cutler, both of which were widely distributed during the period in question.[186] There are, however, some occupational surnames derived from the metal trades that seem to have been largely confined to a few important towns before about 1400. This is true, for instance, of the surnames derived from working in brass (Latoner, Brazier, and Brasman), which occur almost entirely at a few towns. Most bearers of such names to appear in East Anglia before 1400 were inhabitants of Norwich, and the other places where such names occur are mostly towns of some size, such as Ipswich, Lavenham, Bury St. Edmunds, or Sudbury.[187] It is also true of the surnames derived from lock-making (Locksmith, Lokyer, and Lockman), which before 1400 occur at Norwich, Lynn, Thetford, and Bury St. Edmunds, while only two cases have been found of such names occurring outside towns of some size.[188] It is perhaps a fair deduction that some occupations in the metal working trades were confined to the larger towns.

There are many surnames, or bye-names, derived from the metal trades that were always very rare in Norfolk and Suffolk. The majority of these are to be found only in the period *c.* 1250-1350, and it is probable that in most cases they never became stable hereditary surnames at all, but should be considered as bye-names used at times by individuals. Such names that have been found in Norfolk and Suffolk in *c.* 1250-1350 are Aguiller (needle-maker), Ankersmith, Armurer, Blades (bladesmith), Cloer (nailer), Digard (spurrier), Founder, Lolimer (lorimer), Needler, Peutrerer (Pewterer), Pundermaker (maker of balances), Pynne (pin maker), and Rivet (rivetter).[189] Two similar rare bye-names that occur before 1250 are Canner and Paner, and two that have not been found in

Norfolk or Suffolk before the 15th century are Bladesmith and Wyredrawer, though Wyredrawer is a name that occurs earlier in other parts of the country.[190] In addition two obscure compounds of Smith occur, Koosmith and Exsmith (probably for axe-smith).[191] Out of all these, only Ankersmith, Needler, Pynne, and Panner survive to appear in the early 16th-century sources.[192]

The trade of bell-making, which can hardly have employed a great number of persons, has surprisingly given rise to two surnames. The name Belleyeter occurs at Norwich, Lynn, and Bury St. Edmunds.[193] By contrast the surname Senter, which also derives from bell-founding, occurs in the 14th century in south Norfolk and north Suffolk, away from large towns.[194] Again, it is surprising to find at an early period in the countryside a surname derived from such a specialised occupation. The surname Belyet, which occurs in Norfolk in 1524, may be a survival of Belleyeter, but otherwise there is no trace of either surname in the early 16th-century sources. The surname Billiter, a corruption of Belleyeter, has not been found in Norfolk or Suffolk, either in the Middle Ages or in the early 16th-century sources.[195]

One other rather uncommon surname is Enginour, sometimes abbreviated to le Ginour, or Jenour. A William Enginur is mentioned in Suffolk at the beginning of the 13th century, and he later appears as holding land at Market Weston, in north Suffolk, and at Thorney and Creeting, in the centre of the county.[196] A family called le Ginour, who appear during the 14th century holding land in central Suffolk, were probably his descendants.[197] By about 1280 another family called l'Engenour, probably also descended from William, were freeholders at Market Weston and elsewhere in north Suffolk, and probably to be classed as franklins. This family continued to hold land in the area into the 14th century, and a Robert Jenour who appears in the Suffolk 1327 subsidy roll is probably the same person as the Robert L'engynur or le Ginur who appears holding land at Weston and elsewhere.[198] There are scattered occurrences of the name in Norfolk during the 13th and 14th centuries, which appear to relate to the family that held land at Weston.[199] In this case there seems to be good grounds for suspecting that all the bearers of the name in the 13th and 14th centuries in Norfolk and Suffolk were related. The surname Genour, or Jener, which occurs in Suffolk in the 16th century, is probably derived from this family.[200]

There are numerous occupational surnames derived from the food trades, but they do not show any clear regional or local characteristics. The surnames Millor, Mylyur, Milner, Melner, Meller, and Muner, for examples, all occur in Norfolk and Suffolk in the period *c.* 1250-1400, but do not show any very distinct local distribution, though the forms Melner and Meller are perhaps more usual in Suffolk than in Norfolk.²⁰¹ Moliner, a rare name everywhere, has only been found once in East Anglia during the Middle Ages in Suffolk, Grinder, also rare, has also been found only once, in Norfolk, and Milward has not been found at all, though it existed in Essex, and seems to have been fairly common in some parts of England.²⁰² Numerous occupational terms connected with the food trades appear as surnames or bye-names in medieval East Anglia. There are those connected with spices and flavourings, such as Kanell, Spicer, Peper, Mustarder, Mustardman, Sauser, Salter, and Saltman.²⁰³ There are those connected with the production of various types of bread, Blankpayn, Bonpain, Wafre, Wastel, Saltwastel, Reybred, Fresschebred, Whetelof, Wygger (bun-maker), and Whitbred.²⁰⁴ There are also the more general terms derived from baking, Baker and Baxter, which are discussed below, and Pestur, which occurs occasionally in Norfolk and Suffolk.²⁰⁵ There are surprisingly few names derived from butchery, Butcher being quite rare in any form, Fleshhewere being even less common, and the very rare Ketmonger (meat-seller) occurring only once, in Norfolk. Slaughter is a rare name that seems to have originated in Suffolk and Essex. It occurs occasionally in Suffolk, but has not been found in Norfolk.²⁰⁶ It is curious that the name Pulter (a dealer in poultry) is rather more common than Butcher.²⁰⁷ There are also two rare names, Hennemongere and Geliner, that derive from poultry dealing.²⁰⁸ Apart from Brewer and Brewster, which are discussed below, all the names derived from the production of drink are rare. Vintner is the most common.²⁰⁹ Maltster is a rather rare surname, and Maltmilnere, Medemaker, and Medeman (which may be a toponymic), occur in isolated cases, and should probably be ranked as bye-names rather than as stable surnames.²¹⁰.

Of the names mentioned in the preceding paragraph, Miller and Meller survive in the early 16th-century sources for both Norfolk and Suffolk, but surprisingly Milner and Melner had disappeared by that time.²¹¹ Of the other names mentioned, Peper, Spicer, and Salter survived, and were fairly numerous in both counties in the early 16th century. Butcher remained rare, with only one occurrence in the early 16th-century sources in Norfolk, and none in Suffolk.²¹² Buckmonger, Pulter, Maltster, Vintner, and Whitbred all survived into the 16th century as rare surnames, but the remaining names mentioned had been lost.²¹³ In this group, as in others, there was clearly a high casualty rate among occupational surnames. Milner and Melner may well have been absorbed by Miller and Meller, and Saltman may have been absorbed by Salman, a fairly common name in 16th-century Norfolk and Suffolk, but the remainder seem to have become extinct in the two counties.

The most widespread, and perhaps the most celebrated, of the occupational surnames in East Anglia connected with the food trade is of course Cook, or Coke. This was already a very common name in Norfolk and Suffolk by the 14th century, and widely distributed in both counties.[214]

When the various occupational surnames derived from retailing, or mercantile, trades are examined, it is obvious that while as might be expected early occurrences are found mostly in boroughs or market towns, by the 16th century no such distribution can be detected. The surname Mercer, for example, occurs before 1400 in Norfolk and Suffolk at Norwich and Bury St. Edmunds, at East Dereham, Reepham, and Beccles, all market towns, at the Norfolk villages of Tattersett, and South Creake, and the Suffolk village of Gazeley. The Mercer occurring at Reepham is known to have been a Londoner, and the occurrences at Tattersett and South Creake, which are neighbouring parishes, probably all relate to members of one family.[215] Similarly the surname Draper has been found before 1400 at Norwich, at Shipden, then a port, at the Suffolk market towns of Beccles, Brandon, and Haverhill, and at the Norfolk villages of Tilney, Kettlestone, Smallworth and Shernbourne, while early in the 15th century the name occurs at both Lynn and Thetford.[216] This group of names is perhaps the only category of occupational surnames where there is an obviously close connection between the distribution of early occurrences of the surname, and the distribution of the occupations from which the surnames were derived. In the early 16th-century sources the distribution of such names had changed. At that period the surname Mercer has not been found in Suffolk, though it was certainly present later in the century, and in Norfolk it only occurs once, at the village of Wighton. In the same sources the surname Draper occurs eight times in Norfolk and six times in Suffolk. The places concerned included Ipswich and the small town of Market Weston, but otherwise were all villages.[217] There are also a number of rarer words for retail occupations which occur as surnames, or perhaps just as bye-names, at Norwich but not elsewhere in East Anglia so far as has been discovered. Hennemongere, Waxmongere, Fisshmongere, and Lyndraper are examples.[218] It is true that there are exceptions to the usual distribution of occupational names derived from trading or retailing. The surnames Merchant and Chapman were both common and widely distributed throughout Norfolk and Suffolk by the 14th century, though as sometimes both names were borne by bondmen it is likely that there were occasionally really nicknames rather than occupational surnames.[219] A few surnames or bye-names derived from retailing, such as Hukestere, Melman, or Hirynmonger make isolated appearances in villages,[220] and there are a few cases of surnames derived from retailing that were established in rural areas at an early date and ramified there.

One group of such names worth a brief examination is that derived from tallow-chandling. In the first half of the 14th century Talghmongere appears as a surname at Dilham and Tottington, two widely-separated Norfolk villages. It has been suggested that this name is derived from the selling of tails (meaning probably a dealer in horsehair) but it seems much more likely that it derives from the selling of tallow, and the spelling of the name as it occurs at Dilham seems to confirm this. The surname Talughman or Talweman, which occurs in the 16th century at two Norfolk villages, Grimston and Bawdeswell, clearly also means a dealer in tallow, and the surname Talman, which occurs at Congham, near Grimston, and also in the adjoining Smithdon Hundred, is almost certainly a slightly corrupted form of Talughman, though Talman also has been understood to mean a seller of horse-tails. These names all appear in Norfolk villages. They have not been found in Suffolk, and seem to have become extinct by the 16th century.[221]

Few surnames connected with the building trades show any special characteristics, though it is interesting that the commoner names derived from building crafts, Mason for example, are to be found in the 14th century widely scattered in East Anglia, and not confined to large towns of any one district.[222] It is however worth examining the East Anglian surnames derived from the various crafts connected with roofing. One of these is Reder, derived from the thatching of roofs with reeds. The use of reeds or rushes for thatching was certainly not confined to East Anglia, but the name Reder seems to have been much more common in Norfolk than anywhere else, though it does occur in Suffolk and Essex from the 13th century onwards. In medieval Suffolk the name has only been found in a limited district in the north west of the county, but in Norfolk the name was not confined to any one area such as present district of the Broads, or the fens in the west of the county.[223] This should probably be reckoned as primarily an East Anglian surname, much more common in that area than elsewhere.

Of the other occupational surnames connected with the roofing trades, Coverer occurs during the 13th century in Norfolk, but it is rare at that period, and seems to have become extinct subsequently.[224] It has not been found in Suffolk. The surnames Thatcher and Thacker occur in Norfolk and Suffolk from the 13th century onwards. Both names are uncommon, and in Norfolk the occurrences

C

during the 13th and 14th centuries are mostly in the west of the county.[225] Thaxter (or Thakester) on the other hand appears to be a surname confined to Norfolk, where during the 13th and 14th centuries it was an uncommon name, occurring in several parts of the county. This is in marked contrast to the position in the early 16th century, when the name was more numerous, and largely confined to north-east Norfolk.[226] In the early 16th-century sources for Norfolk, Thatcher has not been found, possibly because it was assimilated to the rather more common Thaxter, but Thakker survived.[227] Slater has not been found in Norfolk or Suffolk during the Middle Ages but Tiler or Tyeler occurs as a rare surname in both counties, from the 13th century onwards.[228]

There remain a great variety of occupational surnames or bye-names that have not been discussed, many of them rare. There are however, some quite common names that have not been mentioned. Cooper, Carpenter, and Turner, for example, were all both common and widespread in Norfolk and Suffolk from the 13th century onwards, but none of them was peculiar to the region, and there seems to be nothing of especial significance about the distribution of any of them in East Anglia. Very many occupational terms occur as surnames or bye-names in medieval Norfolk and Suffolk; there were, for instance, a group of names signifying actor, musician, and so forth, Leyker, Jestour, Chanter, Harper, Sytoler, Tabour, Tabourer, Synger, Ruter, Gleiwman, Rimer, and possibly, Solfa;[229] there are a few names derived from basket-making, Skepper, Skippe, Skeppe, and Lepmaker;[230] names derived from various forms of transport, Driver, Carter, Berere, Saylur, Boatman, Sumpter, Sterman, Shipman, and Coger;[231] names from grinding and polishing. Grater, Fourbour, and Furbisher;[232] and names derived from hunting and hawking, Veneur, Hunt, Hunter, Hunteman, Hauker, Fauconer, and Ostricier.[233] Other groups could be cited from amongst the very numerous and varied occupational terms that occur as surnames or bye-names. Many individual names in this category, however, were always very rare, and in some cases seem never to have become hereditary. Few were peculiar to East Anglia, and it is unwise to draw deductions from the distribution of the few known occurrences of a very rare name. Many occupational surnames that occur in Norfolk and Suffolk during the Middle Ages will therefore not be discussed. Middle English terms for occupations have of course been extensively discussed in print elsewhere.[234]

There are, however, some general deductions that can be made from the foregoing consideration of East Anglian occupational surnames. In most cases it is not possible to draw conclusions about the distribution of any industry from the occurrences of occupational surnames. There are obvious instances in which the distribution of occupational surnames does coincide with the distribution of actual occupations, in a broad way, as is the case with the surnames derived from the retail trades, discussed above,[235] but usually such coincidence is lacking, and many occupational surnames are too rare for any safe conclusions to be drawn from the sparse occurrences. Furthermore, two factors complicate any attempt to use occupational surnames as evidence for the location of any given trade. One of these is the very local distribution of some occupational surnames, such as those derived from weaving, or dyeing, already discussed.[236] Even within a single county, some occupational terms seem to have been largely confined to certain districts. The geographical spread of occupational surnames, and indeed of occupational terms in general, has been as yet insufficiently explored. The valuable work done by Fransson and Thuresson did include some consideration of the way in which such terms, and surnames derived from them, were distributed, but both these scholars confined the more intensive parts of their researches to a limited number of counties.[237]

The other factor that affects the distribution of surnames is the apparent origin of some less common occupational surnames from a single family. The case of the surname Enginour has already been considered,[238] and other examples could be given. To take one further example, the surname Shipman appears in Norfolk before 1350 only in one area, at Burnham on the north coast of the county.[239] At the end of the 14th century it occurs at Norwich, but it may be suspected that this is due to a migration from the Burnham area to the city.[240] The same surname also occurs in Suffolk in one particular district, the hundred of Blackbourne, where it is found in the townships of Langham and Bardwell from the late 13th century onwards.[241] It may be suspected that here, too, there was a single family in each county which bore the name. Other examples could be given of similar cases where an occupational surname appears for a considerable period in only one or two townships in a county, and where it may be strongly suspected that all the bearers of the name in the county descended from a single family, even though the obscurity of most families with occupational surnames during the Middle Ages makes this impossible to prove.

The very local character of some occupational surnames is made the more marked by the absence of any significant influx of such surnames into East Anglia from other regions. Walker, for example, though common in the north of England including Lincolnshire, has not been found in Norfolk or Suffolk during the Middle Ages.[242]

It is possible to find examples of uncommon occupational surnames which are said to have been confined to other regions occurring in Norfolk and Suffolk during the Middle Ages. Sedeman, for instance, has been said to have been confined to the north and the west Midlands, but it occurs in medieval Norfolk,[243] and the surname Plater, which has been said to occur only at London, is found in Norfolk.[244] These may be immigrant surnames, but with such rare names it is difficult to say anything certain about their distribution, or about the regions where they originated. In fact it has not been possible to discover any clear case in which an occupational surname from outside East Anglia came into the region during the Middle Ages and established itself there. In this occupational surnames contrast markedly with locative ones, for locative surnames from other regions are found in Norfolk and Suffolk in fair numbers from the 13th century onwards.[245]

There is a great difference between the distribution of many occupational surnames in the period *c.* 1250-1400, and the distribution in the early 16th century. Some surnames which are to be found widely dispersed in *c.* 1250-1400 are to be found in the early 16th century much more concentrated, and grouped together in a way making it seem likely that all the bearers of the surnames in question were members of the same family. The surname Thaxter, discussed above, is an example of this. The contrast in the distribution at different periods is no doubt due to the fact that many of the names occurring during *c.* 1250-1400 never became hereditary, and that in other cases families possessing hereditary occupational surnames became extinct. The disappearance during the later Middle Ages of many rare occupational surnames is no doubt due to the same causes.

One group of surnames remains to be dealt with, those that are derived from office or status. Something has already been said about surnames derived from the classes in the agricultural community.

Many surnames derived from exalted ranks were clearly nicknames. This applies to such relatively common names as King, Bishop, or Earl, as well as to such rare names as le Emprur, le Cunte, or Prince, all of which occur in medieval Norfolk or Suffolk.[246] In some cases such names may have been used as personal names in the first instance, and then have been inherited as surnames by the descendants of the original bearer. Prince, for example, was used during the 14th century as a personal name at Wymondham, Norfolk, where the son of a bondman called Prince appears as William *filius Prynce* or William 'Pryncissone'.[247] In the majority of cases, however, surnames in this category no doubt originated as nicknames. *Hugo Pseudo Archidiaconus*, A norfolk tenant of Ramsey Abbey in the 12th century, was presumably nicknamed Archdeacon, and was perhaps referred to thus to distinguish him from a contemporary Hugh who was in actual fact an archdeacon.[248]

Some other surnames derived from less exalted ranks, such as Knight, Squire, and Page, were clearly sometimes at least nicknames too, Page, for example, occurs in the 13th century as the surname of a serf. This cannot have been his actual rank or occupation, nor did he inherit it, since his father's name was Ralph Coket.[249] In this case Page can hardly have been anything else but a nickname. William 'le Knyght', a customary tenant at Bardwell, Suffolk, in the 13th century, was clearly no knight, and can hardly have been descended from one.[250] There are many other cases of persons surnamed Knight or Page during the 13th or early 14th centuries whose status was clearly humble.[251] In such cases the names involved are unlikely to have been hereditary for any long period, if indeed they were hereditary at all, and it is improbable that persons who were only a generation or two from knightly ancestors could have been reduced to the status of unfree tenants. Such names as Page and Knight must therefore have originated sometimes, perhaps frequently, as nicknames. No doubt there were surnames that in some instances were derived from the actual holding of office, while in others they originated as nicknames. A Norfolk man, William Justyse, was a constable in 1273, and very probably derived his name from that office. On the other hand, in the 13th and early 14th centuries the surname Justice was borne in Suffolk by peasants, one of whom was holding land in villeinage, and in these cases the surname probably originated as a nickname.[252]

Though there are many surnames derived from rank or office to be found in East Anglia, they are not peculiar to the region, and do not require discussion here. Even some common and widespread surnames in this category, however, were very unevenly distributed throughout the country. To take one example, the fairly common name Chamberlain was borne by 10 persons listed in the Suffolk assessments for the lay subsidy granted in 1523; if the surviving Norfolk assessments for the same subsidy are conflated with the returns for the 1522 'Military Survey' in the same county, then there are 31 persons called Chamberlain in the two sources combined, although the Norfolk lists contain only a slightly larger number of names than the Suffolk assessments. In the Buckinghamshire returns for the same subsidy, there is only one person called Chamberlain listed, and in the corresponding returns for Sussex there are only two, though the Sussex lists contain well over half the number of persons that appear in the Norfolk lists cited, and the Buckinghamshire lists slightly less than half.[253] It does not seem that this situation is the result of one family called Chamberlain, or even several, gradually spreading through Norfolk, for the name was already widespread there in the early 14th century.[254]

It was pointed out many years ago by Fransson that occupational surnames of the forms ending in -ster (Brewster, Webster, Baxter, etc.) were much more common in some counties than others, and that Norfolk was one county where such surnames were especially common.[255] It is generally true that the occupational surnames ending in -ster are more common in Norfolk than the corresponding surnames without that suffix. In Suffolk, too, this is generally the case, though not to quite the same extent. In the Norfolk subsidy returns for 1329-30, for example, Brewster occurs six times as a surname, while Brewer does not occur at all. In the Suffolk subsidy for 1327, Brester occurs nine times, and again Brewer does not occur. In Norfolk in 1329-30, Baxter occurs twelve times, and Baker only three, while in Suffolk in 1327, Baxter occurs eleven times, and Baker thirteen. Similarly Webster occurs five times in the Norfolk 1329-30 returns, while Weaver, Webbe, and Webber do not occur at all. In the Suffolk returns for 1327, Webster occurs five times, Webbe seven times, and Webber three, while Weaver does not occur.[256] Similar figures could be given for other surnames of the same types, though many of the names involved are too rare for much significance to be attributed to statistics about their incidence.

In the absence of a sufficient body of Middle English texts from East Anglia it is difficult to say whether this occurrence of the two categories of surnames corresponded with the general usage of occupational terms in Norfolk and Suffolk. However, in the Norwich Free Book, which records the names of those admitted to the freedom of the city, forms in -ster (webestere, litestere, backestere or baxtere) are usually employed to give freemen's occupations up to the early 15th century.[257] In the early 15th century the usage is for a short time very varied. Robert Sterve, baxtere, and Thomas Denys, baker, appear in consecutive entries in 1402-3, and Roger Starlyng, wevere, and John Bennes, webster, in two other consecutive entries at the same date.[258] Later in the 15th century, however, such forms as weaver, lister, baker, and so forth are generally used, with words ending in -ster only exceptionally.[259]

Little need be said about the other suffixes used in occupational surnames. -maker occurs as a suffix to a limited number of surnames, all of them rare. Names found in Norfolk or Suffolk with this suffix, which are not included in the list of such surnames published by Fransson, are Colermaker, Gerthmakere, and Mitenmaker, which are self-explanatory;[260] Patynmaker, probably a maker of wooden shoes;[261] Tassemakere, which probably means a stacker of hay or peat in cocks;[262] Cardemakere, probably a maker of 'cards' for wool-combing;[263] Heynngmakere, probably a maker of hinges;[264] Slyngmaker, no doubt a maker of slings, perhaps for use against birds;[265] Euermaker, probably a maker of water vessels;[266] Pantermaker, probably a maker of bird snares;[267] and Cherchemakere, whose occupation remains obscure.[268] All these names are rare. The majority of surnames ending in -maker found in East Anglia during the Middle Ages occur in connection with Norwich, and many names in this group are only found in the late 13th and 14th centuries.

Of other suffixes occurring in occupational surnames, -monger appears in a small number of names, most of which have already been mentioned. All the names in this category were rare, and many are only found in the late 13th and early 14th centuries, often with only one known instance. -wright occurs as a suffix in a small number of surnames. Huelwrihte occurs as a surname or bye-name in the late 11th century,[269] but both the surname Wright, and surnames formed from compounds of -wright, are rarely found before the late 13th century, probably because the very common Latin word *Carpentarius* was used to translate such names.

None of the three groups of surnames just discussed (those compounded from -maker, -monger, and -wright) were at all numerous in East Anglia, and indeed most of the individual surnames involved were rare. None of the three groups presented any distinctive characteristics in East Anglia.

References

[1] D. C. Douglas, ed., *Feudal Documents from the Abbey of Bury St. Edmunds*, pp. 25-8, 32

[2] *Ibid.*, pp. 28-30, 37-8

[3] Davis, ed., *Kalendar of Abbot Samson, passim*

[4] W. H. Hart and P. A. Lyons, ed., *Cartularium Monasterii de Ramesia* (Rolls Series) (1893), vol. iii, pp. 261-9, 285-91

[5] W. Stubbs, ed., *Great Roll of the Pipe for the 12th Year of Henry II* (Pipe Roll Society, vol. ix) (1888), pp. 21-30

[6] Anon, *Calendar of the Freemen of Lynn* (1913), pp. 1-51; J. L'Estrange, ed., *Calendar of the Freemen of Norwich, 1317-1603* (1888), *passim*; R. A. McKinley, *Norfolk Names in the Sixteenth Century* (1969) p. 34

[7]*See*, e.g. Douglas, *op. cit.*, pp. 27, 32, 40; W. Stubbs, ed., *Great Roll of the Pipe for the 12th Year of Henry II*, p. 34; J. H. Round, ed., *Great Roll of the Pipe for the 34th Year of Henry II* (Pipe Roll Society, vol. xxxviii) (1925), p. 62

[8]*See*, e.g. Douglas, *op. cit.*, pp. 24, 29, 30, 169-70; J. H. Round, ed., *Great Roll of the Pipe for the 23rd Year of Henry II* (Pipe Roll Society, vol. xxvi) (1905), p. 139; Hart and Lyons, *op. cit.*, vol. iii, p. 264; Davis ed., *Kalendar of Abbot Samson*, pp. 48, 49

[9]*See*, e.g. W. Stubbs, ed., *Great Roll of the Pipe for the 12th Year of Henry II*, p. 24; J. H. Round, ed., *Great Roll of the Pipe for the 23rd Year of Henry II*, p. 137; Davis, ed., *Kalendar of Abbot Samson*, pp. 95, 137

[10]*See*, e.g. Douglas, *op. cit.*, pp. 120, 169-70; Stubbs, *op. cit.*, p. 22; D. M. Stenton, ed., *Great Roll of the Pipe for the 5th Year of Richard I* (Pipe Roll Society, New Series, vol. iii) (1927), pp. 21, 25; Davis, *Kalendar of Abbot Samson*, pp. 49, 62; B. Dodwell, ed., *Feet of Fines for the County of Norfolk, 1201-15, and for the County of Suffolk, 1199-1214*, pp. 246-7

[11]*See*, e.g. Stubbs, *op. cit.*, pp. 23-4; D. M. Stenton, ed., *Great Roll of the Pipe for the 5th Year of Richard I*, p. 22; Davis, ed., *Kalendar of Abbot Samson*, pp. 77, 85; Dodwell, *op. cit.*, pp. 239-40; Bedingfeld, ed., *Cartulary of Creake Abbey*, pp. 37, 43, 50, 51

[12]Anon., ed., *Great Roll of the Pipe for the 14th Year of Henry II* (Pipe Roll Society, xii) (1890), p. 32; Hart and Lyons, *op. cit.*, vol. iii, p. 268

[13]P.R.O. E179/149/7, mm. 13, 18, 23, 27, 29, 44, 47, 49, 50, 52, 63-4

[14]Anon., *Suffolk in 1327* (Suffolk Green Books, vol. ix) (1906), pp. 11, 12, 15, 23, 27, 37, 44, 47, 58, 62, 69, 85, 105, 113, 119, 122, 131, 136, 138, 155, 158, 162, 173, 174, 180, 189, 190, 194, 204, 206

[15]*See*, e.g., D. C. Douglas, *op. cit.*, pp. 26, 40; J. H. Round, ed., *Great Roll of the Pipe for the 27th Year of Henry II* (Pipe Roll Soc., vol. xxx) (1909), p. 89; D. M. Stenton, ed., *Great Roll of the Pipe for the 11th Year of John* (Pipe Roll Soc. New Series, vol. xxiv) (1949), p. 46; E. Powell, ed., *A Suffolk Hundred in the Year 1283* (1910), tables 1, 3, 7, 12, 14, 22, 23, 25; Davis, ed., *Kalendar of Abbot Samson*, p. 44; *Rotuli Hundredorum* (Record Commission) (1812), vol. i, pp. 439, 444

[16]Powell, *A Suffolk Hundred in the Year 1283*, p. 69, tables 7, 26; *Suffolk in 1327*, p. 65; B. Thuresson, *Middle English Occupational Terms* (1950), 168; W. Rye, *Calendar of Deeds Relating to Norwich 1285-1306*, pp. 85, 94, 109; Rye, *Cal. Norf. Fines*, vol. i, p. 73

[17]P.R.O. E179/149/7, mm. 7, 10, 11, 19, 36, 42, 43, 48, 56, 59, 62, 64, 65

[18]*Suffolk in 1327*, pp. 3, 6, 13, 35, 49, 66, 70, 84, 87, 97, 104, 118, 133, 134, 135, 145, 156, 159, 169, 170, 173, 178, 184, 185, 191, 195, 205, 206

[19]*See*, e.g. P.R.O. E179/149/7, mm. 3, 16, 22, 33, 42, 44, 50, 51, 54, 62, 68; Powell, ed., *A Suffolk Hundred in 1283*, tables 3, 16, 18; *Rotuli Hundredorum*, vol. i, pp. 435, 453, 487, 497; vol. ii, p. 159

[20]Parker occurs as a surname 12 times in the Norfolk subsidy for 1329-30 (P.R.O. E179/149/7, mm. 29, 49, 51, 53, 57, 62) and 17 times in the Suffolk subsidy for 1327 (*Suffolk in 1327*, pp. 29, 32, 35, 57, 82, 86, 103, 109, 146, 153, 156, 209, 213, 222)

[21]Warner occurs as a surname nine times in the Norfolk subsidy for 1329-30 (P.R.O. E179/149/7, mm. 8, 11, 22, 27, 36, 37, 58) and 19 times in the Suffolk subsidy for 1327 (*Suffolk in 1327*, pp. 11, 54, 57, 68, 73, 78, 79, 91, 110, 117, 157, 169, 170, 196, 209)

[22]Forester occurs eight times in the Norfolk subsidy for 1329-30 (P.R.O. E179/149/7, mm. 6, 15, 50, 56, 57) and five times in the Suffolk subsidy for 1327 (*Suffolk in 1327*, pp. 17, 143, 146)

[23]Shepherd occurs as a surname eight times in the Norfolk subsidy for 1329-30 (E179/149/7, mm. 8, 23, 29, 40, 62, 64) and 16 times in the Suffolk subsidy for 1327 (*Suffolk in 1327*, pp. 7, 24, 45, 48, 95, 105, 117, 139, 147, 155, 156, 164, 168, 220). For other occurrences, *see* e.g. Powell, *Rising in East Anglia in 1381* (1896), pp. 70, 94, 105, 106, 110, 118; Rye, *Cal. Norf. Fines*, vol. i, p. 169; vol. ii, pp. 306, 352, 411; W. Rye, ed., *Calendar of the Feet of Fines for Suffolk* (1900), pp. 115, 150, 164, 171, 227, 238, 252, 260-1

[24]*See*, e.g. P.R.O. E179/149/7, mm. 16, 33, 50, 51, 52, 64, 65; D. M. Stenton, ed., *Great Roll of the Pipe for the 9th Year of Richard I* (Pipe Roll Soc. New Series, vol. lxvi) (1931), p. 245; *Rotuli Hundredorum*, vol. ii, p. 167; *Suffolk in 1327*, p. 97

[25]*See*, e.g. P.R.O. E179/149/7, mm. 23, 25, 50, 65; *Rotuli Hundredorum*, vol. i, p. 447; Powell, *A Suffolk Hundred in 1283*, pp. 42, 92, tables 12, 21, 25, 34; P.R.O. C.133/89/8

[26]*See*, e.g. P.R.O. E179/149/7, mm. 4, 6, 15, 33, 36, 41, 42-5, 50-1, 58, 62-3; Douglas, *op. cit.*, p. 35; Rye, *Cal. Suff. Fines*, pp. 23, 88, 98, 114, 117, 128, 141, 178, 180. The Latin word *oppilio* is used occasionally: Hart and Lyons, *op. cit.*, vol. iii, p. 268

[27]*See* the numerous references cited by Thuresson, *op. cit.*, pp. 62-3

[28]*See*, e.g. Rye, *Cal. Norf. Fines*, vol. i, pp. 122, 134; vol. ii, pp. 432, 434; D. M. Stenton, ed., *Great Roll of the Pipe for the 11th Year of John*, p. 32; P.R.O. E179/149/7, mm. 23, 56; W. Rye, *Calendar of Deeds Relating to Norwich, 1285-1306* (1903), p. 18. The Latin *Bouarius*, which occurs as a surname in the 12th century is perhaps a translation of Bulman: J. H. Round, ed., *Great Roll of the Pipe for the 23rd Year of Henry II*, p. 138

[29]*See*, e.g. Norfolk and Norwich R.O., N.R.S. 18476, court held Tues. before Michaelmas, 8 Edward III; Rye, *Cal. Norf. Fines*, vol. ii, 274, 276; P.R.O. E179/149/7, mm. 6, 17, 22, 35, 40, 54, 60, 62; *Rotuli Hundredorum*, vol. i, pp. 451, 514; Rye, *Cal. Suff. Fines*, pp. 156, 312. The surname Wodehynd, probably with the same significance as Woodherd, has been found once (P.R.O. E179/149/7, m. 6), but does not seem to have survived

[30]*See* below, p. 117

[31]Rye, *Cal. Norf. Fines*, vol. i, p. 167; vol. ii, p. 310; W. Hudson, 'Three Manorial Extents of the Thirteenth Century', *Norfolk Archaeology* (1901), vol. xiv, p. 29; P.R.O. E179/149/7, m. 42; *Suffolk in 1327*, pp. 5, 24, 98, 154; *Rotuli Hundredorum*, vol. i, p. 478

[32]Norfolk and Norwich R.O., N.R.S. 18476, m. 30; P.R.O. E179/149/7, m. 43; Thuresson, *op. cit.*, p. 113; Ipswich and East Suffolk R.O., HA/12/C2/7, m. 10

[33]Powell, *Rising in East Anglia in 1381*, p. 111; Rye, *Cal. Suff. Fines*, p. 190

[34]P.R.O. E179/149/7, m. 66. The only examples of this name recorded by Thuresson (*op. cit.*, p. 64) are in Herts.

[35]P.R.O. E179/149/7, m. 59. Three persons with this surname occur in one township, presumably all related

[36]*Suffolk in 1327*, pp. 7, 166, 198; Thuresson, *op. cit.*, p. 58; P.R.O. E179/149/53, m. 11

[37]Powell, *A Suffolk Hundred in 1283*, p. 80; *Suffolk in 1327*, p. 202

[38]Hudson, *Leet Jurisdiction in Norwich*, pp. 63, 77; L'Estrange, *op. cit.*, p. 100

[39]Rye, *Cal. Suff. Fines*, p. 285. Only one occurrence found, at Mildenhall (Suff.)

[40]P.R.O. E179/149/7, m. 42; Norfolk and Norwich R.O., N.R.S. 18476, mm. 11, 12; N.R.S. 8708, Court held at St. Peter ad Vincula, 11th year of King Edward; Thuresson, *op. cit.*, p. 65

[41]Thuresson, *op. cit.*, p. 66

[42]*Suffolk in 1327*, p. 71. Only one occurrence found, at Huntingfield (Suff.)

[43]Rye, *Cal. Suff. Fines*, p. 177. Only one occurrence found, at Long Melford (Suff.)

[44]*Suffolk in 1327*, p. 195. Only one occurrence found, at Ingham (Suff.)

[45]P.R.O. E179/149/7, m. 51. Only one occurrence found, at Mattishall (Norf.)

[46]Bedingfeld, ed., *Cartulary of Creake Abbey*, p 123. Only one occurrence has been found, at Burnham Thorp (Norfolk)

[47]*Rotuli Hundredorum*, vol i, pp. 440, 481

[48]Hudson, *Leet Jurisdiction in Norwich*, p. 45; *Suffolk in 1327*, p. 47; Rye, *Cal. Suff. Fines*, p. 243

[49]Thuresson, *op. cit.*, p. 112. Only one occurrence for East Anglia found, in Suffolk

[50]*Ibid.*, pp. 67-8

[51]For occurrences as a surname, *see* W. Stubbs, ed., *Great Roll of the Pipe for the 12th Year of Henry II*, p. 33; *Suffolk in 1327*, p. 56; but see also *Great Roll of the Pipe for the 9th Year of Richard I*, p. 247 (Richard the son of Hirdman) and Bedingfeld, ed., *Cartulary of Creake Abbey*, pp. 34, 54 (Hirdeman son of Richard Mortimer). The personal name Aerdman, which occurs in Suffolk in the late 11th century (Douglas, *op. cit.*, p. 32), is possibly a variant of the name elsewhere rendered Hirdman

[52]W. Rye, *Cal. Norf. Fines*, vol. ii, p. 421; *Suffolk in 1327*, p. 200; Thuresson, *op. cit.*, p. 69

[53]J. R. West, ed., *Cartulary of St. Benet's, Holme*, vol. i, pp. 58, 90, 94, 134. (John de Neteshird, Stephen de Neteshirde)

[54]Anon., *Suffolk in 1524* (Suffolk Green Books, vol. x) (1910); for the Norfolk returns mentioned, *see* R. A. McKinley, *Norfolk Surnames in the Sixteenth Century* (1969), p. 9

[55]*Suffolk in 1524*, p. 259. More probably this name is a form of Woodard

[56]Thuresson, *op. cit.*, pp. 55, 274

[57]P.R.O. E179/149/7, mm. 22, 71; *Suffolk in 1327*, pp. 93, 185; Thuresson, *op. cit.*, p. 31

[58]*Suffolk in 1327*, p. 70; Rye, *Cal. Norf. Fines*, vol. ii, pp. 223, 228; *Rotuli Hundredorum*, vol. i, p. 528. *See* also Powell, *A Suffolk Hundred in 1283*, Table 30

[59]P.R.O. E179/149/7, m. 65

[60]*Ibid.*, m. 59; *Suffolk in 1327*, p. 35

[61]Douglas, *op. cit.*, p. 28

[62]*Suffolk in 1327*, p. 48; Rye, *Cal. Suff. Fines*, p. 287; P.R.O. E36/25; P.R.O. E179/150/239; Thuresson, *op. cit.*, pp. 41-2

[63]*See* note 54 above

[64]Anon., *Calendar of the Freemen of Lynn, 1292-1836* (1913), p. 33; Thuresson, *op. cit.*, p. 38; F. Hervey, *Pinchbeck Register*, vol. i, pp. 68, 69

[65]*Suffolk in 1524*, pp. 32, 38, 70, 249, 283; P.R.O. E179/150/205; E179/150/206; E179/150/227; E179/150/239; E179/150/247; E179/150/262; E179/150/271; E179/150/279; E315/466; E36/25

[66]*Rotuli Hundredorum*, vol. i, p. 484; *Nonarum Inquisitiones* (Record Commission) (1807), p. 70; L'Estrange, ed., *Calendar of the Freemen of Norwich, 1317-1603*, p. 135; and see below, p. 57

[67]P.R.O. E101/61/16. *See* Thuresson, *op. cit.*, pp. 39-40; P. H. Reaney, *Dictionary of British Surnames* (1966), p. 72

[68]*Suffolk in 1327*, p. 116

[69]Granger occurs only once in the Norfolk subsidy for 1329 (P.R.O. E179/149/7, m. 21), and only three times in the Suffolk 1327 subsidy (*Suffolk in 1327*, pp. 16, 36, 192); for the early 16th-century occurrences see P.R.O. E179/150/206, 235. For some other occurrences, *see* Anon., *Great Roll of the Pipe for the 19th Year of Henry II* (Pipe Roll Society, vol. xix) (1895), p. 132 (le Grangier); Rye, *Cal. Norf. Fines*, vol. ii, p. 428; Rye, *Cal. Suff. Fines*, p. 18; Norf. and Norwich R.O., N.R.S. 8708

[70]P.R.O. E179/149/7, mm. 1, 2, 17, 44, 53, 54; *Suffolk in 1327*, pp. 180, 186

[71]*Suffolk in 1524*, pp. 9, 27, 40, 157, 166, 201, 214, 250, 274, 286, 287, 294, 314, 332, 350, 351; P.R.O. E101/61/16; E315/466; E179/150/215; E179/150/281

[72]P.R.O. E179/149/7, mm. 55, 63; Rye, *Cal. Suff. Fines*, p. 142

[73]P.R.O. E36/22; E36/25; E315/466; E179/150/216, 246, 268, 281; *Suffolk in 1524*, pp. 72, 83, 84, 87

[74]P.R.O. E179/149/7, mm. 5, 6; Rye, *Calendar of Deeds relating to Norwich, 1285-1306*, p. 65; Fransson, *op. cit.*, p. 200

[75]*Suffolk in 1327*, p. 129; Thuresson, *op. cit.*, p. 103

[76]P.R.O. E179/149/7, m. 51; Thuresson, *op. cit.*, p. 116

[77]A. M. Kirkus, ed., *Great Roll of the Pipe for the 9th Year of John*; (Pipe Roll Soc., New Series, vol. xxii) (1946), p. 175; Thuresson, *op. cit.*, p. 115

[78]P.R.O. E179/149/7, mm. 25, 71; Norfolk and Norwich R.O., N.R.S. 18476, m. 7; N.R.S. 8708; D. M. Stenton, ed., *Great Roll of the Pipe for the 11th Year of John*, p. 31; Ipswich and East Suff. R.O., HA/12/C2/1, m. 4; *Rotuli Hundredorum*, vol. ii, p. 167; Rye, *Cal. Norf. Fines*, vol. ii, p. 329

[79]*Suffolk in 1327*, pp. 64, 142; *Curia Regis Rolls*, 7-8 *John* (1929), p. 177; *Nonarum Inquisitiones*, p. 105; F. Hervey, ed., *Pinchbeck Register* (1925), vol. i, p. 99; *Book of Fees* (1923), vol. ii, p. 917

[80]B. Dodwell, ed., *Feet of Fines for the County of Norfolk, 1201-15, and for the County of Suffolk, 1199-1214* (Pipe Roll Soc., New Series, vol xxxii) (1956), p. 183; Rye, *Cal. Suff. Fines*, p. 3; J. L'Estrange, ed., *Calendar of the Freemen of Norwich, 1317-1603*, p. 37

[81]*Suffolk in 1524*, pp. 164, 169; P.R.O. E36/22; E179/150/281

[82]*Rotuli Hundredorum*, vol. i, p. 450; *Suffolk in 1327*, p. 93; Rye, *Calendar of Deeds Relating to Norwich, 1285-1306*, pp. 80, 101

[83]J. L'Estrange, *op. cit.*, p. 37

[84]*Suffolk in 1327*, pp. 37, 80; Rye, *Cal. Suff. Fines*, p. 234; *Suffolk in 1524*, p. 255; P.R.O. E179/149/7, m. 56; *Feudal Aids* (1904), vol. iii, p. 440

[85]Thuresson, *op. cit.*, p. 50; Anon., *Feet of Fines of the Reign of Henry II, and the First Seven Years of Richard I* (Pipe Roll Society, vol. xvii) (1894), p. 12

[86]Reaney, *Dictionary of British Surnames*, p. 38; D. M. Stenton, ed., *Preparatory to Anglo-Saxon England* (1970), p. 101

[87]Rye, *Cal. Norf. Fines*, vol. i, p. 86

[88]*Rotuli Hundredorum*, vol. i, pp. 447, 474, 482; *Suffolk in 1327*, p. 79; P.R.O. E179/149/7, mm. 5, 50, 51, 58, 65; E179/149/9, m. 33

[89]P.R.O. E179/150/215. And *see* note 54 above

[90]*Suffolk in 1327*, pp. 130, 162; Rye, *Cal. Norf. Fines*, vol. ii, p. 406

[91]P.R.O. E179/149/7, m. 43

[92]*Suffolk in 1327*, p. 102

[93]*Rotuli Hundredorum*, vol. ii, pp. 149, 198; *Suffolk in 1524*, p. 223; P.R.O. C133/89/8

[94]P.R.O. E179/149/7, m. 15; Ipswich and East Suffolk R.O. HA/12/C2/7, m. 4; L'Estrange, ed., *Calendar of the Freemen of Norwich, 1317-1603*, p. 1

[95]Rye, *Cal. Suff. Fines*, p. 290; *Rotuli Hundredorum*, vol. i, p. 438; H. Pigot, 'Hadleigh', *Proceedings of the Suffolk Institute of Archaeology* (1863), vol. iii, p. 233; *Suffolk in 1524*, p. 269; *Suffolk in 1327*, p. 50

[96]*Rotuli Hundredorum*, vol. i, pp. 461, 467; *Suffolk in 1327*, p. 62; *Suffolk in 1524*, p. 351; W. Stubbs, ed., *Great Roll of the Pipe for the 12th Year of Henry II*, p. 25; Hudson, 'Three Manorial Extents', *Norfolk Archaeology*, vol. xiv, pp. 29, 30; P.R.O. E133/89/8

[97]Powell, *A Suffolk Hundred in 1283*, table 3; F. Hervey, ed., *Pinchbeck Register* (1925), vol. i, p. 436; P.R.O. E179/238/112, m. 1; E179/149/7, mm. 27, 64

[98]P.R.O. E36/22; E315/466; E179/150/215, 247

[99]*Suffolk in 1327*, pp. 9, 148, 183, 198; Powell, *Rising in East Anglia in 1381*, p. 96; Rye, *Cal. Suff. Fines*, pp. 172, 195

[100]*Suffolk in 1524*, pp. 25, 32, 37, 86, 167, 168, 292; P.R.O. E36/22, E179/150/205

[101]*Suffolk in 1524*, p. 51; P.R.O. E179/150/206, 244

[102]P.R.O. E179/149/7, mm. 5, 17, 19, 23, 31, 32, 44, 53, 62; *Suffolk in 1327*, pp. 50, 144, 153, 158, 173, 180, 200

[103]P.R.O. E179/149/7, m. 40

[104]*Suffolk in 1327*, p. 188; *Nonarum Inquisitiones* (1807), p. 71

[105]L'Estrange, ed., *Calendar of the Freemen of Norwich, 1317-1603*, p. 55

[106]Anon., *Calendar of the Freemen of Lynn, 1292-1836* (1913), p. 6

[107]*See*, e.g. Rye, *Cal. Norf. Fines*, vol. ii, p. 382; H. Pigot, 'Hadleigh', *Proceedings of the Suffolk Institute of Archaeology* (1863), vol. iii, p. 241; Rye, *Calendar of Deeds relating to Norwich, 1285-1306*, p. 68; P.R.O. E179/149/7, mm. 5, 6, 16, 52; Powell, *A Suffolk Hundred in 1283*, table 30; *Suffolk in 1327*, pp. 90, 135, 185, 186

[108]P.R.O. E179/149/7, m. 60; Rye, *Calendar of Norwich Deeds, 1307-41*, p. 110; Rye, *Cal. Norf. Fines*, vol. i, p. 108; *Rotuli Hundredorum*, vol. i, p. 507

[109]*See*, e.g. P.R.O. E179/149/7, mm. 3, 21; J. H. Round, ed., *Great Roll of the Pipe for the 23rd Year of Henry II*, pp. 137, 138; Rye, *Calendar of Deeds relating to Norwich, 1285-1306*, pp. 102, 114; *Suffolk in 1327*, p. 199

[110]D. C. Douglas, *Feudal Documents from the Abbey of Bury St. Edmunds* (1932), p. 29

[111]P.R.O. E179/149/7, mm. 3, 26, 32, 35, 40, 42, 44, 48, 49, 52, 64; *Suffolk in 1327*, pp. 22, 25, 42, 48, 55, 109, 140, 161, 183, 189, 208, 211

[112]On the 16th-century sources, *see* no. 54 above

[113]A. C. Chibnall and A. V. Woodman, *Subsidy Roll for the County of Bucks, anno 1524* (Bucks. Record Society, vol. viii) (1950), *passim*; J. Cornwall, *Lay Subsidy Rolls for the County of Sussex* (Sussex Record Society, vol. lvi) (1956), *passim*; the figure for Essex is based on the index to the Essex returns for the subsidy granted in 1523, in the Essex County R.O.

[114]*Suffolk in 1327*, p. 51

[115]*Ibid.*, pp. 59, 76; Ipswich and East Suffolk R.O., HA/12/C2/7, mm. 9, 10; HA/12/C2/11, m. 1; Rye, *Cal. Norf. Fines*, vol. ii, p. 280; G. Fransson, *Middle English Surnames of Occupation, 1100-1350* (1935), p. 84; Norfolk and Norwich R.O., N.R.S. 18476, Court held Wednesday before the Translation of St. Thomas, 8 Edward III; Douglas, *op. cit.*, p. 154

[116]Rye, *Calendar of Norwich Deeds, 1307-41*, pp. 15, 45, 63, 75, 132, 183; Rye, *Cal. Suff. Fines*, pp. 26, 240; Rye, *Calendar of Deeds relating to Norwich, 1285-1306*, pp. 54, 62, 93, 107; Hudson, *Leet Jurisdiction in the City of Norwich*, pp. 51, 65; L'Estrange, ed., *Calendar of the Freemen of Norwich, 1317-1603*, p. 35; *Rotuli Hundredorum*, vol. i, p. 456; Fransson, *op. cit.*, pp. 82-3; P.R.O. E179/149/7, m. 23

[117]*Suffolk in 1524*, pp. 25, 64, 100, 124, 126, 128, 143, 144, 147, 149, 239, 291, 361, 382; P.R.O. E36/22; E101/61/16; E179/150/235

[118]P.R.O. E179/149/7, mm. 23, 26, 40, 49, 59; *Suffolk in 1327*, pp. 82, 185, 189, 196, 201

[119]*See*, e.g. Rye, *Calendar of Norwich Deeds, 1307-41*, p. 215; Rye, *Cal. Norf. Fines*, vol. ii, p. 245; P.R.O. E179/149/53, m. 11; Norfolk and Norwich R.O., N.R.S. 8708, m. 10; *Rotuli Hundredorum*, vol. i, p. 444; Powell, *A Suffolk Hundred in 1283*, tables 13, 24; Hervey, ed., *Pinchbeck Register*, vol. i, pp. 99, 104; L'Estrange, *op. cit.*, p. 147

[120]*Suffolk in 1327*, pp. 36, 113, 145, 150, 155, 157, 217

[121]*See* the sources cited in n. 119 above

[122]The places are Herringswell, Brandon, Barnham, Thelnetham, and Beccles; *Suffolk in 1327*, pp. 82, 185, 189, 196, 201

[123]Powell, *A Suffolk Hundred in 1283*, tables 13, 24

[124]Fransson, *op. cit.*, p. 87

[125]The places where the name occurs are Lavenham, Edwardiston, Hadleigh and Kersey. *Suffolk in 1327*, pp. 145, 150, 155, 157

[126]*Ibid.*, pp. 36, 113, 217

[127]Rye, *Cal. Suff. Fines*, pp. 125, 213, 214, 224, 228, 234, 240, 249, 251, 252, 272, 274

[128]Fransson, *op. cit.*, pp. 87-88

[129]For the sources on which these statements are based, *see* note 54 above. The Essex figures are based on an index to the Essex returns for the subsidy granted in 1523, in the Essex County R.O.

[130]L'Estrange, ed., *Calendar of the Freemen of Norwich, 1317-1603*, p. 148

[131]*See*, e.g. Powell, *A Suffolk Hundred in 1283*, tables 22, 30; *Rotuli Hundredorum*, vol. i, p. 478; W. Stubbs, ed., *Great Roll of the Pipe for the 12th Year of Henry II*, p. 25; S. Smith, ed., *Great Roll of the Pipe for the 7th Year of John* (Pipe Roll Society, New Series, vol. xix) (1941), p. 254; D. C. Douglas, *Feudal Documents from the Abbey of Bury St. Edmunds*, p. 115; P.R.O. E179/149/7, m. 71

[132]Fransson, *op. cit.*, p. 89; *Rotuli Hundredorum*, vol. i, p. 478; B. Dodwell, ed., *Feet of Fines for the County of Norfolk, 1198-1202*, p. 106; Rye, *Cal. Nor. Fines*, vol. i, p. 105

[133]P.R.O. E179/149/7, mm. 3, 6, 7, 16, 20, 21, 22, 29, 33, 36, 42, 45, 48, 49, 51, 52, 57, 60, 62, 69; *Suffolk in 1327*, pp. 4, 5, 7, 16, 34, 37, 38, 46, 57, 64, 67, 129, 130, 157, 172, 174, 186, 202, 203, 204, 212, 215

[134]One doubtful example occurs in Suffolk. *See* F. Hervey, ed., *Pinchbeck Register* (1925), vol. i, p. 76 and Reaney, *Dictionary of British Surnames*, p. 328.

[135]*Suffolk in 1524*, pp. 86, 93, 141, 355, 365, 377; P.R.O. E179/150/216, 227, 239, 265, 268; E36/22; E36/25; E315/466

[136]P.R.O. E179/149/7, m. 22. Walkestr' is not amongst the names of this type listed in Fransson, *op. cit.*, p. 41

[137]Fransson, *op. cit.*, p. 101-102; P.R.O. E179/149/7, m. 64; Rye, *Cal. Norf. Fines*, vol. ii, p. 405

[138]Fransson, *op. cit.*, p. 109; P.R.O. E179/149/7, m. 31; W. Hudson, 'Three Manorial Extents of the Thirteenth Century', *Norfolk Archaeology* (1901), vol. xiv, p. 36; Rye, *Calendar of Norwich Deeds, 1307-41*, p. 34; W. Hudson, *Leet Jurisdiction in the City of Norwich* (1892), pp. 14, 51

[139]*Suffolk in 1327*, pp. 47, 48, 60, 81, 215, 217; Rye, *Cal. Norf. Fines*, vol. ii, pp. 332, 380; L'Estrange, ed., *Calendar of the Freemen of Norwich, 1317-1603*, p. 87; Hervey, ed., *Pinchbeck Register*, vol. i, pp. 98, 106; P.R.O. E179/149/7, m. 50; Norfolk and Norwich R.O., N.R.S. 8708

[140]Rye, *Cal. Norf. Fines*, vol. ii, p. 249; L'Estrange, *op. cit.*, p. 90; Fransson, *op. cit.*, p. 105; *Index of Placita de Banco, 1327-8* (P.R.O. Lists and Indexes, xxxii) (1963), Part ii, p. 634; P.R.O. E179/149/7, m. 5; Hervey, ed., *Pinchbeck Register*, vol. i, p. 99

[141]Fransson, *op. cit.*, p. 104; B. Dodwell, *Feet of Fines for the County of Norfolk, 1198-1202*, p. 166; *Suffolk in 1327*, pp. 139, 145

[142]H. Pigot, 'Hadleigh', *Proceedings of the Suffolk Institute of Archaeology* (1863), vol. iii, pp. 246, 248

[143]*Suffolk in 1327*, p. 16; Powell, *Rising in East Anglia in 1381*, p. 113

[144]Rye, *Cal. Suff. Fines*, pp. 222, 273, 305

[145]Compare Thuresson, *op. cit.*, p. 207, and Reaney, *Dictionary of British Surnames*, p. 94

[146]*Suffolk in 1524*, p. 17; P.R.O. E179/150/235

[147]Fransson, *op. cit.*, p. 106; Rye, *Cal. Norf. Fines*, vol. i, p. 145; Rye, *Cal. Suffolk Fines*, pp. 24, 117, 132; *Index of Placita de Banco, 1327-8* (P.R.O. Lists and Indexes, xxxii), part ii, p. 637

[148]Fransson, *op. cit.*, pp. 106-7; Rye, *Calendar of Norwich Deeds, 1307-41*, p. 27; P.R.O. E179/149/7, m. 61; the name Waderman, probably with the same meaning, occurs in Norfolk, 1296; Fransson *op. cit.*, p. 107

[149]Fransson, *op. cit.*, p. 107; Powell, *A Suffolk Hundred in 1283*, p. 91; *Suffolk in 1327*, p. 31

[150]Rye, *Cal. Norf. Fines*, vol. i, p. 93; *Curia Regis Rolls, 5-6 Henry III* (1949), p. 204; L'Estrange, *op. cit.*, p. 91; *Index of Placita de Banco, 1327-8* (P.R.O. Lists and Indexes, vol. xxxii) (1909), Part i, p. 409

[151]*Suffolk in 1524*, pp. 281, 290

[152]Reaney, *Dictionary of British Surnames*, p. 211; Fransson, *op. cit.*, p. 108; Thuresson, *op. cit.*, p. 208

[153]Rye, *Short Calendar of Deeds relating to Norwich, 1285-1306*, pp. 5, 64; Rye, *Calendar of Norwich Deeds, 1307-41*, p. 44; Powell, *A Suffolk Hundred in 1283*, table 6; *Suffolk in 1327*, p. 191; Rye, *Cal. Suff. Fines*, p. 86

[154]Fransson, *op. cit.*, p. 103; Rye, *Cal. Suff. Fines*, pp. 193, 262; Rye, *Cal. Norf. Fines*, vol. ii, p. 252; P.R.O. E179/149/7, mm. 1, 3, 31, 32; Anon., *Calendar of the Freemen of Lynn* (1913), pp. 29, 42, 80; L'Estrange, ed., *Calendar of the Freemen of Norwich, 1317-1603*, p. 123; F. Hervey, ed., *Pinchbeck Register*, vol. i, pp. 68, 71

[155]*See*, e.g. *Suffolk in 1524*, pp. 4, 15, 18, 29, 81, 156, 180, 328, 356, 358; P.R.O. E179/150/216, 227, 239, 246, 265, 271, 281

[156]P.R.O. E179/149/7, mm. 15, 50; Hudson, *Leet Jurisdiction in the City of Norwich*, p. 11; L'Estrange, ed., *Calendar of Norwich Freemen, 1317-1603*, p. 52

[157]P.R.O. E179/149/7, m. 9

[158]L'Estrange, *op. cit.*, p. 87; Rye, *Cal. Suff. Fines*, p. 125; Thuresson, *op. cit.*, p. 204

[159]P.R.O. E315/466

[160]Fransson, *op. cit.*, p. 91; Hudson, *Leet Jurisdiction in the City of Norwich*, pp. 35, 58; Rye, *Cal. Norf. Fines*, vol. i, p. 171; vol. ii, p. 236

[161]Fransson, *op. cit.*, pp. 84, 85, 89, 94, 98, 112, 113, 116-7, and references there cited; Thuresson, *op. cit.*, pp. 209, 213; P.R.O. E179/149/7, mm. 10, 22, 42, 44; Rye, *Calendar of Deeds relating to Norwich, 1285-1306*, pp. 56, 109; Rye, *Cal. Norf. Fines*, vol. ii, pp. 327, 355; Powell, *A Suffolk Hundred in 1283*, pp. 24, 89, table 22; F. Hervey, *Pinchbeck Register*, vol. i, pp. 68, 70, 77, 99, 259; Hudson, *Leet Jurisdiction in the City of Norwich*, pp. 18, 25, 31; *Rotuli Hundredorum*, vol. i, p. 490; L'Estrange, ed., *Calendar of the Freemen of Norwich, 1317-1603*, p. 27; *Suffolk in 1327*, pp. 2, 137

[162]*Suffolk in 1524*, pp. 6, 199; P.R.O. E36/22; E315/466; E179/150/205, 206, 235.

[163]*See*, e.g., P.R.O. E179/149/7, mm. 1, 3, 7, 13, 15, 17, 19, 27, 31, 34, 44, 48, 55, 57; Hudson, *Leet Jurisdiction in the City of Norwich*, pp. 9, 28, 40, 48, 52; Rye, *Cal. Norf. Fines*, vol. i, pp. 83, 128; vol. ii, pp. 248, 267, 311, 391, 430; Rye, *Calendar of Norwich Deeds, 1307-41*, p. 112; Rye, *Calendar of Deeds relating to Norwich, 1285-1306*, p. 7; *Rotuli Hundredorum*, vol. i, p. 477; *Suffolk in 1327*, pp. 8, 66, 82, 96, 120, 137, 162, 185, 219; Fransson, *op. cit.*, p. 113

[164]On the early 16th-century sources, *see* no. 54 above.

[165]*See*, e.g., Rye, *Cal. Norf. Fines*, vol. i, pp. 27, 32, 83; vol. ii, pp. 307, 356, 401, 410; Powell, *Rising in East Anglia in 1381*, p. 88; P.R.O. E179/149/7, mm. 29, 32; Fransson, *op. cit.*, p. 111; *Rotuli Hundredorum*, vol. i, pp. 443, 459, 485, 486, 515

[166]Fransson, *op. cit.*, pp. 110-111

[167]P.R.O. E179/149/7, mm. 5, 7, 23, 26, 27, 29, 30, 31, 48, 49, 53, 56, 57, 65, 69, 71

[168]*Suffolk in 1327*, pp. 11, 25, 26, 27, 34, 41, 46, 51, 56, 99, 127, 129, 154, 158, 207, 210, 217, 218, 219

[169]*Ibid.*, pp. 65, 147; P.R.O. E179/149/7, mm. 5, 35, 44

[170]*Suffolk in 1327*, pp. 137, 138; P.R.O. E179/149/7, mm. 15, 35, 36, 38, 42, 44, 45, 50, 51, 53, 60

[171]L'Estrange, ed., *Calendar of the Freemen of Norwich, 1317-1603*, pp. 9-10, 135. The name le Tanur does however occur at Norwich in 1288-89; Hudson, *Leet Jurisdiction in the City of Norwich*, p. 22

[172]Bedingfeld, ed., *Cartulary of Creake Abbey*, pp. 43, 47, 50, 67

[173]For the early 16th-century sources *see* note 54 above

[174]P.R.O. E179/149/7, mm. 15, 21, 22, 23, 29, 30, 31, 32, 36, 38, 42, 43, 44, 45, 49, 53, 57, 59, 62, 64, 67, 68; *Suffolk in 1327*, pp. 7, 24, 25, 34, 49, 53, 59, 61, 107, 114, 120, 136, 139, 153, 167, 170, 172, 184, 185, 186, 207, 211, 220

[175]*Suffolk in 1524*, pp. 56, 337; P.R.O. E36/25; E36/22; E179/150/265

[176]*Suffolk in 1327*, p. 176; P.R.O. E179/149/7, mm. 15, 50; Hervey, *Pinchbeck Register*, vol. i, p. 99; Bedingfeld, ed., *Cartulary of Creake Abbey*, pp. 41, 108; Fransson, *op. cit.*, p. 132

[177]*Suffolk in 1327*, pp. 37, 99, 137; *Suffolk in 1524*, p. 380; P.R.O. E179/149/7, mm. 19, 33, 35; E36/25

[178]Fransson, *op. cit.*, p. 131

[179]L'Estrange, ed., *Calendar of the Freemen of Norwich, 1317-1603*, p. 123; P.R.O. E179/150/215

[180]Reaney, *Dictionary of British Surnames*, p. 71; *Suffolk in 1327*, p. 58; *Suffolk in 1524*, pp. 192-3; Anon., *Suffolk in 1568* (Suffolk Green Books, vol. xii) (1909), pp. 139-40; Rye, *Cal. Suff. Fines*, pp. 263, 272

[181]*See Suffolk in 1327, passim*, and P.R.O. E179/149/7, *passim*

[182]*See*, e.g. P.R.O. E179/149/7, mm. 5, 44, 59; C133/89/8; Rye, *Cal. Norf. Fines*, vol. i, pp. 66, 167; Rye, *Cal. Suff. Fines*, p. 280; *Suffolk in 1327*, p. 149; Powell, *A Suffolk Hundred in 1283*, table 31; Hervey, ed., *Pinchbeck Register*, vol. i, p. 98

[183]Rye, *Cal. Norf. Fines*, vol. i, pp. 31, 90, 94, 97, 111, 163; vol. ii, p. 271; Hudson *Leet Jurisdiction in the City of Norwich*, p. 39; Rye, *Calendar of Deeds relating to Norwich, 1285-1306*, p. 5; Rye, *Cal. Suff. Fines*, pp. 96, 99, 126-7, 140, 151, 171

[184]For these sources, *see* note 54 above

[185]*See*, e.g. Rye, *Cal. Norf. Fines*, vol. i, pp. 58, 106, 113; vol. ii, pp. 237, 251, 309, 357, 391; Hervey, ed., *Pinchbeck Register*, vol. i, pp. 62-4, 147, 205; D. C. Douglas, *Feudal Documents from the Abbey of Bury St. Edmunds*, pp. 30, 43; Hudson, *Leet Jurisdiction in the City of Norwich*, pp. 47, 71, 72; L'Estrange, *op. cit.*, p. 61; *Suffolk in 1327*, pp. 28, 36, 137; P.R.O. E179/149/7, mm. 5, 11, 36, 59

[186]*See*, e.g. Rye, *Cal. Norf. Fines*, vol. ii, pp. 298, 308; Bedingfeld, ed., *Cartulary of Creake Abbey*, p. 106; Rye, *Cal. Suff. Fines*, pp. 246, 250; P.R.O. E179/149/7, mm. 23, 26, 50; W. Hudson, 'Three Manorial Extents', *Norfolk Archaeology*, vol. xiv, pp. 38, 43; Norfolk and Norwich R.O., N.R.S. 18476, m. 9; *Index of Placita de Banco, 1327-8* (P.R.O. Lists and Indexes, vol. xxxii) part ii, p. 642

[187]Rye, *Cal. Norf. Fines*, vol. i, p. 107; Rye, *Cal. Suff. Fines*, pp. 272, 279; L'Estrange, ed., *Calendar of the Freemen of Norwich, 1317-1603*, p. 20; *Suffolk in 1327*, pp. 137, 217; Hervey, ed., *Pinchbeck Register*, vol. i, pp. 104, 107, 112; Rye, *Calendar of Norwich Deeds, 1307-41*, pp. 13, 45, 137, 215; Rye, *Calendar of Deeds Relating to Norwich, 1285-1306*, p. 112

[188]L'Estrange, ed., *Calendar of the Freemen of Norwich, 1317-1603*, pp. 87-8; Hudson, *Leet Jurisdiction in the City of Norwich*, p. 31; Hervey, ed., *Pinchbeck Register*, vol. i, pp. 74, 75, 99, 115; Anon., *Calendar of the Freemen of Lynn, 1292-1836*, p. 25; P.R.O. E179/149/7, mm. 5, 9

[189]Hudson, *Leet Jurisdiction in the City of Norwich*, pp. 8, 36, 40; Rye, *Calendar of Deeds relating to Norwich, 1285-1306*, pp. 19, 40; P.R.O. E179/149/7 mm. 3, 43, 68; Rye, *Cal. Norf. Fines*, vol. ii, pp. 301, 385; Powell, *A Suffolk Hundred in 1283*, pp. 16, 17, table 29; *Rotuli Hundredorum*, vol. i, p. 525; Anon., *Calendar of the Freemen of Lynn, 1292-1836*, pp. 9, 12, 17; Rye, *Cal. Suff. Fines*, pp. 97, 192; Fransson, *op. cit.*, p. 148: *Suffolk in 1327*, pp. 50, 77, 79, 114, 125, 152; L'Estrange, *op. cit.*, p. 4; Hervey, ed., *Pinchbeck Register*, vol. i, pp. 104, 132, 266; P.R.O., E179/149/9, m. 71

[190]*Suffolk in 1327*, p. 156; Rye, *Cal. Suff. Fines*, p. 8; Douglas, *op. cit.*, p. 38; L'Estrange, ed., *Calendar of the Freemen of Norwich, 1317-1607*, p. 154; Fransson, *op. cit.*, p. 148; Anon., *Calendar of the Freemen of Lynn*, p. 61

[191]Rye, *Short Calendar of Deeds relating to Norwich, 1285-1306*, pp. 73, 94; Fransson, *op. cit.*, p. 153; Powell, *A Suffolk Hundred in 1283*, p. 80

[192]*Suffolk in 1524*, pp. 72, 73, 244, 249, 334; P.R.O. E36/25; E179/150/227, 244, 281

[193]Rye, *Cal. Norf. Fines*, vol. ii, p. 380; Hudson, *Leet Jurisdiction in the City of Norwich*, p. 42; Hervey, ed., *Pinchbeck Register*, vol. i, p. 115; Anon., *Calendar of the Freemen of Lynn, 1292-1836*, pp. 8, 16

[194]P.R.O. E179/149/7, mm. 3, 5, 6; Ipswich and East Suffolk R.O., H.A./12/C2/1, mm. 2, 4, 5

[195]P.R.O. E179/150/281; on the origin of Billiter, *see* Reaney, *Dictionary of British Surnames*, pp. 32-33

[196]D. M. Stenton, ed., *Great Roll of the Pipe for the 1st Year of John* (Pipe Roll Society, New Series, vol. x) (1933), p. 279; *Curia Regis Rolls, 3-5 John* (1925), p. 116; Rye, *Cal. Suff. Fines*, p. 34

[197]Rye, *Cal. Suff. Fines*, pp. 168, 172, 180, 181, 218; *Suffolk in 1327*, pp. 40, 45, 131, 158

[198]Powell, *A Suffolk Hundred in 1283*, pp. 28, 45, table 22; Hervey, ed., *Pinchbeck Register*, vol. i, p. 59; Rye, *Cal. Suff. Fines*, pp. 34, 39, 50, 61, 71, 79; *Suffolk in 1327*, p. 125

[199]Fransson, *op. cit.*, p. 152; P.R.O. E179/149/7, m. 62

[200]*Suffolk in 1524*, pp. 35, 168; *Suffolk in 1568*, pp. 2, 38, 92, 279

[201]*See*, e.g. Rye, *Cal. Norf. Fines*, vol. ii, pp. 245, 247, 310; Powell, *A Suffolk Hundred in 1283*, pp. 89, tables 29, 31; Powell, *Rising in East Anglia in 1381*, pp. 108, 109, 111, 112; P.R.O. E179/149/7, mm. 1, 5, 7, 13, 19, 43, 51, 56, 57; Ipswich and East Suffolk R.O., HA/12/C2/7, m. 12

[202]Powell, *A Suffolk Hundred in 1283*, tables 11, 27; Fransson, *op. cit.*, pp. 57, 58

[203]*See*, e.g. Powell, *A Suffolk Hundred in 1283*, table 28; Rye, *Calendar of Norwich Deeds, 1307-41*, pp. 12, 43, 63, 75, 85, 166; Rye, *Cal. Norf. Fines*, vol. i, pp. 98, 172; vol. ii, pp. 312, 329; Powell, *Rising in East Anglia in 1381*, p. 118; D. M. Stenton, ed., *Great Roll of the Pipe for the 1st Year of John*, p. 288; C. Morley, 'Catalogue of the Beneficed Clergy of Suffolk', *Proceedings of the Suffolk Institute of Archaeology*, p. 66; P.R.O. E179/149/7, mm. 5, 6, 11, 42, 65

[204]*See*, e.g. Rye, *Cal. Norf. Fines*, vol. i, pp. 78, 114, 155; vol. ii, pp. 264, 310, 318, 388; W. Stubbs, ed., *Great Roll of the Pipe for the 12th Year of Henry II*, p. 29; *Rotuli Hundredorum*, vol. i, pp. 499, 515; Hervey, ed., *Pinchbeck Register*, vol. i, p. 140; P.R.O. E179/149/7, mm. 5, 42, 68; *Suffolk in 1327*, pp. 140, 156, 170, 195, 205

[205]*Suffolk in 1327*, p. 82; Fransson, *op. cit.*, p. 62; Rye, *Cal. Norf. Fines*, vol. ii, p. 266; *Rotuli Hundredorum*, vol. i, p. 514

[206]*Suffolk in 1327*, pp. 9, 103, 181; Rye, *Cal. Suff. Fines*, p. 224. Rye, *Cal. Norf. Fines*, vol. ii, p. 259; Powell, *Rising in East Anglia in 1381*, pp. 68, 82, 93; Hudson, *Leet Jurisdiction in the City of Norwich*, p. 66; *Rotuli Hundredorum*, vol. i, pp. 470, 483; P.R.O. C133/89/8; E179/149/7, m. 59; Fransson, *op. cit.*, p. 74

[207]*See*, e.g. Rye, *Calendar of Norwich Deeds, 1307-41*, p. 129; Hervey, *op. cit.*, vol. i, pp. 99, 138; *Calendar of the Freemen of Lynn, 1292-1836*, pp. 10, 16; Powell, *Rising in East Anglia in 1381*, p. 132; Rye, *Cal. Suff. Fines*, p. 236; *Suffolk in 1327*, p. 216; Fransson, *op. cit.*, p. 75

[208]Rye, *Calendar of Deeds relating to Norwich, 1285-1306*, pp. 20, 40; Rye, *Calendar of Norwich Deeds, 1307-41*, p. 91; Fransson, *op. cit.*, pp. 75, 76; *Rotuli Hundredorum*, vol. i, pp. 470, 539; *Index of Placita de Banco, 1327-8* (P.R.O. Lists and Indexes, vol. xxxii), part i, pp. 389, 398

[209]*See*, e.g. P.R.O. E179/149/7, m. 5; Rye, *Cal. Norf. Fines*, vol. i, pp. 79, 85; *Suffolk in 1327*, pp. 9, 37; Rye, *Cal. Suff. Fines*, pp. 152, 158; L'Estrange, ed., *Calendar of the Freemen of Norwich, 1317-1603*, p. 142; Norfolk and Norwich R.O., N.R.S. 18476, m. 11

[210]*Suffolk in 1327*, p. 33; Hervey, *op. cit.*, vol. i, p. 140; Rye, *Cal. Norf. Fines*, vol. ii, p. 380; P.R.O. E179/149/7, mm. 36, 67; Fransson, *op. cit.*, p. 79

[211]On the early 16th-century sources used, *see* note 54, above

[212]P.R.O. E179/150/247

[213]*Suffolk in 1524*, pp. 142, 178, 242, 256; P.R.O. E315/466; E36/25; E179/150/215, 234

[214]*See Suffolk in 1327*, and P.R.O. E179/149/7, *passim*

[215]*Rotuli Hundredorum*, vol. i, p. 530; Bedingfeld, ed., *Cartulary of Creake Abbey*, p. 40; Rye, *Cal. Norf. Fines*, vol. i, pp. 77, 112, 119, 129, 134-5, 156; Hudson, *Leet Jurisdiction in Norwich*, pp. 15, 16; Rye, *Calendar of Deeds relating to Norwich, 1285-1306*, p. 71; Rye, *Calendar of Norwich Deeds, 1307-41*, p. 12; *Suffolk in 1327*, pp. 210, 216; P.R.O. E179/149/7, mm. 22, 23, 50; Hervey, ed., *Pinchbeck Register*, vol. i, pp. 137, 138, 350; *Index of Placita de Banco, 1327-8* (P.R.O. Lists and Indexes, vol. xxxii), part ii, p. 620

[216]L'Estrange, ed., *Calendar of the Freemen of Norwich, 1317-1603*, p. 45; Rye, *Calendar of Deeds relating to Norwich, 1285-1306*, p. 94; Rye, *Cal. Norf. Fines*, vol. i, p. 115; vol. ii, pp. 377, 418-20; *Suffolk in 1327*, pp. 82, 158, 196, 206; P.R.O. E179/149/7, m. 26, 57, 64; Ipswich and East Suffolk R.O., HA/12/C2/20, m. 2

[217]On the early 16th-century sources, *see* note 54 above; and *see Suffolk in 1568* (Suffolk Green Books, vol. xii) (1909), p. 59

[218]Rye, *Calendar of Deeds relating to Norwich, 1285-1306*, p. 40; Rye, *Calendar of Norwich Deeds, 1307-41*, pp. 19, 33, 34, 42, 91, 101; *Index to Placita de Banco, 1327-8* (P.R.O. Lists and Indexes, vol. xxxii) part i, p .389

[219]*See Suffolk in 1327*, and P.R.O. E179/149/7, *passim*; on serfs' names, see below p. 144

[220]P.R.O. E179/149/7, mm. 31, 34, 48

[221]Rye, *Cal. Norf. Fines*, vol. ii, pp. 274, 294 (where the name is given as Falghmongere in error), 331, 357, 378; Fransson, *op. cit.*, p. 99; P.R.O. E179/149/7, mm. 27, 67; *Index of Placita de Banco, 1327-8* (P.R.O. Lists and Indexes, vol. xxxii) part i, p. 379

[222]*See*, e.g. *Suffolk in 1327*, pp. 3, 16, 37, 135, 196; E179/149/7, mm. 3, 19, 32, 34, 48, 51, 58, 59

[223]L. F. Salzman, *Building in England* (1952), pp. 225-8; Powell, *A Suffolk Hundred in 1283*, p. 72; Hervey, ed., *Pinchbeck Register*, vol. i, p. 72; Rye, *Calendar of Norwich Deeds, 1307-41*, p. 109; Powell, *Rising in East Anglia in 1381*, pp. 87, 106; *Suffolk in 1327*, p. 25; L'Estrange, ed., *Calendar of the Freemen of Norwich, 1317-1603*, pp. 115-6; P.R.O. E179/149/7, m. 5; Fransson, *op. cit.*, p. 179; Rye, *Cal. Norf. Fines*, vol. ii, pp. 320, 405; Hudson, *Leet Jurisdiction in the City of Norwich*, p. 73

224Fransson, *op. cit.*, p. 177; Rye, *Cal. Norf. Fines*, vol. i, p. 67

225Rye, *Cal. Norf. Fines*, vol. ii, p. 263; Powell, *Rising in East Anglia in 1381*, pp. 87, 89; Hervey, ed., *Pinchbeck Register*, vol. i, p. 159; Fransson, *op. cit.*, p. 178; *Suffolk in 1327*, pp. 155, 166, 218; L'Estrange, ed., *Calendar of the Freemen of Norwich, 1317-1603*, p. 136; P.R.O. E179/149/53, m. 11; Hudson, 'Three Manorial Extents', *Norfolk Archaeology*, vol. xiv, p. 48

226Rye, *Cal. Norf. Fines*, vol. ii, p. 332; L'Estrange, ed., *Calendar of the Freemen of Norwich, 1317-1603*, p. 136; P.R.O. E179/149/7, mm. 7, 69; E179/149/53, m. 11; Fransson, *op. cit.*, p. 178; McKinley, *Norfolk Surnames in the Sixteenth Century*, p. 38

227P.R.O. E179/150/227, 262, 265, 271, 275, 281

228*Suffolk in 1327*, pp. 93, 185; Rye, *Cal. Suff. Fines*, pp. 287, 290, 302; Rye, *Calendar of Deeds relating to Norwich, 1285-1306*, p. 51; L'Estrange, *op. cit.*, p. 141; Fransson, *op. cit.*, p. 180

229Rye, *Cal. Norf. Fines*, vol. i, pp. 34, 56; vol. ii, pp. 240, 251, 328, 426; *Suffolk in 1327*, p. 163; *Index to Placita de Banco, 1327-8* (P.R.O. Lists and Indexes, vol. xxxii) part i, p. 138; part ii, pp. 635, 637; Rye, *Calendar of Norwich Deeds, 1307-41*, p. 165; Thuresson, *op. cit.*, pp. 183, 186; P.R.O. E179/149/7, mm. 1, 16, 51; Ipswich and East Suffolk R.O., HA/12/C2/1, m. 3; HA/12/C2/2, m. 1; HA/12/C2/7, mm. 10, 11

230P.R.O. E179/149/7, m. 64; Hudson, *Leet Jurisdiction in the City of Norwich*, pp. 6, 45; P. M. Barnes, ed., *Great Roll of the Pipe for the 14th Year of John* (Pipe Roll Soc., New Series, vol. xxx) (1955), p. 182; Rye, *Calendar of Norwich Deeds, 1307-41*, p. 215; Anon., *Calendar of the Freemen of Lynn, 1292-1836*, p. 17

231Hudson, *Leet Jurisdiction in the City of Norwich*, pp. 1, 23, 25, 48, 74; Thuresson, *op. cit.*, pp. 95-6; *Suffolk in 1327*, pp. 13, 14, 18, 162, 164; Rye, *Cal. Norf. Fines*, vol. ii, pp. 335, 406, 415, 434; Powell, *Rising in East Anglia in 1381*, pp. 71, 108; P.R.O. E179/149/7, mm. 5, 7, 15-18, 22, 23, 38, 42, 44; Ipswich and East Suffolk R.O., HA/12/C2/2, m. 9; HA/12/C2/7, mm. 10, 11; P.R.O. E179/238/112; *Index to Placita de Banco, 1327-8* (P.R.O. Lists and Indexes, vol. xxxii), part i, p. 97

232Rye, *Cal. Norf. Fines*, vol. ii, pp. 311, 415; Hervey, ed., *Pinchbeck Register*, vol. i, pp. 70, 143; *Suffolk in 1327*, p. 138; L'Estrange, ed., *Calendar of the Freemen of Norwich, 1317-1603*, p. 56; Rye, *Calendar of Deeds relating to Norwich, 1285-1306*, pp. 3, 5; Rye, *Calendar of Norwich Deeds, 1307-41*, p. 68

233Rye, *Cal. Norf. Fines*, vol. i, p. 63, 148; vol. ii, pp. 233, 236, 269, 282, 327, 332, 350-51, 354, 403-5, 422; Powell, *A Suffolk Hundred in 1283*, pp. 32, 195; tables 3, 4, 21, 35; *Rotuli Hundredorum*, vol. i, pp. 453, 494-5, 516; *Suffolk in 1327*, pp. 60, 70; P.R.O. E179/

149/7, mm. 5, 7, 23, 33, 35, 43, 45, 48, 50-1, 54, 57, 62, 68; Ipswich and East Suffolk R.O., HA/12/C2/7, mm. 9, 14

[234]*See* Thuresson, *op. cit.*, and Fransson, *op. cit.*

[235]*See* above, p. 50

[236]*See* above, pp. 39-44

[237]G. Fransson, *Middle English Surnames of Occupation, 1100-1350* (1935); B. Thuresson, *Middle English Occupational Terms* (1950)

[238]*See* above, p. 48

[239]Rye, *Cal. Norf. Fines*, vol. ii, p. 335; P.R.O. E179/149/7, mm. 7, 23. The name was used in the area in the 12th century as a personal name. *See* Hart and Lyons, eds., *Cartularium Monasterium de Rameseia* (Rolls Series) vol. iii, p. 269

[240]L'Estrange, ed., *Calendar of the Freemen of Norwich, 1317-1603*, p. 123

[241]Powell, *A Suffolk Hundred in 1283*, p. 5; tables 4, 20; Powell, *Rising in East Anglia in 1381*, p. 108; *Suffolk in 1327*, pp. 87, 190

[242]*See* above, p. 42

[243]Thuresson, *op. cit.*, p. 274; L'Estrange, ed., *Calendar of the Freemen of Norwich, 1317-1603*, p. 121; P.R.O. E179/149/7, m. 47

[244]Thuresson, *op. cit.*, p. 275; Rye, *Cal. Norf. Fines*, vol. ii, p. 432

[245]On locative surnames, *see* below, pp. 75-101

[246]Rye, *Cal. Norf. Fines*, vol. i, pp. 77, 173; Hervey, ed., *Pinchbeck Register*, vol. i, p. 426; *Rotuli Hundredorum*, vol. i, p. 489

[247]Norfolk and Norwich R.O., N.R.S. 18476, mm. 7, 8

[248]Hart and Lyons, eds., *Cartularium Monasterium de Rameseia*, vol. iii. p. 263

[249]Bedingfeld, *Cartulary of Creake Abbey*, p 15

[250]Hudson, 'Three Manorial Extents', *Norfolk Archaeology* (1901), vol. xiv, p. 50

[251]*See*, e.g. *ibid.*, p. 25; *Suffolk in 1327*, pp. 3, 10, 187, 189; Bedingfeld, *op. cit.*, pp. 69, 75, 101; Norfolk and Norwich R.O., N.R.S. 18476, m. 3; Hudson, *Leet Jurisdiction in the City of Norwich*, p. 18

[252]*Rotuli Hundredorum*, vol. ii, p. 161; J. H. Bullock, ed., *The Norfolk Portion of the Chartulary of the Priory of St. Pancras of Lewes* (Norfolk Record Society, vol. xii) (1939), p. 70; Norfolk and Norwich R.O., N.R.S. 18476, m. 7

[253]*Suffolk in 1524, passim*; A. C. Chibnall and A. V. Woodman, eds., *Subsidy Roll for the County of Buckingham, Anno 1524* (Bucks. Record Society, vol. viii) (1950); J. Cornwall, ed., *Lay Subsidy Rolls for the County of Sussex, 1524-5* (Sussex Record Society, vol. lvi) (1956); for the Norfolk sources concerned, *see* McKinley, *Norfolk Surnames in the Sixteenth Century*, p. 9

[254]P.R.O. E179/149/7, mm. 7, 12, 31, 48-9, 58; Rye, *Calendar of Deeds relating to Norwich, 1285-1306*, p. 7; L'Estrange, ed., *Calendar of the Freemen of Norwich, 1317-1603*, p. 29

255Fransson, *op. cit.*, pp. 41-5

256*Suffolk in 1327, passim*; and P.R.O. E179/149/7

257Norfolk and Norwich R.O., Norwich Free Book, ff. xxxi-xxxix

258*Ibid.*, f. xl

259*Ibid.*, ff. xlii *et seq.*

260Fransson, *op. cit.*, p. 209; Powell, *Rising in East Anglia in 1381*, p. 114; Hudson, *Leet Jurisdiction in the City of Norwich*, pp. 18, 25, 31

261Anon., *Calendar of the Freemen of Lynn, 1292-1836*, p. 37; Thuresson, *op. cit.*, p. 219

262L'Estrange, ed., *Calendar of the Freemen of Norwich, 1317-1603*, p. 135; R. E. Latham, *Revised Medieval Latin Word List* (1965), p. 476; A. Way, ed., *Promptorium Parvulorum* (Camden Society, 1st series, vol. lxxxix) (1865), p. 487

263L'Estrange, *op. cit.*, p. 27; Rye, *Cal Suff, Fines*, p. 232

264Norfolk and Norwich R.O., N.R.S. 8708, Court held, Feast of St. Peter ad Vincula, 14 Edward II

265L'Estrange, *op. cit.*, p. 125

266*Suffolk in 1327*, p. 61; A. Way, ed., *Promptorium Parvulorum* (Camden Society, 1st series, vol. xxv) (1843), vol. i, p. 143

267Hudson, *Leet Jurisdiction in the City of Norwich*, p. 52; Way, ed., *Promptorium Parvulorum* (Camden Society, 1st series, vol. liv) (1853), vol. ii, p. 381; P.R.O. E179/149/7, m. 50

268P.R.O. E179/149/53, m. 11

269D. C. Douglas, *Feudal Documents from the Abbey of Bury St. Edmunds*, p. 32

CHAPTER 3

LOCATIVE SURNAMES

Surnames derived from place names are an important group in terms of numbers, but are chiefly interesting for the evidence that their distribution at varying dates provides for population movements. A prime necessity in studying surnames in this category is to ascertain with care the place from which each surname is derived, and to examine the way that early occurrences of each surname are distributed geographically as one step towards identifying the place in question. A few examples will illustrate how important it is to do this if misleading inferences are to be avoided.

One surname found in Norfolk from the 13th century onwards is Holgate or Holegate, and the presence in East Anglia, then and later, of some surnames undoubtedly derived from Yorkshire place-names might encourage the view that the name is derived from the village of Holgate, near York. In fact the surname, so far as the bearers of it in medieval Norfolk are concerned, originates from two different localities, both within the county. One of these was in the north Norfolk township of North Creake, where from about 1225 onwards a family called Holgate or de Holgate were holding property, some of it actually in Holgate at North Creake.[1] A second was at Norwich, where a street or lane called 'Le Hollegate' gave rise to a surname, Holgate or Attehollegate, in the late 13th century, found at Norwich and in some nearby villages.[2] In addition, there were during the Middle Ages places called Holgate or Holegate at Burnham and Tittleshall in Norfolk, and at Bardwell in Suffolk, not far from the Norfolk border, and an exhaustive search through the minor place names of the two counties might well reveal others.[3]

Another example is the surname Curwen, which is found from the 13th century onwards in south-west Scotland and north-west England, and in those regions is derived from Colvend in Kirkcudbrightshire.[4] There was, however, in the 13th century a place near Tuddenham, Norfolk, called Kerewen, and as it is in the same district that some early instances of the surname Curwen or Cerewan are found, it seems likely that the surname, when it occurs in Norfolk, is derived from the obscure locality near Tuddenham, rather than the Kirkcudbrightshire village, despite the presence in medieval Norfolk of some surnames derived from places in north-west

England.[5] Similarly the surname Ripon, or de Rypun, which occurs in Norfolk from the end of the 13th century onwards, could be derived from the hamlet of Rippon in Hevingham parish, Norfolk.[6]

It is therefore essential to make a careful identification of the place-names from which locative surnames are derived. Inevitably there are cases where certainty is unattainable, and this factor makes it impossible to give precise figures for, say, the number of surnames derived from places in any given region, though it is not usually sufficiently serious to obscure the general trends disclosed by the evidence.

During the 13th and 14th centuries there occur a very large number of surnames or bye-names derived from places in Norfolk and Suffolk. The high proportion of locative names in certain 13th-century lists of military tenants is noted elsewhere in this paper.[7] Such sources, of course, deal with only one class, but locative names are still very numerous, if fewer proportionately, in 13th- and 14th-century sources that cover a larger segment of the population. In the Norfolk portion of the Hundred Rolls, for example, there are more than 350 persons with surnames or bye-names that can be derived with some certainty from localities in Norfolk, and more than 50 with names derived from places in Suffolk. In the same part of the Hundred Rolls surnames or bye-names derived from 290 places in Norfolk occur, and the places concerned are scattered in all parts of the county.[8] None of these figures includes names derived from places outside Norfolk and Suffolk, and the numbers would be larger were it not for the existence of many doubtful cases, where it is impossible to identify reliably the places concerned. The Norfolk returns for the 1329-30 subsidy list persons with locative surnames or bye-names derived from some 351 places within the county.[9] The locative surnames or bye-names derived from places in Suffolk that occur in the Suffolk 1327 subsidy are similarly numerous.[10] In both counties the sources include only part of the total population, and it must be supposed that the number of locative surnames in use was considerably greater than appears from the figures just given. It is also no doubt true that many of the locative names occurring during the 13th century and the first half of the 14th were not hereditary.

If we consider the distribution of locative names, in Norfolk or Suffolk, as it occurs in sources for the 13th century or the first half of the 14th, the most noticeable characteristic is that most such names occur at, or near to, the places from which they are derived. This can be seen most clearly in the subsidy rolls. In the Suffolk 1327 subsidy roll, for example, of all the persons with locative names derived from places within the county that can be identified with reasonable certainty, 15 per cent were listed at the place from which their names were derived, 24 per cent are listed at points less than five miles away from such places, 16 per cent between five and 10 miles away, 24 per cent between 10 and 20 miles, 12 per cent between 20 and 30 miles, and nine per cent over 30 miles away. Well over half were therefore listed within 10 miles of the places from which their names originated.[11] In the case of many other sources, the Hundred Rolls for example, the places where persons resided are often not given, so that it is not possible to produce from them statistics such as those just given for the Suffolk subsidy rolls. It is possible, however, to find in the Hundred Rolls, and in some other sources for the period *c.* 1200-1350 such as the feet of fines for Norfolk and Suffolk,[12] numerous cases where the places of residence of persons with locative names are noted. An examination of many such cases drawn from the Hundred Rolls and the feet of fines shows that rather more than half the persons concerned were living at, or near the places (within 10 miles) from which their names were derived. In such a matter it would be misleading to imply that precise statistics can be given, for there are too many uncertain factors. The places from which some locative surnames originate are doubtful, in some sources the abode of many persons with locative surnames is not stated, and the process of measuring distances between one whole parish and another cannot pretend to any great accuracy. Nevertheless the evidence does suggest that in the 13th century and the first half of the 14th, when most people had names that were either simply bye-names, and not hereditary, or surnames that had not been hereditary for very long, those with locative surnames tended to be living at, or fairly near, the places from which their names originated. No doubt some such persons were lords of manors and other substantial landholders who were living on the lordships from which their surnames or bye-names were derived.[13] The position as it was *c.* 1200-1350 may be contrasted with the early 16th-century situation in Norfolk, when bearers of locative surnames were on the average living much further from the places where their names originated.[14]

The distribution of locative surnames does provide evidence for migration over longer distances, however. So far only locative surnames found in Norfolk and Suffolk, and derived from place-names within the two counties, have been discussed. Undoubtedly there was migration from East Anglia to other regions, particularly to London, and there was also a continuous movement into the region from outside during much of the Middle Ages, though there does not seem to have been a major influx at any one time.

Migration into London during the Middle Ages has been studied by Professor Ekwall and Dr. Reaney. Surnames derived from East Anglian place-names occur in London from about the middle of the 12th century onwards, but only a very few examples have been found before 1200.[15] During the 13th and 14th centuries, however, locative surnames from places in Norfolk and Suffolk became numerous, and indeed during those two centuries more places in Norfolk than in any other county gave rise to locative surnames present in London. Many Suffolk places, too, gave rise to London locative names, though not much more than half the number of those in Norfolk and rather fewer than the number in Essex, Lincolnshire, or Yorkshire. Although it would be foolish to deduce any precise figures for migration into London during the Middle Ages from the incidence of locative surnames there, it seems likely that after the home counties immediately around the capital, Norfolk and Suffolk were the most important source of immigrants.[16] The places from which the names of London migrants were derived are widely distributed in both counties, and there is nothing to suggest a particularly heavy migration from any one part of East Anglia at any one period.[17] It is doubtful if there was any region, apart from London, which received a great many migrants from Norfolk or Suffolk. Short of making a thorough examination of medieval sources for the whole country, it is difficult to be certain of this. An investigation of some sources, including some subsidy rolls and some printed feet of fines, for the east Midlands, Yorkshire, and the home counties has, however, not produced any evidence of an exceptional concentration of locative surnames from Norfolk or Suffolk anywhere. The medieval feet of fines for Essex contain a considerable number of locative surnames derived from places in Suffolk, and a small number from Norfolk, but the numbers involved do not seem greater than would be expected from the propinquity of the counties, their size and populousness. So far as it is possible to judge while the difficulty of identifying the origin of some locative surnames makes it impossible to furnish precise statistics, the number of Suffolk locative surnames in medieval Norfolk was rather greater than the number of Suffolk locative surnames in medieval Essex.

It is rather easier to study the influx into East Anglia of locative surnames from other regions. As early as the 11th and 12th centuries there appear in Norfolk and Suffolk persons with surnames or bye-names that originated outside the two counties, in some cases from remote parts of England. A group of names derived from places in south-east England, such as de Arundell, de Graveney, de Hardres, de Hastings, de Lenham, de Lewes, or de London occur in East Anglia during the 12th and early 13th centuries, and other instances could be given of locative surnames or bye-names derived from places outside East Anglia and its contiguous regions.[18] For this early period the number of locative names occurring in the original sources is too small to enable any firm conclusions to be drawn about migration into Norfolk and Suffolk from other regions, though it is clear that there was at least some movement over relatively long distances. After about the mid-13th century, however, more copious evidence is available, and it is possible to form a general view of migration. It cannot be claimed that any precise figures for population movements can be deduced from a study of locative surnames. There are too many uncertainties about the identification of the places from which locative surnames originated, and about the varying proportions between regions of locative surnames to the whole body of surnames. It is also impossible to suppose that persons with locative surnames were the only ones that migrated, yet it is quite possible that surnames in that category were more readily acquired by persons who migrated than by those who did not. Such factors mean that any conclusions presented must be subject to some reservations. Nevertheless, it is felt that from a study of locative surnames some general trends in population movement can be discovered, and also that the study of some individual surnames in the category may throw light on the way in which surnames ramified.

A list of locative surnames found in Norfolk and Suffolk during the Middle Ages has been drawn up from a variety of sources.[19] It is of course not claimed that this list is at all comprehensive, and had additional sources, printed and unprinted, been searched, no doubt many further locative surnames could have been discovered in either county. It is, however, thought that the list is sufficiently representative to provide evidence for conclusions about the movement into East Anglia of locative surnames originating outside the region. The observations that follow are based on the evidence provided by this list.

It has already been remarked that there is some evidence for movement into the region from fairly distant parts of England during the 12th century. During the 13th, 14th and 15th centuries, the fuller evidence available about locative surnames indicates a continual flow of migrants into East Anglia. So far as can be seen from the appearance of locative surnames in the region, there was no period during the Middle Ages when an exceptionally large inflow of migrants took place. The period after the Black Death, for instance, did not give rise to any major increase of immigration into East Anglia, so far as can be detected. The evidence suggests a steady and long-continued movement into the region.

It is not surprising that Lincolnshire and Essex are the two counties that contributed the greatest numbers of locative surnames appearing in Norfolk and Suffolk from other counties. Though the Essex places concerned are dispersed throughout the county, a high proportion of them are from two districts, the north-west corner of the county, and the district along the Thames estuary. Persons with locative surnames from Essex are to be found widely scattered in East Anglia during the Middle Ages, and do not seem to be particularly concentrated in any one district. Locative surnames from Lincolnshire are almost as common as those from Essex. Numerous Lincolnshire locative surnames occurred during the 13th and 14th centuries in west Norfolk at no great distance from the Lincolnshire border, and many of these came from places in south-west Lincolnshire, so that only a short-range movement was involved. Lincolnshire names were however to be found in other parts of East Anglia, though less commonly. The surnames in question are largely derived from two regions: the area in south-west Lincolnshire near the Norfolk border and the southern part of the Wolds. A survey of Lincolnshire locative surnames occurring in early 16th-century Norfolk showed that most of them came from the same two districts.[20] Locative surnames from other parts of Lincolnshire were much less common during the Middle Ages, but some did occur. This was particularly so at Norwich itself, where those found include names derived from the larger places in Lincolnshire, such as Lincoln, Louth, Grimsby, Spalding, and so forth.[21] The concentration of Lincolnshire locative names in West Norfolk had ceased to exist by the early 16th century.[22]

After Essex and Lincolnshire, Cambridgeshire is the county that provides the most locative surnames. The Cambridgeshire names were derived mostly from the eastern part of the county, especially the districts around Newmarket and Wisbech, and during the Middle Ages they were considerably more common in west Norfolk and in north-west Suffolk than in other parts of East Anglia, so that the movement of population from Cambridgeshire was to a large extent over fairly short distances.

No other county provided locative surnames in East Anglia comparable in numbers to those from Essex, Lincolnshire and Cambridgeshire. Very few locative surnames occurring in East Anglia can be certainly derived from places in the south east Midlands (Bedfordshire, Buckinghamshire, Hertfordshire, Huntingdonshire, and Northamptonshire), despite the nearness of the region to East Anglia. Many of the locative surnames from the south-east Midlands are those derived from boroughs or market towns, such as Bedford, Sandy, Brackley, Hertford, Ware, Huntingdon, Ramsey, St. Neots, Peterborough, Daventry, and Northampton, rather than from smaller places.[23] Considerably more numerous are the locative surnames from places in two more distant counties, Leicestershire and Warwickshire. There are very few locative surnames occurring in medieval East Anglia that can be certainly derived from the west Midlands, the Welsh marches, or south-west England. Indeed, apart from the counties already mentioned the only ones in southern England that gave rise to any substantial number of locative surnames found in Norfolk and Suffolk were Kent and Sussex, each of which produced about the same number as Leicestershire or Warwickshire. The Sussex surnames were mostly from the eastern half of the county, and their relative commonness may owe something to the fact that Lewes Priory had large possessions in Norfolk, and that two large landowning families, the Earls Warenne and the Hastings family (eventually earls of Pembroke) had extensive holdings both in Sussex and in East Anglia.[24] The Kent locative surnames came predominantly from the north west of the county, and particularly from places on or near the Thames estuary.

So far as concerns the north of England, locative surnames derived from all three ridings in Yorkshire appear in East Anglia during the Middle Ages, and indeed the number from each of the ridings is similar to the number derived from Kent or Sussex. The fact that there were so many names from Yorkshire no doubt owes something to the high proportion of surnames there that were of the locative type, but even allowing for this factor, the evidence suggests that there was more migration from Yorkshire than there was from, say, the south-east Midlands. The surnames from the North and East Ridings were not derived from any limited areas, but a high proportion of them were from market towns or larger places. The surnames Pickering, Beverley, York, Whitby, and Thirsk occur in East Anglia, for example.[25] A majority of the surnames derived from West Riding place-names come from the south-eastern part of the Riding, especially from the area around Doncaster and Bawtry. Places in the south-east part that have given rise to surnames in medieval East Anglia include Bawtry, Bilham, Brotherton, Cawood, Conisborough, Doncaster, Drax, Pontefract, Selby, and Trumfleet.[26]

As regards the northern counties, only a fairly small number of surnames appear to be derived from places in Northumberland and Durham, though there are more from these two counties than from the south-east Midlands, or from the west and southwest of England. Places in County Durham and Northumberland that gave rise to surnames found in Norfolk and Suffolk during the 16th century or earlier include Durham itself, Bamborough, Bellingham, Errington, Harbottle, Lesbury, Reaveley, Redesdale, Rumby, and Shaftoe.[27] The number of surnames derived from places in Cumberland and Westmorland is also quite small, but since these two counties are more remote from East Anglia than almost any other part of England, the presence of even a limited number of names from this region is noteworthy. Places in Cumberland and Westmorland that have given rise to surnames occurring in East Anglia not later than the 16th century include Carlisle and Kendal, both of which occur in several places in Norfolk and Suffolk during the later Middle Ages, Blennerhasset, Wetherall, and Strickland.[28] In addition, some surnames occur in East Anglia that are clearly derived from places in the four northernmost English counties, but that cannot be derived confidently from any one place-name. The name Coupeland, for example, which is found at Norwich, may be derived from places in Cumberland, Westmorland, or Northumberland.[29] Similarly the surname Newbiggin, found at Lynn, may be derived from one of several places called Newbiggin in northern England. It is interesting that a man from Newbiggin (unfortunately the place is not further identified in the record) was admitted a freeman of Lynn in 1381-82, though his surname was not derived from the place.[30] There were thus a small but significant number of surnames in East Anglia derived from place-names in the four northern counties, a number sufficient to indicate that there was some migration during the Middle Ages, even from that relatively remote part of England.

The foregoing paragraphs summarise the evidence about locative surnames occurring in the whole of Norfolk and Suffolk, and derived from place-names outside the two counties. These include of course many surnames that appear in rural villages only. An examination of the locative surnames occurring in two of the region's larger towns, Norwich and Lynn, will perhaps illustrate some aspects of the subject in more detail.

One characteristic of both Norwich and Lynn was the high proportion of locative surnames. At Norwich the surviving records of freemens' admissions begin in 1317. Between that date and 1350, 49 per cent of all freemen had locative surnames or bye-names. For the whole period 1317-1400, 38 per cent of freemen had locative names. For the 15th century, the figure was only 17 per cent.[31] At Lynn, where the record of admissions begins in 1292, 56 per cent of those admitted up to 1300 had locative surnames or bye-names, 64 per cent in the period 1301-50, 49 per cent in 1351-1400, 27 per cent in 1401-50, and 24 per cent in 1451-1500.[32] The position at Yarmouth seems to have been similar to that at Norwich. In the period from 1429 (when the record of Yarmouth admissions to the freedom begins) to 1500, 18 per cent of all those admitted had locative surnames.[33] Clearly there was a marked decrease during the later Middle Ages in the proportion of freemen having locative names. The main cause of this decline is a reduction in the number of freemens' surnames or bye-names that were derived from places in Norfolk, and especially from places close to Lynn and Norwich respectively. It has been pointed out by Dr. Reaney that in 1285-1350 inhabitants of Norwich (not only freemen of the city,) can be found who bore names derived from a great number of places within Norfolk, 351 in all, and that these greatly outnumbered those with names from places in all the other English counties put together.[34] At King's Lynn, too, a large majority of the locative names borne by freemen admitted before 1350 were derived either from places in Norfolk, or from places in the neighbouring counties of Cambridgeshire and Lincolnshire within 15 miles of Lynn.[35] The marked decline in the proportion of locative surnames from Norfolk, or in the case of Lynn from Norfolk and the neighbouring parts of Lincolnshire and Cambridgeshire taken together, after the middle of the 14th century was probably due rather to the rise of hereditary surnames than to any change in the pattern of migration. In the late 13th and early 14th centuries, it is probable that many of the migrants into towns did not have hereditary surnames, and there may naturally have been a strong tendency for them to acquire surnames or bye-names from their native villages. The much reduced proportion of locative names at Lynn and Norwich after *c.* 1350 suggests that many such names never became hereditary. When the majority of the rural population acquired hereditary surnames, a position which had probably been reached by *c.* 1350 in East Anglia,[36] then most new migrants into the towns would arrive already in possession of stable surnames, and so far as those from East Anglia were concerned, the proportion of locative surnames would only be as high as amongst the region's population generally.

Dr. Reaney considered the locative names occurring among the inhabitants of Norwich listed in several sources for 1285-1350. His analysis shows that no county apart from Norfolk and Suffolk contributed any substantial number of names. The most important county outside East Anglia was Lincolnshire; Yorkshire, Cambridgeshire, and Essex provided rather fewer names than Lincolnshire; there are a few names from the remaining east Midland counties, and only one or two isolated examples from other regions.[37] The locative surnames of Norwich freemen admitted between 1317 (when the records of admissions commence) and 1500 show the

D

same pattern, with surnames derived from the various counties in much the same proportions as in the sources used by Dr. Reaney. There is little change in the pattern of locative surnames from outside East Anglia occurring amongst the Norwich freemen during the whole period 1317-1500. Surnames from the east Midlands are more common during the 15th century than earlier, but the number of names from that region is small at any period, and not much significance can be given to the alteration.[38]

At Lynn, during the period 1292-1500, the county that after Norfolk gave rise to the greatest number of locative surnames or bye-names among those admitted to the freedom was Lincolnshire, from which throughout the whole period there came consistently more locative names from any other county save Norfolk. Nearly as many locative names came from the three Ridings of Yorkshire, taken together, as from Lincolnshire. More such names came from the south-east part of the West Riding than from any other district in Yorkshire. No other county gave rise to locative names at Lynn in numbers approaching those from Lincolnshire or Yorkshire. Suffolk and Cambridgeshire both provided about a half of the number of names from Lincolnshire, and much smaller numbers again came from Essex, Leicestershire, Northumberland, Westmorland, and Kent. There was no significant number of names from any other county.[39]

One characteristic of the locative surnames that occur in East Anglia but are derived from places outside the region is the high proportion that originate from the names of boroughs or market towns. A populous town would of course be likely to give rise to more surnames than say a small village, except in an unlikely situation where movement was nearly all into the town, and very little out of it. Where locative surnames originate in remote counties or in regions from which few locative surnames occur in East Anglia, the predominance of names derived from the larger places is especially great. Some remarks have already been made about this in connection with the more distant parts of Lincolnshire, the southeast Midlands, and the North and East Ridings of Yorkshire.[40] With more distant counties the characteristic is even more pronounced. In Dr. Reaney's collection of locative surnames occurring at Norwich, for example, the only places listed in Oxfordshire, Berkshire, Worcestershire, Hampshire, Dorset and Sussex are Oxford, Wantage, Evesham, Winchester, Shaftesbury, Wareham, and Chichester, all cities, boroughs, or market towns, while in contrast the same collection includes surnames originating from very numerous Norfolk villages, and a smaller but still considerable number of Suffolk ones.[41] In the list of locative surnames occurring in Norfolk and Suffolk during the Middle Ages, already mentioned,[42] the only place in Hampshire that can certainly be identified as having given rise to a locative surname in Norfolk or Suffolk is Winchester; in Huntingdonshire the places that can be certainly identified are the towns of Huntingdon, Ramsey, and St. Neots, and five villages, though the county is not distant from the Norfolk border; in Somerset the only identifiable places are Bath and Taunton, and in Wiltshire Salisbury.[43]

It is very doubtful if this can have been caused by cities and towns in distant counties being well known in Norfolk and Suffolk, whereas villages from the same counties would be unknown. No doubt cities like Salisbury and Winchester were well known in East Anglia, and some smaller places may have been well known too, because of trading connections. Beverley and Bawtry in York-shire, for example, which both gave rise to locative surnames occurring in Norfolk, though neither of them very large, were river ports, and may have been well known on that account.[44] It is unlikely, however, that market towns in the more distant counties, such as Wantage in Berkshire, or Pickering in North Yorkshire (from both of which as already stated locative surnames found in East Anglia were derived), can have been much better known in Norfolk or Suffolk than villages in the same counties.

It may also be suspected that in some instances where people appear in Norfolk or Suffolk bearing surnames derived from villages in counties some distance away, they are migrants not directly from the villages concerned, but from neighbouring towns. The surname Leicester, for example, occurred fairly frequently in East Anglia.[45] There also occur the surnames Anlep, Ayleston, Humberston, and Kilby, all most probably derived from villages within a few miles of Leicester, though Humberston may be from a Lincolnshire village.[46] All four surnames occur at Leicester during the 13th and 14th centuries, and except for Kilby all were fairly common there.[47] It must be suspected that the bearers of these names were migrants from Leicester itself to East Anglia. Nicholas de Knapetoft of Leicester, mentioned at Ipswich in 1327-8, bore the name of a Leicestershire village, but was an inhabitant of the borough itself.[48] Similar cases can be found in connection with other major towns. Richard de Dodenhale, who occurs in Norfolk under Richard II, came from the city of Coventry, despite his surname, and John Bernes, citizen of London, who occurs at Hunstanton in 1358-9, probably derived his name from Barnes in Surrey.[49]

These cases, and other examples that could be cited, strengthen the impression that migration into East Anglia from any counties that were at all distant came mostly from the towns. There is a very marked difference between the great number of locative surnames occurring in East Anglia that originate from places within the region, many of them villages or small hamlets, and the fewer but still quite numerous locative names derived from places in immediately adjoining areas such as Essex, Cambridgeshire, or south Lincolnshire, also including many derived from small inhabited places, on the one hand, and on the other the locative surnames derived from other parts of England, that include a relatively high proportion of surnames drawn from the names of larger places. It seems that while there was much migration over short distances between villages in East Anglia and the bordering counties, and also movement locally from villages into large towns like Norwich, those involved in movement into East Anglia over longer distances tended to be largely though not entirely from towns and cities.

How far were the persons bearing any one locative surname of East Anglian origin likely to be members of one family, and how far did locative surnames from other parts introduced into the region take root and spread there? In the case of many surnames it is of course impossible to answer such questions, but some examples will perhaps throw light on the processes involved.

One distinctive Norfolk surname is Larwood. The name first occurs at Horstead, north east of Norwich, and is apparently derived from a locality in Horstead parish. A survey of Horstead, made in 1586, mentions Larwode Hyrne and Larwode Lyng Common.[50] The first person of the name to be found is John son of Geoffrey de Larwode of Horstead, who was buying property in Old Swine-market Street at Norwich in 1299, and subsequently. William de Larwode of Horstead, a cleric, who bought property in old Swine-market Street in 1303, must almost certainly have been a relative, though the connection cannot be traced.[51] About 1300 the surname does not seem to have been altogether stable, for although John took his father's name, and was known as John de Larwode, one of his sons, Thomas, a clergyman, was known as Thomas de Horstede.[52] In 1329-30 four persons called de Larwode were listed at Horstead in a subsidy roll, John, who was presumably the same person as the John de Larwode already mentioned, two persons both called Nicholas de Larwode, and a Geoffrey de Larwode, who is perhaps unlikely to have been the same person as the Geoffrey mentioned in 1299.[53] Evidently by that date the surname was well established at Horstead, and since Larwood was a small locality it seems very probable that all those surnamed Larwood were members of the same family. There are occasional references to persons named Larwood at Horstead during the later Middle Ages. In 1379 a John de Larwode, John de Larwode junior, and a Thomas Larwode were listed at Horstead, and John de Larwod junior is mentioned there again in 1382. A Nicholas Larwod of Stratton Parva (Stratton Strawless, a few miles from Horstead) was holding land at Horstead in 1452.[54] A John Larwode, a cleric, who died in 1430, had no known connection with Horstead. His will asks that he be buried at Wiveton, Norfolk. It also mentions his brother, Thomas Larwood. Henry Larwode, mentioned at North Elmham in 1421-22, is also not known to be connected with others of the name.[55] Though the pedigree cannot be traced, the long connection of the name with Horstead, and the recurrence of certain christian names, strongly suggest that all the Larwoods belonged to the same family. By the early 16th century the surname had spread considerably. Certain Norfolk sources for 1522-25 list 16 persons called Larwood in the county. None of them were at Horstead, but 14 were in north-east Norfolk at no great distance from that place, including seven in a group of adjoining parishes. The remaining two were at Fakenham, a market town in north-west Norfolk, and at Carlton Rode, a village in the south east of the county. At the same period two persons called Larwood are mentioned in East Suffolk, the first instances found of the name outside Norfolk.[56] In this instance it is likely that the surname originated with a single family, first appearing in the late 13th century, and becoming a stable hereditary surname in the 14th, but as late as the 1520s still very largely concentrated in the part of Norfolk where it originated.

Other examples could be given of locative surnames originating in Norfolk or Suffolk that seem to have originated with a single family, and then to have spread, mostly in the same neighbourhood as the place of origin. There are also some locative surnames brought into East Anglia by migration, that appear to have belonged to a single family so far as the region itself is concerned, whatever may have been the position in other parts of England. One example of this is the surname Fitling, derived from the East Yorkshire village of Fitling, near Hull. The surname Feiling is derived from the village, but has not been found in Norfolk or Suffolk during the Middle Ages.[57] Fitling occurs as a surname in the 15th century at Hull, from which the village was only 10 miles distant.[58] Pagan Fitting of Ingworth, who was buying property at Norwich in 1290, and Richard Fittyng of Ingworth, who became a freeman of Norwich in 1319-20, may have derived their surname from the village, but that is uncertain, and no connection can be traced between them and the family called Fitling who occur in Norfolk later.[59] The earliest person called Fitlyng found in Norfolk was Thomas Fitlyng, a fishman, who was admitted to the freedom of

Norwich in 1380-81.[60] When Thomas's widow made her will in
1429 the executors included Robert Fyttyng, fishman and citizen
of Norwich who must have been a relative, and was probably
Thomas's son.[61] Robert's own will, dated 1444-5, left property at
Norwich and at Heigham, a village just outside Norwich to the
south, to his widow, with reversion to his son Thomas.[62] The younger
Thomas's descendants have not been traced, but by his day the
family was evidently established in the countryside south of Norwich.

ohn Fitlyng, who in 1484 bequeathed property at Kimberley,
about nine miles from Heigham, was probably a member of the
same family, perhaps a son of the younger Thomas. The Norfolk
returns for the subsidy granted in 1523 list eight persons called
Fitling (Fytlyng, Fyttlyng, etc.), all in a limited area around
Kimberley and Wymondham.[63] The name does not occur in Norwich
at that date, and it does not occur in the Suffolk returns for the
1523 subsidy. This seems to be a case of a surname that was brought
into Norfolk from Yorkshire by a migrant to Norwich, involved in
the fish trade, at the end of the 14th century, present in Norwich
for two generations, and by the early 16th was well established in
one district of Norfolk but no longer found in Norwich. It is an
example of how rapidly, in the course of little more than a century,
a newly-introduced surname could ramify.

Here, too, other examples could be given of locative surnames,
derived from places outside East Anglia, that were so far as can
be seen brought into the region by a single person, and subsequently
became relatively common, compared to other locative surnames,
in one particular district of the region. It would, however, certainly
be an error to suppose that all East Anglian locative surnames
originated with a single family, or that all locative surnames that
occurred in the region but were derived from places outside it
were brought in by a single migrant whose descendants subsequently multiplied. Dr. Reaney has pointed out this in connection
with immigrants to London, some of them from East Anglia,[64] and
examples can be found of locative surnames within the region that
seem clearly to have originated with more than one family. For
instance, the presence in East Anglia of people with surnames
derived from Leicester and its surrounding villages has already
been mentioned. The surname Leicester was present in the region
from the early 13th century onwards, and during that century the
name occurs at various places in both Norfolk and Suffolk, without
any known connection between the persons so named.[65] In the
Norfolk subsidy rolls for 1329-30 11 taxpayers called Leicester
(Leycestr, etc.) are listed, in 11 different places, dispersed in various
parts of the county.[66] There is nothing to suggest that these scattered

individuals were all related, and it is very unlikely that they were. In this case, and in others that could be cited, the surname must have been brought into East Anglia by a number of separate immigrants.

Some conclusions about locative surnames may be briefly summarised. The distribution of the very numerous locative surnames derived from place-names inside East Anglia, many of them villages and smaller localities, suggests a great deal of population movement over short distances. The large numbers of locative surnames found in East Anglia that originate from place-names in neighbouring areas, notably Essex, Cambridgeshire, and south Lincolnshire, should be considered as part of the same short distance movement. Over longer distances, however, much movement of population into the region took place from towns and cities. The nature of the evidence makes it impossible to state any accurate statistics for the proportion of migrants coming from villages and hamlets, or from cities and towns, but the general impression left by the evidence is that the majority of migrants into East Anglia from all parts except those immediately bordering the region came from the larger inhabited places.

The number of surnames or bye-names derived from East Anglian place-names is very large, especially in the period *c.* 1200-1350. Many of the names that occur at that period never became hereditary, in all probability. Of those names that did survive, however, and were still to be found in the 16th century, many are likely to have been borne by the descendants of one common ancestor, though no doubt there were exceptions, and though in the nature of the case it is impossible to be precise about ratios. It seems likely, too, that the majority of locative surnames brought into the region from other parts, were originally brought in as the name of a single individual only, though here too there were certainly exceptions.

The consequences for the distribution of locative surnames of migration over a lengthy period can be seen from an examination of the position in Norfolk early in the 16th century. By that date most surnames in the county had been hereditary for at least several generations, and the changes that had taken place in the distribution of locative surnames by then, as compared with earlier periods, provide a means of estimating the amount of movement amongst the county's population as a whole. In order to obtain a picture of the distribution of locative surnames throughout Norfolk at one particular period, the surnames found in two early 16th-century sources have been listed. The two sources are the returns for the 'Military Survey' of 1522, and the returns for the lay subsidy granted in 1523, which between them cover almost the whole of Norfolk, though of course the returns do not all relate to precisely the same date.[67]

The distribution of locative surnames in Norfolk during the 1520s, as revealed in these sources, was very different from the situation that existed some 200 years earlier, as has already been described.[68] In all, 19 per cent of the surnames listed in the two Norfolk sources just mentioned were derived from place names. This figure only includes surnames of which the origins can be identified without any reasonable doubt. Inevitably some doubtful cases have been found, and the true proportion of locative surnames is no doubt slightly higher. In order to have some firm basis for drawing conclusions, however, it has seemed best to exclude all dubious instances from consideration, and to restrict all calculations to those surnames where there is no reasonable doubt of their origins. The figures given below, therefore, though they do not relate to quite the whole body of locative surnames to be found in the sources concerned, are nevertheless based on an examination of the great majority of such surnames. It is also true that the locative surnames under consideration form less than a fifth of the total number of surnames to be found in the two sources, and that it would be imprudent to assume too readily that where migration is involved figures derived from locative surnames alone can be regarded as completely typical of the whole population. After all these reservations have been made, however, it is unlikely that deductions based on this sizeable body of locative surnames will be misleading in general terms. It is of course not claimed that mathematically precise statistics can be produced by such methods, but the general picture that results should be reasonably accurate.

In the two main sources already mentioned for the 1520s,[69] there are listed surnames that are derived from 179 places in Norfolk, and in addition there are 14 place-names that have given rise to surnames found in the sources, but for which it is impossible to identify the places concerned with certainty because there are more than one place in the county with the same name, or with names so similar as to make identification hazardous.[70] A good many doubtful cases have been excluded; there are in the two sources concerned 56 further surnames that are almost certainly derived from place-names, but for which it is uncertain whether they derived from places inside or outside the county, and there are a further small number of surnames which could be derived from place-names, but which could have some quite different origin. However there are 193 place-names in Norfolk which can be said with reasonable certainty to have given rise to surnames that occur in the two sources concerned.

The two sources do not of course list the whole adult male population of the county, and no doubt there were locative surnames existing in Norfolk during the 1520s that were not mentioned in the two sources. It is also of course true that there were surnames, originating from Norfolk place-names, that were by the 1520s only to be found outside the county. It is hardly feasible to search all possible sources, inside and outside Norfolk, for locative surnames originating inside the county, and surviving into the 1520s. However, the Suffolk returns for the subsidy granted in 1523 record surnames derived from nine places in Norfolk, not included in the 193 places already mentioned.[71] The Essex returns for the same subsidy list surnames derived from six more places in Norfolk, additional to the nine mentioned in Suffolk, and the 193 places occurring in the two Norfolk sources.[72] These figures for two counties that might have been expected to receive more migrants from Norfolk than most areas, do not suggest that there were very large numbers of surnames derived from Norfolk place names to be found outside the county that did not also occur within it, though no doubt a more extensive search through other early 16th-century sources would glean some more examples. As for the existence inside Norfolk of locative surnames derived from Norfolk places other than the 193 already mentioned, Walter Rye's *Norfolk Families*, which admittedly deals only with armigerous families, lists families bearing names derived from more than 30 places in Norfolk that are not among the 193 Norfolk places already mentioned, or in the further 15 places found, as just described, in the Suffolk and Essex subsidy returns. Of the families dealt with by Rye, however, many had become extinct by about 1520, and some of the names involved had possibly never become established as hereditary surnames. If only families listed in Rye's work continuing to exist after 1500 are taken into account, then surnames can be found derived from no more than eight further Norfolk place-names, additional to the 193 place names already mentioned, and the 15 found in the Suffolk and Essex subsidies.[73] In all, these various sources provide a list of 216 Norfolk places from which surnames surviving into the 1520s were derived.

These 216 places were only a small proportion of the inhabited places existing in Norfolk during the 16th century, perhaps very roughly about a quarter. It does not appear that the places concerned fall predominantly into any one category of settlement. It is not the case, for example, that the places from which the 16th century locative surnames are derived are mostly the more populous ones such as boroughs and market towns. Nor is it true that the places concerned were predominantly those villages, most of them always small, that became depopulated during or before the 16th

century, though it might be thought that people migrating away
from such villages would be particularly likely to acquire locative
surnames derived from their former homes.[74] What seems clear is
that although places from which Norfolk locative surnames were
derived can be found in all parts of the county, there were two areas
from which a significantly high proportion of such surnames were
derived. One of these was the part of north-east Norfolk lying around
North Walsham. Twenty-nine places in this area gave rise to surnames, and there are a further four places in the area that may
have originated surnames, but about which there is some uncertainty.[75] The second area was the coastal district of north-west
Norfolk, where 11 places certainly and a further four places possibly,
gave rise to surnames.[76] To delve into possible economic causes for
this situation would go beyond the scope of a study concerned
essentially with the history of surnames, though it must be supposed
that there were features in the economic or social arrangements of
the two areas that produced this result.

The main interest, however, in the locative surnames to be found
in the two early 16th-century sources under discussion is the
evidence they provide about migration during the preceding period.
The surnames may be divided into two main categories, those
derived from the names of places inside Norfolk, and those derived
from places outside the county.

The two main sources list 739 persons with surnames derived from
Norfolk places, if doubtful instances are excluded. When the distribution of these surnames is considered, the most obvious fact is the
small number that were still resident at, or very near to, the places
from which their surnames originated. The following table shows
how far persons with locative surnames listed in the two sources
were from the places that gave rise to their surnames. The distances
have been arrived at by the admittedly rather rough and arbitrary
method of measuring distances between the centres of inhabited
places on a modern Ordnance Survey map, but it is thought that
the table gives a reasonably accurate picture of the general position.

> Persons, in Norfolk, listed in the two 16th-
> century sources,[77] with surnames derived
> from Norfolk place-names, showing the
> distance between the places where they were
> listed in the two sources, and the places from
> which surnames were derived.

Listed at place of surnames' origin	23
Listed within 5 miles from origin	81
Listed 6–10 miles from origin	123

Listed 11–20 miles from origin   239
Listed 21–30 miles from origin   151
Listed over 30 miles from origin   122

Total   739

These figures only deal with migration inside Norfolk, and consequently do not give any indication of how much longer range migration took place, across the county's borders. The only way in which a full picture could be obtained would be by making a thorough search through all available source material for the period, to track down all occurrences of people with surnames derived from places in Norfolk. This would be an impossibly large task. However, the Suffolk and Essex returns for the subsidy granted in 1523 have been searched,[78] the persons with locative surnames derived from Norfolk have been noted, and the distances between the places where such persons occurred, and the places from which their surnames were derived, have been measured. The following table shows the result when the Suffolk and Essex figures are added to those already given for Norfolk. (Percentages are out of the total of 900.)

	Norfolk	Suffolk	Essex	Total
Listed at place of surnames' origin	23 (3%)	0	0	23 (3%)
Listed within 5 miles from origin	81 (9%)	1 (0%)	0	82 (9%)
Listed 6–10 miles from origin	123 (14%)	4 (·5%)	0	127 (14%)
Listed 11–20 miles from origin	239 (26%)	16 (2%)	0	255 (28%)
Listed 21–30 miles from origin	151 (17%)	20 (2%)	0	171 (19%)
Listed over 30 miles from origin	122 (13%)	66 (7.5%)	54 (6%)	242 (27%)
Totals	739 (82%)	107 (12%)	54 (6%)	900

Suffolk and Essex are likely to have been the two counties that received more migrants from Norfolk than any others. Nevertheless, if a similar search had been made through all the other counties, and the resulting figures added to the above table, then the proportion of persons migrating over long distances would obviously be shown as considerably larger.

Considerations of time have prevented similar figures being produced for Suffolk, though a preliminary survey of the Suffolk returns for the subsidy granted in 1523[79] indicates that the position in that county was very similar to the position in Norfolk. The

figures given in the preceding table may be compared with the
distribution of persons with locative surnames occurring in the
Suffolk 1327 subsidy roll.[80]

It would be rash to assume that the proportion of people with
locative surnames that migrated from their native towns or villages
was exactly the same as the proportion for the population as a
whole. Some persons with locative surnames, though not by any
means all, appear to have acquired them on moving away from
their native settlements. In consequence the proportion of migrants
amongst people with locative surnames may have been rather
higher than the average for the whole population. The evidence
summarised in the above tables does, however, suggest that between
the time when most surnames became hereditary, and the 1520s, a
period of perhaps 200 years very approximately, most Norfolk
families changed their place of residence at least once. That there
was considerable geographical mobility among the rural population
during the later Middle Ages has been shown in a study of the
Ramsey Abbey estates (mostly in Huntingdonshire), using an
entirely different type of evidence.[81] The evidence put forward here
concerning locative surnames perhaps shows how general such
mobility was in a clearer way than could be done by using any
other approach.

The migration within and outside Norfolk of persons bearing
locative surnames originating in the county is only one aspect of the
matter. The migration into East Anglia of persons with locative
surnames originating in other counties has already been discussed
with reference to the medieval period.[82] It may be useful to summarise here the position that had been reached by the early 16th
century, as evidenced in Norfolk by the two main sources that have
already been described.[83] In these sources there occur 1,260 persons
with locative surnames derived from English places, outside Norfolk.
This figure excludes doubtful cases, and is therefore in the nature
of a minimum. It also excludes persons with surnames derived from
places outside England. This figure of 1,260 persons must be compared with the 739 persons with locative names derived from places
in Norfolk, already mentioned, and with a total of about 18,500
persons listed in the two sources. The 1,260 persons are about seven
per cent of the total number listed in the two sources, but it obviously
cannot be supposed that only those with locative surnames migrated
into Norfolk, while those with surnames of other types punctiliously
remained outside the county's border. About 17 per cent of all those
listed in the two sources had locative surnames, and if, calculating
on this basis, it could be safely assumed that the 1,260 persons just
mentioned were 17 per cent of the total number of migrants, or

descendants of migrants, into Norfolk, then the total of migrants or their descendants would be about 7,400. Such a calculation, however, involves some rash assumptions. In the first place it cannot be taken for granted that persons with locative surnames were not more likely to migrate than persons with surnames in other categories. As has been stated already, there are some grounds for thinking that persons with such surnames may have been more likely than others to be migrants. Secondly, it cannot be assumed that in the regions from which the migrants came the proportion of locative surnames was the same as in early 16th-century Norfolk. In West Yorkshire, for example, it is known that the proportion was considerably higher,[84] and this was an area that contributed some migrants to Norfolk. It is therefore impossible to calculate accurately what proportion of the Norfolk population in the 1520s were migrants into the county, or the descendants of migrants. It would probably be a conservative estimate to suppose that the 1,260 persons mentioned above were one half of the total number of migrants, or descendants of migrants, among the 18,500 individuals listed in the two sources. On the basis of such a supposition, about 14 per cent of the whole 18,500 would be migrants, or their descendants. This figure is at best a very rough estimate, but it does perhaps give some impression of the proportion of the county's population that by the early 16th century were either migrants themselves, or were descended from migrants who had entered the county at or after the period when surnames became hereditary. This situation of course implies a considerable geographical mobility during the later Middle Ages, with sizeable numbers of people making moves at least sufficiently far to take them into a new county, but it also has certain implications for the history of surnames. It is clear that if a surname is found in East Anglia in the 16th century, even if it has been established there for many years and has ramified in the region, it cannot be taken for granted that the name is East Anglian in origin.

What were the principal regions from which the migrants entering Norfolk came? The number of locative surnames derived from each of the other counties, or from the various main regions of England outside East Anglia, should indicate with reasonable accuracy the areas from which the migrants came. Judging from such evidence, the most important source for immigrants into Norfolk was Suffolk. Locative surnames derived from places in the latter county are widespread in Norfolk, and are not in any way concentrated in the area just north of the Norfolk and Suffolk border. The surnames in question, however, did not come in equal proportions from all parts of Suffolk. The district from which most of the surnames came was the inland part of East Suffolk, the hundreds of Hartismere, Hoxne, Bosmere and Claydon, Thredling, Carlford, and Wangford. There were few from the coastal area, and not many from any part of West Suffolk. In the great majority of cases the places from which the surnames were derived were only villages,[85] in contrast to the locative surnames drawn from more distant counties. In the two sources there are listed in Norfolk about a hundred persons whose surnames can be confidently derived from Suffolk place-names, and about a further hundred whose names might be derived from Suffolk place-names, but which might possibly have other origins. In view of the important part clearly played by migration from Suffolk it must be considered likely that many of these doubtful cases were in fact of Suffolk origin, but it is impossible to be certain.

After Suffolk the next most important county was Lincolnshire. Most of the Lincolnshire locative surnames listed in Norfolk were derived from places in Holland and Kesteven. The only places in Lindsey that certainly gave rise to surnames found in the two sources for Norfolk were Grimsby and Manby.[86] Among the Lincolnshire surnames those from the towns of Lincoln, Boston, Grantham, Spalding, Stamford, and Tattershall form about a quarter of the total number. Apart from these six towns, the other Lincolnshire surnames came mostly from two limited areas, in the south of the county, the district around the south-west part of the Wash, near the Norfolk border, and the southern part of the Lincolnshire wolds. Lincolnshire locative surnames, like those from Suffolk, were widespread in Norfolk in the early 16th century. There was no particular concentration in the parts of Norfolk adjoining Lincolnshire. The two sources list about 90 persons in Norfolk with Lincolnshire locative surnames, and there are about 70 further persons whose names might be derived from Lincolnshire place-names, but where there is some doubt as to origins.

The whole of the East Midlands region provided remarkably few locative surnames in early 16th-century Norfolk. Even Cambridgeshire, provided very few, many less than Suffolk or Lincolnshire. Cambridgeshire apart, the only county in the East Midlands that provided any significant number of surnames was Leicestershire, which though relatively distant provided nearly as many surnames as Cambridgeshire. In view of the nearness of the East Midlands, the lack of surnames from the region in Norfolk is surprising. It may well be due to the attraction of London for emigrants from the East Midlands during the Middle Ages.[87]

There were, however, three other counties from which substantial numbers of locative surnames found in Norfolk were derived, Essex, Kent, and Yorkshire. Essex and Kent each produced a little less than half of the number of locative surnames produced by Suffolk. The places from which the Essex locative surnames were derived are distributed in all parts of the county, without being noticeably concentrated in any one area,[88] but the Kent names come mostly from places lying within a few miles of the county's north coast, with markedly fewer from the districts adjoining the east coast, and only a very few from the inland district of Kent. The Kent places that gave rise to locative surnames found in Norfolk are mostly villages near the coast, but not actually upon it. It may be conjectured that early bearers of these names first migrated from the villages that gave rise to their surnames to Kentish ports, and that subsequently they, or perhaps more probably their descendants, migrated to Norfolk. Locative surnames originating in Kent and Essex are widely spread in Norfolk, and are not limited in any one area, nor are they confined to the larger towns.

All three Ridings of Yorkshire gave rise to substantial numbers of locative surnames found in early 16th-century Norfolk. From each of the three Ridings there occur in the two sources already described about 40 persons whose names can be derived with reasonable certainty from places in the Riding, and about another 40 which could possibly be derived from places in the Riding, but for which there are other possible origins. The ramification in Norfolk of one surname from the East Riding, Fitling, has already been discussed.[89] It has been shown that the surname Fitling appeared in Norfolk at Norwich, and then in the course of rather more than a century became established in the south-east part of the county. By the early 16th century Yorkshire locative surnames were widespread in Norfolk, and it seems probable that in many cases such surnames first arrived at one of the main Norfolk ports, and later spread into the countryside over a period of several generations. Even allowing for the fact that locative surnames form an unusually high proportion of surnames in Yorkshire,[90] a factor that tends to make Yorkshire locative surnames in Norfolk look rather more important, relative to those from other counties, than in fact they were, the existence in Norfolk of numerous surnames originating in Yorkshire must indicate more migration from Yorkshire than from most other counties.

Many English counties provide a few locative surnames occurring in early 16th-century Norfolk, but apart from the counties already dealt with, the only region that has provided enough locative surnames to be of any significance in this context is the north-west of England, the counties of Lancashire, Cumberland, and Westmorland. Despite the remoteness of this region from Norfolk, there are distinctly more surnames from the north-west than, for instance, from the west Midlands, a rather nearer region. It seems likely that many of the surnames from the north-west found in Norfolk arrived here not as a result of direct migration, in one stride, from one region to another, but after settlement for a time in some intermediate district. Surnames derived from the north-west of England often occurred in medieval Yorkshire, and it is likely that many north-western locative names arrived in Norfolk as a result of migration from Yorkshire.[91]

The position about English locative surnames from outside Norfolk, present in the county during the early 16th century, has been surveyed in the preceding paragraphs. This is the position reached after almost all surnames had been hereditary for several generations, and many had been hereditary for some two centuries, or more in a limited number of cases. This is a sufficiently long period for a quite considerable amount of migration to have taken place, but at the same time the period covered is not so long for it to be likely that many surnames had undergone a complicated series of migrations. It is indeed quite possible that some surnames found in Norfolk in the early 16th-century sources may well have made more than one migration after leaving the district of origin, but it is improbable that this was true in the majority of cases. In a region like East Anglia, however, which is not geographically isolated, and where there are no major physical barriers to movement within the region, it is evident that the longer the passage of time since surnames became hereditary, the greater the possibility that surnames of all categories had made a series of migrations, perhaps long ones, from their places of origin. For later periods, therefore, it might be risky in such a region to base arguments about migration on the incidence of locative surnames from outside the region.

In the early 16th century locative surnames from outside Norfolk were to be found in all parts of the county, and indeed this had been a characteristic of their distribution for many years previously. The Norfolk subsidy roll for 1329–30, for example, shows that by that date locative surnames from outside the county were already widespread throughout Norfolk.[92] When the relatively copious information in the early 16th-century sources is examined, however, it can be seen that there was at that period one region of Norfolk where an unusually high proportion of the inhabitants had surnames derived from places outside the county. This was the part of north-east Norfolk around Aylsham and North Walsham. Some parishes in this area have a much larger than average proportion of persons listed in the sources, bearing locative surnames, with unusually high ratios both of locative surnames originating inside Norfolk, and of ones from outside the county.[93] One other characteristic of the surnames of this region is that locative surnames originating within it tend to be concentrated closer to the places from which they originated than is the case for the county as a whole.[94] The obvious explanation for this state of affairs is that this was a region which, for some time before the early 16th century, had attracted immigrants from elsewhere, while at the same time losing fewer of its own population through emigration than did other parts of Norfolk. Certain factors in the economic history of the region provide an explanation, but these cannot be discussed here.

There was in the early 16th century one other part of Norfolk, a small area around Great and Little Walsingham, where there was an unusually high proportion of locative surnames derived from other parts of Norfolk. In this case, however, there was no corresponding concentration of locative surnames from outside the county. The existence of so many locative surnames from other parts of Norfolk may probably be ascribed to the opportunities for commerce created by the flow of pilgrims to the Little Walsingham shrine.[95]

One topic that remains to be dealt with is the presence in East Anglia of locative surnames originating outside England. Locative surnames of foreign origin, mostly French, occur in the region from the late 11th century onwards. It is, however, impossible in many cases to identify with certainty the places from which such surnames originated, and it is also not possible to estimate the extent of migration into the region by noting the numbers of locative surnames from outside England, or even by considering all the surnames to which foreign origins may on any grounds be attributed. The dangers of attempting to estimate the number of aliens, or descendants of aliens, in the region by such methods can be seen from the position as it was in the 15th and early 16th centuries, when several sources provide a good deal of useful information. It is clear that in the 15th century aliens were residing in many parts of Norfolk, not only in the ports and large towns, where they might perhaps be expected, but in many rural villages as well. In 1436, for example, when many aliens took oaths of allegiance that were noted in the Patent Rolls, 146 of those who swore allegiance were noted as residing in Norfolk, and between them these 146 aliens were living at 40 different places in Norfolk.[96] This is certainly a very incomplete list of aliens in the county at that date, since many foreigners then living in England did not swear allegiance, and out of those who did, the places of residence are in many cases not recorded on the Patent Rolls.[97] The 15th-century inquisitions into aliens provide a similar picture of a widely dispersed alien population, although the inquisitions are known to have omitted some aliens who were in fact residing in the county, and although the places of residence of those who were listed are not always given.[98] An inquisition of 1440, for instance, which covers in the existing returns just over half the county (18 hundreds, and the boroughs of Yarmouth and Bishop's Lynn), lists 205 aliens. The residences of some are not given, but the remainder were resident at 62 different places.[99] When it is remembered that this was an incomplete list of aliens living in not much more than half of Norfolk, the very widespread nature of alien settlement in Norfolk at this period is evident. There was, however, no corresponding diffusion of foreign surnames, whether locative surnames of foreign origin, or surnames plainly of alien character, in other categories. Thirty-nine of those in the 1440 inquisition were not listed as having surnames at all. These were mostly servants, and it is probable that they had no surnames in fact, rather than that they possessed surnames that were omitted from the returns for the inquisition. Of those that had surnames, many were purely English, such as for instance Capper, Taylor, Couper, Andrew, Hamond, Hobart, and many others.[100] Similarly a separate return of the aliens living in Norwich in 1440 lists persons with such surnames as Rider, Johnson, Forest, Skynner, Couper, Bush, Goldsmyth, and Glasier, which have every appearance of being English.[101] More confusing still, some aliens appear with locative surnames derived from places in England. To give one example from the early 16th century, 11 persons named Duffield or Duffeld are listed in the Norfolk subsidy rolls for 1524 and 1525, 10 of them grouped together in one part of south-east Norfolk. The surname seems to be derived from one or other of the places called Duffield (in Derbyshire, and in East Yorkshire), and in all probability most of the Norfolk Duffields did derive their surnames from one of those two places. However, one of the 10 Duffields listed in south-east Norfolk is noted in the subsidy rolls as an alien. It can only be conjectured that the individual in question possessed when he immigrated to England a surname that somewhat resembled Duffield, and that when he settled in Norfolk his own surname was distorted into the form of a surname already well established locally.

Up to and including the early 16th century, very few surnames (whether locative surnames, or ones in other categories) that can be definitely identified as Welsh, Scots, or Irish occur in East Anglia. No surnames that can be derived with certainty from Welsh place names occur in the two early 16th-century sources already mentioned. The surnames Walsh and Wallis do occur, but in East Anglia these names might well have been bestowed originally upon Breton immigrants, rather than upon Welshmen.[102] The name Welsh occurs only once in the same two sources.[103] In the same two sources there are very few locative surnames of Scots origin.[104] The surname Scot or Scott was well established in East Anglia at an early date. There were, for example, 35 persons called Scot listed in the Suffolk subsidy rolls for 1327, and at least six persons with the same name in the Norfolk Hundred Rolls.[105] In the two main sources for early 16th-century Norfolk, already described, there are 23 persons so named, and in the Suffolk returns for the subsidy granted in 1523, there are at least sixteen.[106] These persons were presumably all ultimately of Scots descent, though not necessarily all direct migrants from Scotland to East Anglia. There are, however, many Scots and Welsh surnames that also occur independently in England, so that it is not possible to estimate the extent of Scots and Welsh migration into East Anglia from surnames with any accuracy.

It is clear that in these circumstances any attempt to estimate the extent of foreign immigration by examining the incidence of identifiably foreign surnames must produce unreliable results. A wide dispersal of foreign immigrants in East Anglia during the Middle Ages did not result in a correspondingly extensive dispersal of alien surnames.

References

[1]Bedingfeld, ed., *Cartulary of Creake Abbey*, pp. 10, 29, 35, 39, 43, 46

[2]Rye, *Calendar of Deeds Relating to Norwich, 1285-1306*, pp. 34, 74; Rye, *Cal. Norf. Fines*, vol. i, p. 111; P.R.O. E179/149/7, m. 3

[3]Hudson, 'Three Manorial Extents', *Norfolk Archaeology*, vol. xiv, p. 46; B. Dodwell, ed., *Feet of Fines for the County of Norfolk, 1198-1202*, p. 194; B. Dodwell, ed., *Feet of Fines for the County of Norfolk, 1201-1215, and for the County of Suffolk, 1199-1214*, p. 12; and see W. Rye, *Index to Norfolk Topography* (Index Society) (1881), pp. 153-4

[4]Reaney, *Dictionary of British Surnames*, p. 85

[5]Rye, *Calendar of Deeds Relating to Norwich, 1285-1306*, p. 52; Rye, *Calendar of Norwich Deeds, 1307-41*, p. 41; Rye, *Cal. Norf. Fines*, vol. i, pp. 67, 75; P.R.O. E179/149/7, mm. 3, 55

[6]K. Allison, 'Lost Villages of Norfolk', *Norfolk Archaeology*, vol. xxxi, p. 162; Rye, *Cal. Norf. Fines*, vol. i, p. 153

[7]*See* pp. 141-42

[8]*Rotuli Hundredorum*, vol. i, pp. 434-543

[9]P.R.O. E179/149/7, *passim*. Some doubtful cases, where identification is uncertain, have been excluded from this figure. Compare the much smaller number of locative surnames surviving in Norfolk in the 16th century: McKinley, *Norfolk Surnames in the Sixteenth Century*, pp. 17-18

[10]*Suffolk in 1327, passim*

[11]*Ibid.*

[12]Rye, *Cal. Norf. Fines*, vols. i and ii, and Rye, *Cal. Suff. Fines*

[13]*See* p. 142

[14]McKinley, *op. cit.*, pp. 21-23

[15]E. Ekwall, *Early London Personal Names* (1947), p. 120; P. H. Reaney *Origin of English Surnames* (1967), p. 346

[16]Reaney, *op. cit.*, p. 346

[17]*Ibid.*, pp. 349, 350

[18]J. H. Bullock, ed., *Norfolk Portion of the Chartulary of the Priory of St. Pancras of Lewes*, p. 37; B. Dodwell, ed., *Feet of Fines for the County of Norfolk, 1201-15, and for the County of Suffolk, 1199-1214*, pp. 4, 5, 221, 232; J. R. West, ed., *St. Benet of Holme*, vol. i, pp. 80, 82, 83, 92; B. Dodwell, ed., *Feet of Fines for the County of Norfolk, 1198-1202*, p. 96.

[19]The sources concerned are: Hart and Lyons, eds., *Cartularium Monasterii de Rameseia*; J. W. West, ed., *St. Benet of Holme, 1020-1210*; J. H. Bullock, ed., *Norfolk Portion of the Chartulary of the Priory of St. Pancras of Lewes*; Bedingfeld, *op. cit.*; *Rotuli Hundredorum*, vols. i and ii; Rye, *Calendar of Deeds Relating to Norwich, 1285-1306*; Rye, *Calendar of Norwich Deeds, 1307-41*; Rye, *Cal. Norf. Fines*, vols. i and ii; L'Estrange, *op. cit.*; Anon., *Calendar of the Freeman of Lynn, 1292-1836*; P.R.O. E179/149/7; E179/149/9; E179/149/49, 50, 51, 53; E179/238/112; *Suffolk in 1327*; Powell, *Rising in East Anglia in 1381*; Powell, *A Suffolk Hundred in 1283*; Rye, *Cal. Suff. Fines*; Davis, ed., *Kalendar of Abbot Samson of Bury St. Edmunds*; and the printed Pipe Rolls for the reigns of Henry II, Richard I, and John.

[20]McKinley, *op. cit.*, p. 26, and see below, p. 96

[21]*See*, e.g. L'Estrange, *op. cit.*, pp. 65, 88, 89, 128; Rye, *Calendar of Deeds Relating to Norwich, 1285-1306*, p. 17, 35, 44, 55

[22]McKinley, *op. cit.*, p. 26

[23]*See* e.g. L'Estrange, *op. cit.*, pp. 19, 41, 72, 114, 100, 102; *Rotuli Hundredorum*, vol. i, p. 474, 475, 482, 495; P.R.O. E179/149/7, mm. 5, 11, 26, 29, 53; Anon., *Calendar of the Freeman of Lynn, 1292-1836*, pp. 3, 5, 69

[24]Bullock, *op. cit.*, *passim; Calendar of Inquisitions Post Mortem*, vol. ix, (1916) nos. 54, 55, 118; vol. vi (1910), pp. 385-93

[25]L'Estrange, *op. cit.*, pp. 15, 109, 112, 155; P.R.O. E179/149/7, m. 59; Rye, *Cal. Norf. Fines*, vol. i, pp. 55, 59, 163, 168; vol. ii, pp. 269, 414, 435

[26]*Rotuli Hundredorum*, vol. i, p. 448; Bullock, *op. cit.*, pp. 37, 48, 63, 69; Rye, *Cal. Norf. Fines*, vol. ii, pp. 250, 388; L'Estrange, *op. cit.*, pp. 40, 121; Anon, *Calendar of the Freeman of Lynn, 1292-1836*, pp. 18, 89; P.R.O. E179/149/7, mm. 3, 4, 25, 29, 53, 54

[27]*Rotuli Hundredorum*, vol. i, pp. 447, 448, 471, 484, 505; L'Estrange, *op. cit.*, pp. 46, 87; Rye, *Cal. Norf. Fines*, vol. i, pp. 143, 151; Rye, *Calendar of Deeds Relating to Norwich, 1285-1306*, p. 105; Rye, *Calendar of Norwich Deeds, 1307-41*, p. 71; Anon, *Calendar of the Freemen of Lynn, 1292-1836*, pp. 54, 75, 79, 86, 92, 96, 116

[28]*Rotuli Hundredorum*, vol. i, p. 471; L'Estrange, *op. cit.*, pp. 81, 132, 148; Rye, *Cal. Norf. Fines*, vol. i, pp. 143, 151; Anon, *Calendar of the Freemen of Lynn, 1292-1836*, pp. 101, 117; P.R.O., E179/150/281

[29]Rye, *Calendar of Deeds Relating to Norwich, 1285-1306*, p. 105; Rye, *Calendar of Norwich Deeds, 1307-41*, p. 71

[30]Anon., *Calendar of the Freemen of Lynn, 1292-1836*, pp. 23, 122

[31]L'Estrange, *op. cit.*, *passim*. And see p. 148

[32]Anon., *Calendar of the Freemen of Lynn, 1292-1836*, pp. 1-73

[33]Anon., *Calendar of the Freeman of Great Yarmouth* (1910), pp. 1-18

[34]Reaney, *Origin of English Surnames*, pp. 331-337

[35]Anon., *Calendar of the Freemen of Lynn, 1292-1836*, pp. 1-11

[36]*See* above, p. 20

[37]Reaney, *op. cit.*, pp. 336-7. A few of Dr. Reaney's identifications of places may be disputable

[38]Because of various inaccuracies and duplications in L'Estrange, *op. cit.*, this paragraph has been based on the Norwich Old Free Book (in the Norfolk and Norwich R.O.). The study of Norwich locative surnames has been greatly assisted by an index of freemen's names, compiled by Miss M. Grace

[39]Anon., *Calendar of the Freemen of Lynn, 1292-1836*, pp. 1-73

[40]*See* above, pp. 80-82

[41]Reaney, *Origins of English Surnames*, pp. 336-7

[42]*See* above, n. 19

[43]*See* sources listed in n. 19 above

[44]L'Estrange, *op. cit.*, p. 15; Rye, *Cal. Norf. Fines*, vol. ii, pp. 349, 388; Anon., *Calendar of the Freemen of Lynn, 1292-1836*, p. 7; P.R.O. E179/149/7, m. 59

[45]*See*, e.g., Rye, *Cal. Norf. Fines*, vol. i, p. 99; vol. ii, p. 311; *Rotuli Hundredorum*, vol. i, p. 478; L'Estrange, *op. cit.*, p. 87; P.R.O. E179/149/7, mm. 22, 23, 27, 29, 31, 32, 33, 40, 49; Hervey, ed., *Pinchbeck Register*, vol. i, p. 98

[46]Anon., *Calendar of the Freemen of Lynn, 1292-1836*, p. 40; Rye, *Cal. Norf. Fines*, vol. ii, pp. 322, 404, 408; Bullock, *op. cit.*, p. 14

[47]*See*, e.g. H. Hartopp, ed., *Register of the Freemen of Leicester, 1196-1770* (1927), pp. 6, 7, 11, 12, 13, 16, 19, 23, 28, 29, 30, 32, 44; M. Bateson, ed., *Records of the Borough of Leicester, 1103-1327* (1899), pp. 30, 69, 144, 210, 255, 260, 263, 272, 356

[48]*Index of Placita de Banco, 1327-8* (P.R.O. Lists and Indexes, xxxii), part ii, p. 631; Bateson, *op. cit.*, pp. 274, 313, 355, 397

[49] Rye, *Cal. Norf. Fines*, vol. ii, pp. 334, 377; M. D. Harris, ed., *Coventry Leet Book, 1907-13*, p. 5

[50] P. Millican, *History of Horstead and Stanninghall, Norfolk* (1937), pp. 208, 210

[51] Rye, *Calendar of Deeds Relating to Norwich, 1285-1306*, pp. 74, 94, 95

[52] Rye, *Calendar of Norwich Deeds, 1307-41*, p. 58

[53] P.R.O. E179/149/7, m. 62

[54] Rye, *Cal. Norf. Fines*, vol. ii, p. 374; Norfolk and Norwich R.O., N.R.S. 3543; Millican, *op. cit.*, p. 37; P.R.O. E179/238/112

[55] Norfolk and Norwich R.O., Norwich Consistory Court Records, Register Surflete, f. 62; Rye, *Cal. Norf. Fines*, vol. ii, p. 405

[56] P.R.O. E101/61/16; E36/25; E179/150/204, 281; *Suffolk in 1524*, pp. 73, 365

[57] Reaney, *Dictionary of British Surnames*, p. 117

[58] K. J. Allison, ed., *A History of Yorkshire East Riding* (Victoria County History) (1969), vol. i, pp. 31, 39, 84

[59] Rye, *Calendar of Deeds Relating to Norwich, 1285-1306*, p. 31; L'Estrange, *op. cit.*, p. 52

[60] Norfolk and Norwich R.O., Norwich Old Free Book, p. 31. Thos. Fitling at one time possessed land in Essex. See Anon., ed., *Feet of Fines for Essex*, (1929-49), vol. iii, pp. 86, 87, 166

[61] Norfolk and Norwich R.O., Norwich Consistory Court Records, Register Surflete, f. 45

[62] *Ibid.*, Register Wylbey, f. 15

[63] P.R.O. E179/150/234, 235

[64] Reaney, *Origins of English Surnames*, pp. 337-42

[65] Davis, ed., *Kalendar of Abbot Samson*, p. 147; Hervey, ed., *Pinchbeck Register*, vol. i, p. 98; Rye, *Cal. Norf. Fines*, vol. i, p. 99; Rye, *Calendar of Deeds Relating to Norwich, 1285-1306*, p. 3

[66] P.R.O. E179/149/7, mm. 22, 23, 27, 29, 31, 32, 33, 40, 49

[67] For a detailed list of the manuscript sources involved, and for a discussion of their value, *see* R. A. McKinley, *Norfolk Surnames in the Sixteenth Century* (1969), pp. 9-16. The returns for the 'Military Survey' are P.R.O. E.36/22; E101/61/16; E36/25; and E315/466. The lay subsidy rolls used are P.R.O. E179/150/265; E179/150/227; E179/150/280; E179/150/281; E179/150/222; E179/150/215; E179/150/234; E179/150/247; E179/150/284; E179/150/271; E179/150/235; E179/150/246; E179/150/268; E179/150/213; E179/150/244; E179/150/204; E179/150/262; E179/150/206; E179/150/279

[68] *See* above pp. 76-77

[69] That is, the sources listed in n. 67 above

[70]In arriving at these figures, places that are contiguous and of which the names have the same main element (e.g. Great and Little Massingham, Great and Little Walsingham) have been treated as if they were a single place. This has not been done where places have the same main element in their names, but are not contiguous (e.g. Wood Dalling and Field Dalling)

[71]Anon., *Suffolk in 1524, Being a Return for a Subsidy Granted in 1523*, Suffolk Green Books, vol. x (1910), *passim*

[72]Based on transcripts of the Essex Subsidy, in the Essex County Record Office, made available by courtesy of the County Archivist

[73]W. Rye, *Norfolk Families* (1913), *passim*

[74]*See* the fuller discussion on these points in McKinley, *Norfolk Surnames in the Sixteenth Century*, pp. 18-20

[75]The 29 places concerned are: Alby, Antingham, Aylsham, Bacton, Banningham, Bradfield, Brampton, Bromholme, Buxton, Calthorpe, Cawston, Colby, Felmingham, Gunton, Gimingham, Hanworth, Heydon, Knapton, Marsham, Oxnead, Paston, Scottow, Skeyton, Sloley, Suffield, Trunch, Tungate, Woodrow (near Cawston), and Worstead. The four doubtful places are: North Walsham, Keswick (near Bacton), Swanton Abbot, and Witton (near Bacton)

[76]The 11 places concerned are: Congham, Docking, Harpley, Ringstead, Shernborne, Sandringham, Stanhoe, Titchwell, Ingoldisthorpe, Massingham (Great and Little) and Waterden. The four doubtful places are: Appleton, Barwick, Burnham and Thornham

[77]i.e., the sources listed in n. 67 above

[78]Anon., *Suffolk in 1524, Being a Return for the Subsidy Granted in 1523*; transcript of the Essex returns for 1523 subsidy, in Essex County Record Office

[79]Anon., *Suffolk in 1524, Being a Return for the Subsidy Granted in 1523*

[80]*See* above, p. 77

[81]J. A. Raftis, *Tenure and Mobility* (1964), pp. 129-182

[82]*See* above, pp. 78-82

[83]i.e., the sources listed in n. 67 above

[84]G. Redmonds, *Yorkshire, West Riding* (English Surnames Series, vol. 1) (1973), pp. 63-64

[85]Mildenhall and Bungay were the only places certainly involved that were more than villages. The surnames Dedham, Clare and Clere, and Bury also occur, and may be derived from Debenham, Clare, and Bury St. Edmunds respectively, but in all three cases other origins are possible

[86]Lindsey or Linseye also occurs as a surname, but might well be derived from Lindsey (Suff.)

[87]P. H. Reaney, *Origin of English Surnames*, pp. 344-351

[88]Contrast the position as it was in the Middle Ages, for which *see* above, p. 80

[89]*See* above, pp. 87-88

[90]Redmonds, *op. cit.*, pp. 63-64

[91]R. A. McKinley, *Norfolk Surnames in the Sixteenth Century*, p. 27; G. Redmonds, *op. cit.*, pp. 63, 125, 139-40, 264

[92]P.R.O. E179/149/7, *passim*

[93]*See* the examples given in R. A. McKinley, *Norfolk Surnames in the Sixteenth Century*, p. 28

[94]*Ibid.*, pp. 28-29

[95]*Ibid.*, p. 29

[96]*Calendar of Patent Rolls, 1429-36* (1907), pp. 541-88

[97]*Ibid.*; Nellie J. M. Kerling, 'Aliens in the County of Norfolk, 1436-85', *Norfolk Archaeology*, vol. xxxiii (1962), p. 200

[98]For the general character of the Norfolk inquisitions into aliens, *see* Kerling, *op. cit.*, pp. 200-215

[99]P.R.O. E179/149/126

[100]*Ibid.*

[101]P.R.O. E179/149/130

[102]P.R.O. E179/150/206; E179/150/211; E179/150/235; E179/150/239; E179/150/247; E36/25; E101/61/16; P. H. Reaney, *Dictionary of British Surnames*, p. 341

[103]P.R.O. E179/150/239

[104]R. A. McKinley, *Norfolk Surnames in the Sixteenth Century*, p. 30

[105]Anon., *Suffolk in 1327*, Suffolk Green Books, no. IX (1906), pp. 18, 32, 38, 49, 52, 56, 58, 59, 60, 69, 82, 99, 104, 111-113, 115, 124, 145, 149, 172, 188, 192, 201, 202, 204, 217, 221; *Rotuli Hundredorum*, vol. i, pp. 450, 451, 453, 462, 482, 498, 500

[106]Anon., *Suffolk in 1524, Being a Return for a Subsidy Granted in 1523*, pp. 24, 32, 33, 35, 36, 38, 42, 52, 124, 128, 148, 186, 210, 225, 230, 327, 328, 329, 351, 360, 385. (It is difficult to be certain of the precise number, as some persons appear to be listed more than once in this subsidy.) P.R.O. E179/150/239; E36/22; E179/150/227; E179/150/247; E179/150/204; E179/150/265; E179/150/222; E179/150/246; E315/466; E179/150/271; E36/25; E101/61/16; E179/150/205; E179/150/206

CHAPTER 4

TOPONYMICS

Toponymics may be defined as names derived from the topographical features of the country. The term has sometimes been used to include surnames derived from the names of individual localities, but in this paper it will be used only for surnames arising from words for general topographical elements of the landscape, fens, streams, enclosures, and so forth. Surnames from individual place names have been referred to as locative surnames, and are discussed in another chapter.

The class of toponymics includes some common and widespread surnames that are not confined to East Anglia, and which do not exhibit any local peculiarities in that region. These common surnames were already widely distributed in Norfolk and Suffolk early in the 14th century, and clearly there is no possibility that any of them can have originated with a single family in the region. The surname Green and its variants (atte Grene, del Grene, etc.), for example, is borne by 49 different individuals, resident in 38 different places, in the Norfolk subsidy roll for 1329-30.[1] In the same source the less common surname Cross (including variants such as atte Cross and de Cros, and Latin equivalents such as *de Cruce*) is borne by 15 different individuals, listed in 13 different places.[2] Similar figures could be given for other toponymics, Well, Attwater, Hey, Townsend, and Wood, to give only a few examples. It is of course not surprising that words for topographical features should have given rise to surnames that are both common and widely distributed, and it is hardly worth while enlarging on the point. There are, however, some rare toponymics that seem to have originated with a single family, so far as East Anglia is concerned, and there are also some more common surnames that seem to be peculiar to the region or at least much more common there than in other parts of the country. There is also to be considered the connection between the growth of some toponymics, and the geography of the regions where such surnames originate.

There are some relatively rare toponymics that are each to be found only in one very limited area in East Anglia, at least so far as early references, before *c.* 1400, are concerned, and in such instances it must be considered probable that all the bearers of each such surname belong to the same family, even though it is usually impossible at such an early period to trace the relationships. One example is the surname Underburgh, which has been found only in one limited area of north-west Norfolk around Burnham. The first known member of the family was a John *de Subburgo*, who was holding land in the Burnham area about the middle of the 13th century.[3] A Robert *de Suburg'*, who appears holding land at Burnham, and also around Norwich, *c*. 1260-80, may have been John's father, and Robert the son of John the son of Robert Underburgh, who had land at North Creake, near Burnham under Edward II, may well have been John's son.[4] At the end of the 13th century, and during the first half of the 14th, others of the same surname appear in and around Burnham. Simon Underburgh, who occurs about 1290, seems to have married a lady called Christiana and to have had two sons, William and Paul Underburgh, and that there was a relationship between Simon and his sons, and others bearing the same name, is shown by a fine about land in North Creake, in which William son of Simon Underburgh, Robert son of John son of Robert Underburgh, and Robert son of Richard Underburgh, whose relationship to the others is unknown, were all involved.[5] The family survived into Edward III's reign, but the name has not been found at any later period, and seems to have become extinct.[6] This seems to be an example of a topographical surname that originated with one family, ramified locally to some extent, and then became extinct.

Other examples could be given of rare topographical surnames that appear to have originated with a single family. The surname Netherhouse, for instance, occurs at Honingham, in Norfolk, early in the 14th century, and it was still in use there at the end of the century. Under Richard II, William atte Netherhous of Honingham became a freeman of Norwich, but the name does not seem to become established in the city. So far as can be seen, the family at Honingham was the only one to bear the surname in Norfolk or Suffolk.[7] A distinctively Suffolk name, still present in the county, that seems to have similarly originated with a single family, is Greengrass. The name first occurs in 1275, in the north-Suffolk hundred of Blackbourne, and in 1283, and again in 1327, it occurs at Fakenham Magna, in the hundred.[8] Presumably the name originated from some locality noted for its lush grass, though it is possible that it may be a nickname. In the Suffolk returns for the subsidy granted in 1523, the name only occurs at Fakenham Magna, and at another village in Blackbourne hundred.[9] No early occurrences of the surname Greengrass outside Suffolk are known, and this does seem to be a clear case of a toponymic with a single origin.

In some other instances, toponymics that are rare in East Anglia, and appear to have belonged to a single family in that region, are probably to be reckoned as surnames brought in from outside the region by migrants. Orchard, for example, is a surname that occurs early in the 13th century in connection with Warham, in north Norfolk. It continues to be found in the same part of the county through the 13th century, and into the 14th, but only one occurrence of it has been found elsewhere in Norfolk, and it has not been found in Suffolk at all, during the Middle Ages.[10] This rarity is the more significant since other toponymics derived from fruit trees, such as Appleyard or Pyrie, were not rare in East Anglia during the Middle Ages.[11] Orchard was a fairly common name in some southern counties during the same period,[12] and it must be suspected that its presence in Norfolk was due to immigration. Another toponymic, the presence of which in East Anglia seems possibly to be due to migration from northern England, is Bothe (or Booth). The earliest occurrence of the name Bothe that has been found in East Anglia is in 1287, when Odo de la Bothe (or atte Bothe) is mentioned.[13] John de la Bothe, who occurs at Norwich from 1290 onwards, was Odo's son, and of two others of the same name who occur in Norfolk at the end of the 13th century, Nicholas de la Bothe of Norwich was John's son, and the other, William atte Bothe, mentioned in 1297, probably belonged to the same family, though the connection cannot be traced.[14] John atte Bothe appears to have left Norwich, and he and others of the same name occur in the 14th century in Happing hundred, in north-east Norfolk.[15] The name Bothe or Booth has not been found in Suffolk during the Middle Ages, and the Norfolk references probably all relate to one family. Booth has long been a fairly common surname in some parts of the North Country, and it seems possible that the surname was introduced to Norfolk by a family that migrated to Norwich, a city that was attracting new inhabitants from many parts of England in the late 13th and early 14th centuries. However, atte Tolbooth occurs as a surname at Lynn, and 'le Botheman' occurs as an occupational term at Norwich, so that it is difficult to be sure if Bothe is an import to Norfolk.[16]

How far do toponymics reflect the landscape characteristic of each district? It might be expected, for instance, that such markedly distinct areas as the fen-lands around the Wash, or the Norfolk Breckland, would each have its own body of topographical surnames. Obviously when considering this question it will be best to concentrate on relatively early occurrences of surnames, say those before *c.* 1400, for once surnames have become hereditary population movements gradually obscure the original distribution. Some

surnames worth examining in this connection are those derived
from the various words for marshy ground, such as Fen, Carr, Marsh,
Sloth, and Moor.

The word carr or kerr had a precise meaning in Norfolk during
the Middle Ages, and later. The *Promptorium Parvulorum*, an English-
Latin dictionary compiled *c.* 1440, probably at Kings Lynn, defines
'Ker' as 'where trees grow by water or fen', and Forby, writing
centuries later, gave the meaning of 'Car' in the East Anglian
dialect as 'a wood or grove on moist soil, generally of alders'.[17]
This meaning of the word no doubt dates back long before *c.* 1440;
at the beginning of the 13th century two alder groves at Caister
St. Edmund, near Norwich, were named Muchelker and Litleker,
which suggests that the meaning of the word was the same *c.* 1200
as later.[18] The distribution of early occurrences of the surname
Carr or Kerr in Norfolk is very largely concentrated in certain
limited areas. The Norfolk subsidy rolls for 1329-30 list 20 tax
payers called de Ker or atte Ker. Sixteen of these are in east
central Norfolk, in an area lying mostly in the hundreds of Forehoe,
Eynsford, and Mitford, and the eastern edge of Launditch hundred.
Three others occur fairly close together in south-east Norfolk, and
there is an isolated occurrence in the north-east of the county.[19]
Other early occurrences (before *c.* 1400) of the name Carr, and of
surnames derived from place-names that are compounds of Carr,
such as de Rydeker, de Mikleker, de Wateker, and so forth, are
distributed in much the same way.[20] In Suffolk Carr was much
rarer as a surname. Only five persons of the name are listed in the
Suffolk subsidy roll for 1327, and three of these are listed in one
township, and so probably belonged to the same family.[21] Other
occurrences of the name in Suffolk during the Middle Ages are
sparse,[22] and the name seems to be too rare, and too dispersed, in
Suffolk for any deductions to be drawn from its distribution there.
In Norfolk, however, the early occurrences of Carr as a surname are
mostly in the Boulder Clay areas of central and south-east Norfolk.[23]
For other parts of the county, such as the area of the Broads in the
east, or the Breckland in the south west, no early references have
been found, and it is perhaps a fair deduction that during the
period in which these early instances have been found, *c.* 1250-1400,
carrs were a common feature of the landscape in the Boulder Clay
areas of Norfolk, but rare or lacking elsewhere, though woods with
the word Ker as part of their names are numerous in the Broads
today. If the distribution of the surnames Carr, Kerr, etc., in
certain early 16th century sources is examined, it can be seen that
the situation had entirely changed by that date, and that the
distribution characteristic of the earlier period had disappeared.[24]

Early Norfolk occurrences of the surname Fen are largely concentrated in the district around the Broads in east Norfolk, with a
smaller number in the fens around the Wash in the west. In the
Norfolk subsidy 'for 1329-30, there are 28 persons called Fen
(including atte Fen, etc.) and of these, 21 are in the Broads area,
especially around Wroxham, three are in the west Norfolk Fenland,
and the remaining four are widely dispersed in other parts of the
county.[25] Other early occurrences of the name Fen, and of surnames
formed from compounds (Overfen, de Westfen, de Blackfen, de
Fenrowe, atte Fenhous, etc.) show a similar pattern of distribution.[26]
The name Fen was also common in Suffolk. Twenty-five persons
of the name occur in the Suffolk 1327 subsidy rolls, and are there
rather widely distributed. Nine are in the extreme north-east of the
county, where there are marshes along the rivers Yare and Waveney,
12 are dispersed in central Suffolk, and three others are in the
coastal areas of the south east. The name is absent in this subsidy
from the Fens in the extreme north west of the county, the Breckland
area in north-west Suffolk, and from the south west of the county.[27]

If the distribution of the name Fen in 1327 is compared with the
distribution of the same surname in the Suffolk returns for the
subsidy granted in 1523, it can be seen that by the 16th century
the situation had largely changed, and that by the later date the
name was widely distributed over most of Suffolk, though still
noticeably absent from the north-west of the county.[28] In certain
early 16th-century sources for Norfolk, the surname was fairly
widespread in the east of the county, though it was still more
common in the Broads district than anywhere else; in the Fenlands
around the Wash the name was rare.[29]

Of the other toponymics derived from terms for marshy ground, the
surnames Marsh and Mareis were much less common in medieval
Norfolk or Suffolk than were Carr and Fen. In the Norfolk subsidy
rolls for 1329-30, for example, Marsh occurs only five times, and
Mareis only three times.[30] Neither name appears to be particularly
characteristic of any district in East Anglia, though in Norfolk
both tend to occur rather more frequently in the fenlands in the
west of the county than elsewhere.[31] Two other toponymics, both
rare, derived from words for quagmire are Sloth (or Sloh) and
Goggell. Most of the medieval references to Sloth or atte Sloth in
Norfolk come from the district around East Dereham, and possibly
relate to a single family.[32] In Suffolk the name occurs from the late
12th century onwards but it was always rare. The name was found
in several parts of Suffolk, and it is unlikely that it was borne by
only one family.[33] The rare surname Goggell or Gogill is probably
derived from a term meaning quagmire.[34] The name appears at

Trunch in 1434, and at Yarmouth in 1437. By the early 16th
century it was established in two areas in Norfolk, at Old.Bucken-
ham in the south-east of the county, and at Aylmerton, Colby,
Gimingham, Trunch, and South Repps in the north east.[35] Rather
later in the same century the name occurs at Norwich.[36] The name
has not been noted in Norfolk or Suffolk before 1434, and this may
be a case of a topographical name which originated outside East
Anglia being brought into the region by migration.

Some other toponymics have a significant distribution, when
early instances are considered. One of these is the surname Damme
(atte Dam, etc.). In the Norfolk subsidy for 1329-30 most instances
of this surname are in the hundreds of Launditch and Mitford, in
the centre of the county. The name at this date is lacking from either
the west Norfolk fenlands, or the Broads district in the east of the
county.[37] The rare surname atte Damesende occurs in Launditch in
the 14th century, but has not been noted anywhere else in East
Anglia during the Middle Ages.[38] This name, like Carr, seems to
have been largely confined in Norfolk to the Boulder Clay area in
the middle of the county up to *c.* 1400. In the 15th century the
name occurs in parts of north-east Norfolk, from which it had
hitherto been absent.[39] In certain 16th-century sources for Norfolk,
the name occurs mostly in north-east and south-east Norfolk, two
areas where it has not been found before 1400.[40] The changes in the
distribution of this surname are similar to those observed in other
cases, and agree with other evidence for a movement of population
into north-east Norfolk during the later Middle Ages.[41]

There is a contrast between the distribution of the name in the
Norfolk 1329-30 subsidy and the Suffolk 1327 subsidy, where the
name is much rarer, and is mostly to be found in the Broads area
in the extreme north-east of the county, with a few instances in the
coastal sandlings further south.[42] The occurrences of the name in
Suffolk are perhaps too few for any conclusions safely to be drawn
from them, and the group of persons named del Dam or atte Dam
in north-east Suffolk could represent the ramification of a single
family in that area.

Dam or Damme was perhaps a surname originally much more
common in East Anglia, and particularly Norfolk, than elsewhere.
The Hundred Rolls, which provide a large though not of course
comprehensive collection of late 13th-century surnames, give only
four occurrences of the name outside Norfolk, one instance each in
Cambridgeshire and Oxfordshire, and two in Sussex, while the very
full collection of Middle English topographical surnames made by
Löfvenberg for Sussex, Surrey, Somerset, and Worcestershire
includes only a single instance of the name, in Sussex.[43] The word

should probably be taken to mean any kind of bank retaining water, not necessarily a dam in the modern sense.

The early distribution of such toponymics as Carr and Dam appears to be linked with the geological characteristics of the sub-regions into which East Anglia may be divided, but it is noticeable that the very distinctive Fenland region in west Norfolk and north-west Suffolk did not produce any large body of toponymics peculiar to the fens. Dam as a surname has not been found in the Norfolk or Suffolk fenland. A few surnames derived from the word 'bank' (at the Benk, Bank, Bencher) occur in Suffolk, but not in the Fenland,[44] and the name Dike, though it occurs in Norfolk and Suffolk, was very rare.[45] A few other surnames are obviously connected with Fenland topography. The name Delf or atte Delf occurs in the Norfolk Fenland during the 14th century, and is no doubt in that area derived from a ditch or artificial channel.[46] The names Syke and Sykes are rare in both Norfolk and Suffolk, and though Syke occurs in the Norfolk Fenlands it seems to be more common in the Broads district than elsewhere, so far as early references go.[47] The surname Hithe, derived from a word for a landing place,[48] does occur in the Suffolk Fenland, but it has not been found in the Norfolk fens, though it occurs in East Norfolk, and though there were certainly landing places called hithes in the Norfolk Fenland, for instance at Fordham, Downham, Wiggenhall, and Stoke Ferry.[49] A few individual banks or channels, like the great bank in the Norfolk Fenland called the Podike, for example, gave rise to surnames,[50] but in general surnames derived from marshland topography were mostly lacking in the Norfolk and Suffolk fens.

A few East Anglian surnames are derived from words for enclosure, or field divisions, but most of these are rare. The term 'wong' occurs once or twice as an element in surnames derived from compounds (de Estwong, Bomwong), but otherwise it has not been found as a surname.[51] The surname Tye (atte Ty, de Ty, de Tey, etc.), derived from a word meaning a small enclosure that was perhaps most commonly used in east and south-east England, was moderately common in Suffolk during the Middle Ages, and it occurs occasionally in Norfolk. In Suffolk the name appears mostly in the south of the county, in places not far from the Essex border.[52] Pihtel, also derived from a word meaning a small close, has been found as the name of a single family, at Hempnall in Norfolk, but no other instances have been found.[53] A few instances occur of surnames derived from a hide of land (de la Hyde, etc.) in both Norfolk and Suffolk.[54] As the hide was not a unit normally employed in East Anglia during the period when such names are likely to have arisen, names such as de la Hyde or atte Hyde may well be those of families that migrated into the region. Surnames derived from 'inland' occur in Norfolk during the 13th and 14th centuries, but these (usually 'de Inlonde') seem in all cases to be derived from a locality called Inland in the Norfolk parish of Gateby, and not from any agricultural term.[55]

All the names mentioned in the last paragraph were rare in medieval Norfolk and Suffolk. A much more common surname in Norfolk was Herne (atte Hirne, del Hyrne, etc.), derived from a word meaning a corner, or nook of land.[56] Sixteen persons of the name occur in the Norfolk 1329 subsidy, and occurrences in other sources are fairly numerous.[57] The name is much less common in Suffolk, and it only occurs once in the Suffolk 1327 subsidy.[58] It is unlikely in this case that the distribution of the name, very largely absent from Suffolk in the Middle Ages, and absent so far as early references (before *c.* 1400) are concerned from some parts of Norfolk such as the Broads district, can be due to geological or geographical factors, and the uneven distribution of the surname in East Anglia is perhaps rather caused by local usages prevailing during the Middle Ages respecting the employment of terms such as 'hyrne' in certain areas. It may perhaps be deduced that the term was much more generally used in speech in parts of Norfolk than it was in Suffolk. The Latin phrase *de Angulo* is usually a translation for the vernacular atte Hirne in Norfolk;[59] at North Elmham in the 14th century, for example, the phrase *de Angulo* seems to be used for a family which is also called atte Hirne or en le Hirne.[60]

The lack of early instances of Hirne as a surname in parts of east Norfolk may be connected with the distribution of another name, Wend, which is also, like Hirne, derived from a word meaning a bend or angle.[61] In Norfolk, the early instances of this surname are nearly all to be found in the Broadlands, although there are a few examples in other parts of the county.[62]

Of all the surnames derived from the various words for enclosure of one kind or another, the most common in both Norfolk and Suffolk is the name Hawe (atte Hawe, atte Hagh, etc.). If the distribution of this name in Norfolk sources for the period before 1400 is examined, it too can be seen to occur almost exclusively in two areas, the Broadlands and the part of east central Norfolk around Wymondham and East Dereham. Compounds such as de Suthagh, de Westhagh, de Fulsurghawe also occur mostly in the same areas.[63] In medieval Suffolk, Hawe was a rare surname, and its occurrences were scattered.[64] The surname Hay or Hey, derived from another word for enclosure, is distinctly less common in either Norfolk or Suffolk. In Norfolk it appears mostly in the west of the county, in places where Hawe is largely lacking in early sources.[65] In Suffolk its appearances are too scarce and dispersed for any conclusions to be drawn.[66]

No other surnames derived from words for fields or enclosures were at all widespread in East Anglia. Surnames derived from meadow (atte Medwe, in the Medwe, *de Prato*) were uncommon in both Norfolk and Suffolk; nine persons with such names appear in the Norfolk 1329 subsidy, and 16 in the Suffolk 1327 subsidy. The Norfolk instances are dispersed, but in Suffolk the name was chiefly to be found in the sandy coastal belt.[67] Surnames derived from Lea, or Legh, and from Gore or Gare, are rare in both counties during the Middle Ages.[68] Names derived from Field (atte Feld, *de Campo*), Acre, or Croft are similarly uncommon.[69]

It seems clear that the distribution of some toponymics was originally limited in East Anglia to certain districts. In some instances this is probably connected with the surface topography of the region as it was when most surnames were being formed, and becoming hereditary, during the 13th and 14th centuries. In others it is more likely to be linked with the very local use of particular words for topographical features, parallel to the local use of particular occupational terms. Clearly it would be useful if evidence from surnames as they were in the 13th and 14th centuries, when most surnames were either not hereditary, or had not been hereditary for more than a generation or two, could be used together with field names, locality names, and similar evidence, from the same period.

Any use of evidence from surnames to throw light either on the topography of a region, or on the terms locally employed for topographical features, is of course complicated by the possibilities of topographical surnames being brought into the region by immigration. By the 13th century surnames derived from identifiable place-names were being brought into the region by immigrants, and some such names became hereditary, and well established in East Anglia. Clearly topographical names could have been introduced in the same way. Surnames that were at all common in East Anglia at an early period are likely to have originated within the region, but some of the rarer topographical surnames may be introductions from elsewhere. The surnames Bothe and Hide, discussed above, are probably examples of this process. The surname Shaw, common in parts of northern England, occurs in Suffolk at the end of the 14th century, and in Norfolk during the 15th, but remained rare in East Anglia.[70] This is probably another instance of a surname brought into the region by migration. It is, however, difficult to be certain in some cases whether particular surnames are native to the region or not. The surname Lathe, or atte Lathe, for example, derived from a word for 'barn' used in the north of England,[71] occurs at Ketteringham, Norfolk, at the end of the 13th century, and early in the 14th when it occurs in West Norfolk around King's Lynn. As two of the persons called atte Lathe (or atte Lathes) who occur at Ketteringham also appear in west Norfolk, it seems likely that all the bearers of this surname in Norfolk belonged to the same family.[72] It might seem that this was a case of a surname that had been introduced into East Anglia by the migration of one family and had subsequently ramified there to some extent, but the word 'lathe' is given in the *Promptorium Parvulorum*, a Norfolk compilation, as a synonym for the English 'barn', and a translation for the Latin *horreum*, so that there is little reason to suppose that the surname is not native to Norfolk, though evidently rare in the county.[73] Surnames derived from 'barn' are rare in Norfolk during the Middle Ages.[74] In Suffolk, on the other hand, where the surname Lathe, or atte Lathe, has not been found in early references, Barn is a fairly common surname during the Middle Ages.[75]

East Anglian evidence can throw light on the origins of some toponymics. One name of obscure origins, and one that seems originally to have been confined to Norfolk, Suffolk, and Essex, is Gannock, or atte Gannock. The origins of the word 'gannok' are very uncertain.[76] During the Middle Ages, however, the word 'gannoker' was used to mean an alehouse keeper in the three counties just mentioned,[77] and consequently at that period, and in that region, the word 'gannok' almost certainly meant an alehouse. The surnames Gannok (atte Gannok, or del Gannok), and Gannoker occur in Norfolk and Suffolk from the late 13th century onwards. Gannocker has also been found in medieval Essex, but neither name is known to occur elsewhere, and both were probably surnames originally confined to one part of England.[78] Most of the early references to both names come from south-west Norfolk and north-west Suffolk, but they are too dispersed for it to be likely that all relate to one family. The name Gannok still survived in west Norfolk in the 16th century.[79]

A much more common surname than Gannok was Childerhouse. Sixteen persons of the name are listed in the Norfolk 1329 subsidy and eight in the Suffolk 1327 subsidy.[80] Indeed this seems to have been mainly an East Anglian name, and much more common in the region than in other parts of England. There were, for example, 11 persons of the name in the Suffolk returns for the subsidy granted in 1523, and 10 in certain fairly comprehensive Norfolk sources of about the same date, while the Sussex and Buckinghamshire returns for the 1523 subsidy list no persons of the name.[81] It has been suggested that the surname is derived from residence at or near an orphanage, but there are difficulties in accepting this view.[82] Although medieval England possessed institutions which cared for children amongst other religious or charitable activities, it is doubtful if anything which can accurately be described as an orphanage existed, and no case of the word 'childerhouse' being applied to such an institution has been cited. The derivations proposed for some other surnames may also be questioned. The surname Nabb has been derived from a personal name, and this is no doubt the correct derivation in some cases.[83] In Norfolk, however, the name occurs as atte Nab, and must in this instance be derived from some topographical feature, probably a knoll or hill.[84] The surname Goter has been explained, as an occupational name, meaning goatherd.[85] In Suffolk, however, it appears as atte Goter, and is in this case at least derived from residence beside a water course, or possibly, since the name occurs in north-west Suffolk, from a dike in the fens.[86]

There has been some dispute about the origins of the surname Woodruff, fairly common in Norfolk and Suffolk during the Middle Ages. No forms have been found that support the suggestion that the name is an occupational one, from 'wood-reeve'. In 13th- and 14th-century sources for East Anglia the name Woderove or Woderowe is fairly common; it occurs, for instance, as the name of several persons in the Suffolk 1327 subsidy, and in the Norfolk 1329 subsidy;[87] other occurrences are numerous.[88] In some instances the name occurs as de Woderove or atte Woderove, which suggests that the name derives from some topographical element, or possibly from a place-name.[89] Woodruff, or similar forms, has not been found in East Anglia in any period before *c.* 1400. By the early 16th century, however, Woodruff or Woodrofe has become fairly common, and it also occurs in Suffolk, though less frequently, while forms such as Woodrove are rare.[90] It seems likely that Woodruff has evolved from an earlier Woderove, or atte Woderove, derived either from Woodrow, near Cawston, Norfolk, or from other places where there were rows of cottages in a wood. It may be compared with surnames like de Fenrow or Del Wro.[91]

Another surname with a somewhat similar origin is Budde. This has been derived from an old English personal name, and it may so originate in some cases, but the name del Bude occurs at Bardwell, Suffolk, in 1283, a place where the name Budd (or Bude, Boude) occurs both at that date, and later, while in Norfolk the name atte Bud occurs in Stalham in 1329, and the name Budde occurs at the same date in the adjoining township of Sutton.[91] It is probable that in these instances the name is derived from the Old English word 'bold', a building.[93]

One characteristic of East Anglian, and especially Norfolk, surnames in the Middle Ages was the large number of names ending in the suffix -gate. In some cases such names are derived from residence at or near a gate, in some cases a town gate. This is clear from the use of the Latin *ad Portam* to translate surnames like In the Gate, atte Yate, and so forth, and by the use of Latin phrases such as *ad Portam Bosci*, or *ad Portam Ecclesie* to translate names like de Woodgate, de Churchgate, and so forth.[94] Some surnames, too, are derived from identifiable town gates; Henry atte Barreyates, for example, a 14th-century freeman of Norwich, derived his name from one of the city gates.[95] It seems likely that the plural forms, At the Gates, atte Yates, and so forth, are derived from town gates.[96] There are cases, however, where surnames ending in -gate were clearly derived from the names of streets or roads. Hamo son of Simon Attehollegate, who occurs at Norwich in 1290, is the same person as Hamo son of Simon de Berestrete, and Hollegate was an old name for a Norwich street running off Bere Street.[97] The surname Gatesend must also be derived from the end of a street or road.[98] In many cases it is difficult to be sure if names ending in -gate are derived from gates, or whether they are derived from street or road names incorporating the Scandinavian word for a road or street, 'gata'. Names such as de Nethergate, de Estgate, de Northgate, etc., could originate in either way, though the commonness and wide distribution of such names makes it unlikely that all are derived from town or castle gates. Two points, however, may be made. One is that names ending in -gate are much more common in Norfolk than in Suffolk, though not rare in the latter county.[99] The other point is that there are in Norfolk a number of hamlets with names ending in -gate; around North Walsham and Worstead, for example, are the hamlets of Lingate, Tungate, Bengate, Lyngate, Withergate, and Briggate. It would be going beyond the bounds of this paper to investigate the origin of such place-names, but it may be suggested that they were derived from streets or roads, and that their names may be compared with those of the numerous East Anglian hamlets with names such as Cake Street, Wood Street, Market Street, and so forth. Surnames ending in -gate are probably derived in many cases from the names of hamlets. The surnames de Tungate, de Bengate, and de Briggate all occur during the 14th century in north-east Norfolk, not far from the hamlets so named.[100]

The surname Street (atte Strete, etc.) occurs in both Norfolk and Suffolk, but rarely.[101] A few compounds, such as atte Stretesend, de Sowstrete, de Wodestret, de Bradestret, etc., also occur:[102] In some cases such names, de Cakestrete for instance, are clearly derived from the names of hamlets.[103]

Gustav Fransson has drawn attention to a class of rare toponymics formed by the addition of the suffixes -er or -man to topographical terms.[104] Such surnames are rare everywhere, and are not especially characteristic of East Anglia, but some further instances of the class can be added to those listed by Fransson. One of these is Bencher, which occurs as a surname in Suffolk in 1327, no doubt meaning 'dweller on the bank',[105] as do similar names such as At the Benk.[106] Oker, which occurs in 15th-century Norfolk is probably a topo-nymic similar to Oakman, derived from the oak tree.[107] Stather, which occurs in Norfolk at the same period, must be derived from residence near a staithe or landing place, and have the same meaning as atte Stathe, which also occurs as a Norfolk surname.[108] Stronder, a 14th-century Suffolk surname, is derived from the strand or sea-shore, and may be compared to the contemporary Suffolk surnames del Stronde and de Stronde.[109] Wyndaler, which occurs as a Suffolk surname in 1327, is probably derived from Windale in Gillingham (Norfolk). The surname de Windhil or del Wyndhel occurs in Suffolk at about the same period.[110] Two other names in the same class, occurring in East Anglia, Heller and Knotter, have been noted by P. H. Reaney.[111]

A few toponymics ending in -man, not listed by Fransson, have also been noted. One of these is Slademan; Thos. Sclademan, who occurs in Suffolk in 1327, is almost certainly the same person as the Thomas del Slade, who appears in the county at about the same date.[112] The surname Sikman occurs in Norfolk in the 14th cen-tury.[113] Names such as de Sick, atte Syk, de Estsike, etc., are to be found in Norfolk at the same period.[114] Spitelman occurs in Suffolk, probably from residence near, or employment in, a hospital.[115] And Suchman, which occurs in 13th-century Norfolk, is probably to be connected with the surname Such, Sutch, de la Zouche, etc.[116] Two more common names of this type, both occur-ring in East Anglia, not listed by Fransson, are Dykman and Moorman.[117]

There remain very many topographical names that have not been mentioned. Many of these were always rare, and some never became stable hereditary surnames. Such names as atte Fold, atte Holm, de Tothill, Ferye, de la Penne, or atte Drove each occur once or twice only, and in all probability were never hereditary.[118] There are other toponymics that are much more common, Lane, Style, Cross, Stone, and so forth, but none of these are in any way peculiar to East Anglia, nor does the distribution of them within the region have any particular significance, though investigation of the forms assumed by such surnames at different periods might throw light upon the sound changes that occurred regionally in certain words. The study of topographical surnames is closely connected with other disciplines, in particular with historical geography and with the study of place-names. It is hoped that enough has been said here to suggest that investigation of toponymics may produce results useful for other fields of research.

References

[1]P.R.O. E179/149/7, *passim*

[2]*Ibid.*

[3]A. L. Bedingfeld, *Cartulary of Creake Abbey*, p. 103

[4]*Ibid.*, pp. 129-30; Rye, *Cal. Norf. Fines*, vol. ii, p. 247

[5]Rye, *Cal. Norf. Fines*, vol. i, p. 156; vol. ii, p. 247; *Rotuli Hundredorum*, vol. i, p. 484; Bedingfeld, *op. cit.*, p. 133; *Abbrevatio Placitorum* (Record Commission) (1811), pp. 225, 292; *Calendar of Close Rolls, 1302-07* (1908), p. 462

[6]*Index of Placita De Banco, 1327-8* (P.R.O. Lists and Indexes, xxxii), (1963) part i, p. 441; *Feudal Aids* (1904), vol. iii, p. 405; *Calendar of Patent Rolls, 1327-30* (1891), p. 157

[7]P.R.O. E179/149/7, m. 69; L'Estrange, ed., *Calendar of the Freemen of Norwich, 1317-1603*, p. 100

[8]*Rotuli Hundredorum*, vol. ii, p. 157; Powell, *A Suffolk Hundred in 1283*, table 10; *Suffolk in 1327*, p. 185; Reaney, *Dictionary of British Surnames*, p. 145; Reaney, *Origins of English Surnames*, p. 230

[9]*Suffolk in 1524*, pp. 51, 58

[10]B. Dodwell, ed., *Feet of Fines for the County of Norfolk, 1201-15, and for the County of Suffolk, 1199-1214*, p. 96; W. Rye, *Cal. Norf. Fines*, vol. i, pp. 70, 80-81, 169; P.R.O. E179/149/7, m. 58

[11]*See*, e.g., *Suffolk in 1327*, pp. 14, 162, 216; L'Estrange, ed., *Calendar of the Freemen of Norwich, 1317-1603*, p. 4; Rye, *Cal. Norf. Fines*, vol. ii, pp. 340, 341

[12]M. T. Löfvenberg, *Studies on Middle English Local Surnames* (1942), p. 143

[13]Hudson, *Leet Jurisdiction in the City of Norwich*, p. 15; Rye, *Calendar of Deeds relating to Norwich, 1285-1306*, p. 13

[14]Rye, ed., *Calendar of Deeds relating to Norwich, 1285-1306*, pp. 35, 37, 50; Rye, *Calendar of Norwich Deeds, 1307-41*, pp. 54, 159, 166; W. P. W. Phillimore, ed., *Placita Coram Domino Rege* (British Record Society) (1898), p. 61

[15]P.R.O. E179/149/7, m. 49

[16]P. H. Reaney, *Origin of English Surnames*, pp. 331-37; Norfolk and Norwich R.O., Norwich Old Free Book, f. xxxviii; Rye, *Cal. Norf. Fines*, vol. ii, pp. 335, 357, 419

[17]A. Way, ed., *Promptorium Parvulorum sive Clericorum* (Camden Soc., 1st Series, vol. xxv) (1843), vol. i, p. 272; R. Forby, *Vocabulary of East Anglia* (1830), vol. ii, p. 159. *See* also A. H. Smith, *Place-Name Elements* (English Place-Name Society, vol. xxvi), (1970), part ii, p. 4

[18]R. H. C. Davis, ed., *Kalendar of Abbot Samson*, p. 154

[19]P.R.O. E179/149/7, mm. 3, 6, 9, 10, 11, 25, 30, 38, 50, 51, 53, 71

[20]*See*, e.g. *ibid.*, mm. 32, 69, 70; E179/149/9, m. 71; Rye, *Cal. Norf. Fines*, vol. i, pp. 78, 118; vol. ii, pp. 244, 358; Norfolk and Norwich R.O., N.R.S. 18476, mm. 2, 12

[21]*Suffolk in 1327*, pp. 71, 177, 216

[22]*See*, e.g. Powell, *A Suffolk Hundred in 1283*, p. 58; table 27; Rye, *Cal. Suff. Fines*, p. 303

[23]On the geological sub-regions of Norfolk, *see* H. C. Darby, *Domesday Geography of Eastern England* (1952), pp. 147-51

[24]On the early 16th-century sources, *see* above, pp. 89-90

[25]P.R.O. E179/149/7, mm. 5, 21, 26, 27, 40, 43, 48, 58, 62, 63

[26]*See*, e.g. *ibid.*, mm. 12, 27, 58, 62; E179/149/9, m. 30; *Rotuli Hundredorum*, vol. i, pp. 438, 451, 508; Rye, *Cal. Norf. Fines*, vol. i, pp. 136, 171; vol. ii, 233, 238, 330, 337, 357, 380, 387

[27]*Suffolk in 1327*, pp. 16, 29, 44, 68, 74, 79, 86, 87, 91, 96, 98, 101, 113, 120, 122-3, 128, 146, 156, 160, 187-8

[28]*Suffolk in 1524*, pp. 14, 103, 132, 133, 143, 152, 167, 168, 171, 205, 255, 266, 285, 317, 333, 355

[29]On the 16th-century sources, *see* above, pp. 89-90

[30]P.R.O. E179/149/7, mm. 3, 26, 35, 43, 53, 54, 58

[31]*See* e.g. references cited in n. 30 above, and also Rye, *Cal. Norf. Fines*, vol. i, pp. 93, 109; vol. ii, pp. 231, 235, 287, 293; A. L. Bedingfeld, ed., *Cartulary of Creake Abbey*, p. 90; J. H. Bullock, ed., *The Norfolk Portion of the Chartulary of the Priory of St. Pancras, Lewes*, pp. 17, 46, 55, 67; B. Dodwell, ed., *Feet of Fines for the County of Norfolk, 1198-1202*, p. 59

[32]*Rotuli Hundredorum*, vol. i, pp. 480, 489, 494; Rye, *Cal. Norf. Fines*, vol. i, p. 39; *Index of Placita de Banco, 1327-8*, part i, pp. 387, 422; P.R.O. E179/149/7, mm. 36, 50

[33]P.R.O. C.133/89/8; *Suffolk in 1327*, pp. 71, 86, 162; Powell, *A Suffolk Hundred in 1283*, p. 82; D. M. Stenton, ed., *Great Roll of the Pipe for the 7th Year of Richard I* (Pipe Roll Society, New Series, vol. vi) (1929), p. 78

34Löfvenberg, *op. cit.*, p. 78; A. H. Smith, *The Place-Name Elements*, part i, p. 205

35A. Campling, ed., *East Anglian Pedigrees*, (Harleian Society, vol. xci) (1939), p. 80; P.R.O. E179/150/211; E179/150/235; E101/61/16; Anon., *Calendar of the Freemen of Great Yarmouth* (1910), pp. 3, 18; M. A. Farrow, ed., *Index to Wills proved in the Consistory Court at Norwich, 1370-1550* (1945), p. 172

36L'Estrange, ed., *Calendar of the Freemen of Norwich, 1317-1603*, p. 61

37P.R.O. E179/149/7, mm. 26, 29, 31, 33, 34, 36, 43, 50, 52, 54, 71. There is, however, one early occurrence of the name in the Broads area: Rye, *Cal. Norf. Fines*, vol. i, p. 75

38P.R.O. E179/149/7, m. 38; Rye, *Cal. Norf. Fines*, vol. ii, pp. 354, 355

39Rye, *Cal. Norf. Fines*, vol. ii, pp. 406, 408, 412, 419, 422, 432

40On these early 16th-century sources, *see* above, pp. 89-90

41*See* McKinley, *Norfolk Surnames in the Sixteenth Century*, p. 29

42*Suffolk in 1327*, pp. 91-3, 99, 111, 135, 175

43*Rotuli Hundredorum*, vol. ii, pp. 218, 503, 804; Löfvenberg, *op. cit.*, p. 49

44Hervey, ed., *Pinchbeck Register*, vol. i, p. 138; *Suffolk in 1327*, pp. 62, 191

45D. M. Stenton, ed., *Great Roll of the Pipe for the 7th Year of Richard I*, p. 75; *Suffolk in 1327*, pp. 201, 214; P.R.O. E179/149/7, m. 53. On the name Dikeman, *see* below, p. 119

46Rye, *Cal. Norf. Fines*, vol. ii, p. 280; P.R.O. E179/149/7, m. 42

47*Suffolk in 1327*, p. 60; L'Estrange, ed., *Calendar of the Freemen of Norwich, 1317-1603*, pp. 6, 134; Rye, *Cal. Norf. Fines*, vol. i, p. 99; Anon., *Great Roll of the Pipe for the 12th Year of Henry II*, p. 26; *Rotuli Hundredorum*, vol. i, p. 511; P.R.O. E179/149/7, mm. 1, 20, 29, 43; Ipswich and East Suffolk R.O., HA/12/C2/1, m. 2

48A. Way, ed., *Promptorium Parvulorum*, vol. i, p. 242

49*Suffolk in 1327*, p. 197; *Rotuli Hundredorum*, vol. i, pp. 441, 488, 513; Rye, *Cal. Norf. Fines*, vol. i, pp. 128, 140; vol. ii, p. 341; Rye, *Calendar of Deeds Relating to Norwich, 1285-1306*, p. 7; H. C. Darby, *Medieval Fenland* (1940), p. 58; *Index of Placita de Banco, 1327-8* (P.R.O. Lists and Indexes, xxxii), part i, p. 437

50P.R.O. E179/149/7, m. 42; Bullock, ed., *The Norfolk Portion of the Chartulary of the Priory of St. Pancras of Lewes*, pp. 49, 57, 61; *Rotuli Hundredorum*, vol. i, p. 460

51Rye, *Cal. Norf. Fines*, vol. ii, p. 288; P.R.O. E179/149/7, m. 42

52*Suffolk in 1327*, pp. 18, 139, 144, 146, 147, 158, 159, 217; Rye, *Cal. Suff. Fines*, pp. 44, 66, 99, 129, 184, 186, 200, 222, 237, 247, 269, 271, 286, 287; Bullock, *op. cit.*, pp. 4, 11; Rye, *Calendar of Deeds Relating to Norwich, 1286-1305*, pp. 78, 87; Rye, *Cal. Norf.*

Fines, vol. ii, pp. 279, 297; A. H. Smith, *The Place-Name Elements*, part ii, p. 177

[53]Rye, *Calendar of Norwich Deeds, 1307-41*, pp. 27, 108; Rye, *Calendar of Deeds Relating to Norwich, 1285-1306*, p. 96; Smith, *op. cit.*, part ii, p. 64

[54]Rye, *Cal. Norf. Fines*, vol. i, p. 118; Hervey, *Pinchbeck Register*, vol. i, p. 312; *Suffolk in 1327*, pp. 49, 153, 213; Rye, *Cal. Norf. Fines*, pp. 5, 45, 88, 224, 246, 273. The surname Fifhide, which occurs in Norfolk in the 15th century, possibly means 'Five Hides', Rye, *Cal. Norf. Fines*, vol. ii, p. 293

[55]B. Dodwell, ed., *Feet of Fines for the County of Norfolk, 1198-1202*, p. 196; Rye, *Cal. Norf. Fines*, vol. ii, p. 297; P.R.O. E179/149/7, m. 35; *Book of Fees*, vol. ii, p. 909

[56]A. H. Smith, *The Place-Name Elements*, part i, p. 276; Reaney, *Dictionary of British Surnames*, p. 162; Forby, *op. cit.*, vol. ii, p. 157

[57]P.R.O. E179/149/7, mm. 5, 10, 16, 38, 39, 42, 45, 50, 58, 67; and *see*, e.g., *Rotuli Hundredorum*, vol. i, p. 498; Bullock, *op. cit.*, p. 73; Rye, *Cal. Norf. Fines*, vol. ii, pp. 304, 310, 321, 349; L'Estrange, *op. cit.*, pp. 72, 78

[58]*Suffolk in 1327*, p. 79

[59]Way, *op. cit.*, vol. ii, p. 241

[60]P.R.O. E179/149/7, m. 38; and *see* Forby, *op. cit.*, vol. ii, p. 157

[61]Reaney, *Dictionary of British Surnames*, p. 346

[62]P.R.O. E179/149/7, m. 25, 26; Rye, *Cal. Norf. Fines*, vol. ii, p. 384; L'Estrange, *op. cit.*, pp. 6, 147; *Rotuli Hundredorum*, vol. i, p. 497

[63]*See*, e.g., P.R.O. E179/149/7, mm. 27, 38, 40, 49, 50, 51, 52, 55, 62, 63; Rye, *Cal. Norf. Fines*, vol. i, pp. 96, 162; vol. ii, pp. 245, 257, 282, 284, 309, 321, 351, 358, 395; *Rotuli Hundredorum*, vol. i, p. 490

[64]*See* e.g., *Suffolk in 1327*, pp. 39, 50, 79, 81, 84, 109, 113, 127, 163, 166, 168; Rye, *Cal. Suff. Fines*, pp. 185, 214; Ipswich and East Suffolk R.O. HA/12/C2/1, mm. 3, 4; HA/12/C2/2, mm. 2, 9

[65]P.R.O. E179/149/7, mm. 25, 32, 53; E179/149/9, m. 49; Rye, *Cal. Norf. Fines*, vol. ii, pp. 240, 242, 349, 362, 365; *Rotuli Hundredorum*, vol. i, pp. 465, 469, 496, 498

[66]*Suffolk in 1327*, pp. 9, 32, 40, 128, 153, 163; Hervey, ed., *Pinchbeck Register*, vol. i, pp. 99, 141

[67] P.R.O. E179/149/7, mm. 20, 21, 26, 27, 28, 31, 34, 51, 69; *Suffolk in 1327*, pp. 61, 65, 92, 109, 114, 116, 122, 125, 126, 155, 177, 183, 187, 201

[68]*See*, e.g. P.R.O. E179/149/7, mm. 38, 50; Ipswich and East Suffolk R.O., HA/12/C2/7, mm. 9, 10, 12; Rye, *Cal. Norf. Fines*, vol. i, pp. 22, 84, 158; vol. ii, 269, 309; Hudson, *Leet Jurisdiction in the*

City of Norwich, p. 19; *Suffolk in 1327*, pp. 31, 81, 96, 98, 101, 142, 143, 215

[69]*See*, e.g. P.R.O. E179/149/7, m. 15, 46, 47, 48, 49, 51, 64, 69; SC.2/192/75; SC.2/192/80; Ipswich and East Suffolk R.O., HA/12/C2/20, m. 2; Rye, *Cal. Norf. Fines*, vol. ii, p. 284, 324, 415; Rye, *Cal. Suff. Fines*, pp. 214, 241

[70]Rye, *Cal. Suff. Fines*, pp. 272, 282; Rye, *Cal. Norf. Fines*, vol. ii, p. 413

[71]A. H. Smith, *op. cit.*, part i, p. 248; Reaney, *Dictionary of British Surnames*, p. 195

[72]*Feudal Aids*, vol. iii, p. 395; Rye, *Cal. Norf. Fines*, vol. i, pp. 135, 147; vol. ii, pp. 232, 249, 331, 332, 343, 350, 399, 400; *Index of Placita de Banco, 1327-8* (P.R.O. Lists and Indexes, xxxii), part i, p. 428; P.R.O. E179/149/9, m. 49

[73]A. Way, *Promptorium Parvulorum*, vol. i, p. 288. There are localities called Lathe Street and Lathe Green in Saxlingham (Norf.)

[74]*Rotuli Hundredorum*, vol. i, p. 477 (Henry de le Berne)

[75]*See* e.g. Powell, *A Suffolk Hundred in 1283*, table 5; *Suffolk in 1327*, pp. 29, 36, 37, 42, 72, 104, 119, 123, 138-9, 140, 147, 178

[76]A. H. Smith, *op. cit.*, part i, pp. 193-4

[77]F. Blomefield, *An Essay towards a Topographical History of the County of Norfolk* (1806), vol. iii, p. 138; Way, *op. cit.*, vol. i, p. 185; Fransson, *op. cit.*, p. 80; Ipswich and East Suffolk R.O., Flixton Priory Court Rolls, Court held 1st Nov., 1305 (I owe this reference to Mr. J. M. Ridgard)

[78]Rye, *Calendar of Norwich Deeds, 1307-41*, pp. 140, 156; Rye, *Cal. Norf. Fines*, vol. ii, pp. 239, 339, 354; *Suffolk in 1327*, p. 193; Rye, *Cal. Suff. Fines*, p. 292; Fransson, *op. cit.*, p. 80; P.R.O. E179/149/7, m. 5, 22, 43; P.R.O. C.133/89/8

[79]P.R.O. E179/150/205

[80]*Suffolk in 1327*, pp. 41, 92, 93, 97, 113, 176; P.R.O. E179/149/7, mm. 7, 9, 21, 26, 35, 50, 51, 62. On the surname becoming hereditary, *see* above, p. 11

[81]*Suffolk in 1524*, pp. 76, 81, 86, 90, 258, 263, 264, 377; A. C. Chibnall and A. V. Woodman, *Subsidy Roll for the County of Buckingham, Anno 1524, passim*; J. Cornwall, *Lay Subsidy Rolls for the County of Sussex, 1524-25, passim*; on the Norfolk sources *see* above

[82]P. H. Reaney, *Dictionary of British Surnames*, p. 67

[83]*Ibid.*, p. 228

[84]L'Estrange, ed., *Calendar of the Freemen of Norwich, 1317-1603*, pp. 6, 100; Rye, *Cal. Norf. Fines*, vol. ii, pp. 234, 292; P.R.O. E179/149/7, m. 38; A. H. Smith, *op. cit.*, part ii, p. 48. There is

a locality called The Nab at Burgh St. Margaret, Norfolk: Ordnance Survey, sheet TG.41

[85]*See* above, p. 34

[86]*Suffolk in 1327*, p. 200; A. H. Smith, *op. cit.*, part i, p. 206

[87]*Suffolk in 1327*, pp. 32, 96, 98-101; P.R.O. E179/149/7, mm. 10, 35, 40, 42, 44, 48, 68

[88]*See*, e.g. Davis, ed., *Kalendar of Abbot Samson*, p. 85; Rye, *Calendar of Deeds Relating to Norwich, 1285-1306*, p. 58; Rye, *Calendar of Norwich Deeds, 1307-41*, pp. 27, 61, 173; Hudson, *Leet Jurisdiction in Norwich*, p. 8; P.R.O. E179/149/9, mm. 49, 71

[89]P.R.O. E179/149/7, mm. 10, 35; *Index of Placita de Banco, 1327-8*, (P.R.O. Lists and Indexes, xxxii), part ii, p. 617

[90]*Suffolk in 1524*, pp. 20, 240, 381; P.R.O. E36/22; E179/150/205, 213, 227, 239, 265; E315/466; E36/25; E101/61/16

[91]For other views of the derivation of Woodruff, *see* P. H. Reaney, *Dictionary of British Surnames*, p. 359, and E. Ekwall, *Early London Personal Names* (1947), p. 176; and see for comparable names, P.R.O. E179/149/7, mm. 4, 13, 16, 50, 57, 58, 60

[92]Powell, *A Suffolk Hundred in 1283*, tables 3, 4; W. Hudson, 'Three Manorial Extents', *Norfolk Archaeology* (1901), vol. xiv, p. 44; Reaney, *Dictionary of British Surnames*, p. 51; P.R.O. E179/149/7, m. 49

[93]Reaney, *Dictionary of British Surnames*, p. 38; A. H. Smith, *op. cit.*, part i, p. 41

[94]*See*, e.g., *Suffolk in 1327*, pp. 67, 215; Powell, *A Suffolk Hundred in 1283*, p. 21; Bullock, *op. cit.*, p. 8; P.R.O. E179/149/7, m. 49

[95]L'Estrange, *op. cit.*, p. 5; J. Kirkpatrick, *Streets and Lanes of the City of Norwich* (1889), p. 87

[96]*See*, L'Estrange, *op. cit.*, p. 154; Hudson, *Leet Jurisdiction in the City of Norwich*, pp. 4, 12

[97]Rye, *Calendar of Deeds Relating to Norwich, 1285-1306*, pp. 34, 35; Kirkpatrick, *op. cit.*, p. 10

[98]*See*, e.g., Rye, *Calendar of Norwich Deeds, 1307-41*, p. 11; L'Estrange, *op. cit.*, pp. 58, 73; *Index of Placito de Banco, 1327-8* (P.R.O. Lists and Indexes, xxxii), part i, p. 412. But Gatesend was also an alternative name for the village of Tattersett; Blomefield, *op. cit.*, vol. vii, p. 192.

[99]*See*, e.g., *Suffolk in 1327*, pp. 23, 24, 29, 37, 39, 112, 183, 198

[100]Rye, *Cal. Norf. Fines*, vol. i, p. 168; vol. ii, p. 248; P.R.O. E179/149/7, mm. 27, 48, 67

[101]*See*, e.g., Rye, *Cal. Norf. Fines*, vol. ii, pp. 351, 359, 362; *Suffolk in 1327*, pp. 47, 109, 178; D. M. Stenton, ed., *Great Roll of the Pipe for the 9th Year of Richard I* (Pipe Roll Society, New Series, vol. viii) (1931), p. 245; P.R.O. E179/149/7, mm. 19, 29, 34, 43, 62

102*Suffolk in 1327*, pp. 42, 43, 45; C. Morley, 'Catalogue of the Beneficed Clergy of Suffolk, 1086-1550', *Proceedings of the Suffolk Institute of Archaeology* (1936), vol. xxii, p. 77; Hervey, *Pinchbeck Register*, vol. i, p. 104; Powell, *A Suffolk Hundred in 1283*, p. 81; table 17

103*Suffolk in 1327*, p. 43

104Fransson, *op. cit.*, pp. 190-208

105*Suffolk in 1327*, p. 191

106Hervey, *Pinchbeck Register*, vol. i, p. 138

107Rye, *Cal. Norf. Fines*, vol. ii, p. 435; Fransson, *op. cit.*, p. 206

108Rye, *Cal. Norf. Fines*, vol. ii, pp. 326, 435

109*Suffolk in 1327*, pp. 4, 9, 71; Reaney, *Dictionary of British Surnames*, p. 310

110*Suffolk in 1327*, pp. 184, 194; Powell, *A Suffolk Hundred in 1283*, pp. 26, 89; W. Rye, *Norfolk Topography* (1881), p. 392

111Reaney, *op. cit.* pp. 160, 192

112*Suffolk in 1327*, p. 136; *Index of Placita de Banco, 1327-8* (P.R.O. Lists and Indexes, xxxii), part ii, p. 635

113Rye, *Calendar of Norwich Deeds, 1307-41*, p. 221

114*See*, e.g. Rye, *Cal. Norf. Fines*, vol. i, p. 99; P.R.O. E179/149/7, mm. 1, 7, 20, 29

115*Index of Placita de Banco, 1327-8* (P.R.O. Lists and Indexes, xxxii), part ii, p. 608. Compare Ralf le Spitel skinnere, cordwainer (Hervey, ed., *Pinchbeck Register*, vol. i, pp. 142, 148)

116Rye, *Cal. Norf. Fines*, vol. i, p. 40

117*Suffolk in 1327*, pp. 29, 197, 202; Hervey, ed., *Pinchbeck Register*, vol. i, p. 146; Rye, *Cal. Norf. Fines*, vol. ii, p. 362; *Feudal Aids*, vol. iii, p. 447

118P.R.O. E179/149/7, mm. 39, 44, 45, 50, 58; Rye, *Cal. Norf. Fines*, vol. ii, p. 332

CHAPTER 5

SURNAMES DERIVED FROM PERSONAL NAMES

Surnames derived from personal names were in the 16th century borne by a larger proportion of the East Anglian population than surnames in any other category, and the number of different names in the class was very great, greater probably than for any other class.[1] In the 13th century, when for the first time it is possible to find evidence for the surnames or bye-names used by large numbers in various social classes, the personal names then current in East Anglia included names of Anglo-Saxon, Scandinavian, and French origin, and each of the three groups formed a substantial proportion of the total. The linguistic origins of the surnames derived from personal names in the region are naturally mixed in a similar way. Any attempt to estimate the proportion of English, Scandinavian, and Norman elements in the population from the personal names or surnames in use at this relatively late period would be futile. After the Conquest French personal names spread rapidly through most parts of England, and well before 1200 there is evidence that both Scandinavian and Anglo-Saxon personal names were being used within single families.[2]

The tendency for personal names of Anglo-Saxon or Scandinavian origin to fall into disuse after the Conquest has frequently been remarked upon, and the impression is sometimes given that by c. 1275 they had almost ceased to be employed. It is important not to put the date at which such names disappeared earlier than the evidence warrants, because it affects the date at which the many surnames derived from the personal names in question were first formed and became hereditary. In Norfolk and Suffolk there are many Anglo-Saxon or Scandinavian personal names to be found still surviving during the first half of the 14th century. In the Suffolk 1327 subsidy roll, for instance, there are 115 persons called Edmund (a name especially common in the county), three called Edward, 59 called Seman, and five called Sewal.[3] In the Wymondham (Norfolk) court rolls for 1328-9, four different men called Sewal appear.[4] Alfred, Goda, Sewal, Godmann, Godwin, Osbert, Leveday, Bonde, and Ketel all appear as personal names in the Norfolk 1329-30 subsidy.[5] In 1348-56 four men with the personal name Semannus appear on a manor at South Elmham in Suffolk.[6] Many other instances could be given of Anglo-Saxon and Scandinavian personal names surviving into the 14th century, some of the names involved being ones that never seem to have been common at any period.[7]

This is all the more significant when considered in relation to the rise of hereditary surnames from personal names. Some cases suggest that surnames were particularly likely to evolve from the rarer personal names in places where these survived until a relatively late period. No doubt if a personal name continued in use in, say, one or two adjoining villages, after it had ceased to be employed in most other places, it would be all the more distinctive, and so perhaps more likely to give rise to a surname.

One example is the unusual surname Edman or Ediman, derived from an Old English personal name. In the Norfolk subsidy rolls for 1329-30, only three persons surnamed Ediman are listed, two at Dunham Magna in central Norfolk, and one at East Bilney, about six miles away. In the same source two persons with the personal name Edman occur, and both of these are at Dunham Magna.[8] At about the same date a Philip Edman was admitted to the freedom of Norwich.[9] His origins have not been traced, though it would be interesting to know if he came from Dunham Magna or its vicinity. In this case a rare personal name had evidently continued to be used at Dunham long after it had disappeared over most of the country, and had given rise to a surname there at a late period. Ediman has not been found as a surname in Norfolk before 1329-30. In the same subsidy rolls Gamel appears as a surname or bye-name in only two Norfolk villages, at Titchwell where there were three persons of the name recorded, and at Hempstead in Happing Hundred, where there are again three. Hempstead is the only place at which Gamel occurs as a personal name in the subsidy.[10] By the 14th century Gamel was rare as a baptismal name. In the Norfolk 1329-30 subsidy there is only the one instance, and it does not occur at all as a baptismal name in the Suffolk 1327 subsidy, though it occurs there as a surname or bye-name, and though it occurs about the same date as a personal name at Bury St. Edmunds.[11] Titchwell and Hempstead are about 40 miles apart, and there are no known grounds for suspecting a relationship between the groups named Gamel at the two parishes (probably a single family at each). It does appear, however, that at Hempstead a rare personal name, surviving in use to an unusually late period, had given rise to a surname. Another example of the same phenomenon occurs in the Norfolk hundred of South Greenhoe. There in the 1329-30 subsidy the surname Conen or Conon occurs in three different townships, all close together, and in one of them there appears also Conan used as a personal name.[12] Conan is a Breton personal name, never common in East Anglia, and by the 14th century rare.

Apart from the survival locally of some rare personal names, and the connected rise of certain surnames, it was also true in the 13th and 14th centuries that there was a tendency, natural enough, for a personal name to become unusually common amongst the inhabitants of a particular place. In the Suffolk 1327 subsidy, for example, out of 21 persons, one a woman, listed at Euston, six had the personal name Peter; at Bradwell, in the same subsidy out of 22 persons listed, including six women, five had the personal name Henry.[13] It is less easy to find examples of the same situation where women's names are concerned, if only because references to women were comparatively rare, but at Foulden, in the Norfolk 1329-30 subsidy, out of 10 women listed three were called Petronilla.[14] There are places where it can be seen that such situations affected the development of surnames. For instance, in the late 13th and early 14th centuries the personal name Abel was in use at Ingham in north Suffolk. In the same parish Abel appears as a surname or bye-name in the late 13th century, and in the 14th century it occurs at Bury St. Edmunds, about four miles away and the nearest large town, and at Pakenham, about four miles from Ingham.[15] At Hopton, not far from Ingham, the personal names Haylot, Moyse (or Moses) and Guderam (or Godram) occur in the 13th century, and at the same place Haylot, Moyse, and Guderam all occur as surnames from the late 13th century onwards.[16] The evolution of surnames was thus affected by local habits in the giving of personal names, whether in the preservation of certain personal names in one or two villages long after they had been discarded generally, or in the common use within a limited area of personal names rare in other parts.

The origin of surnames formed by the addition of the suffix -son to personal names, and to occupation terms, has been the subject of some discussion.[17] The existence in East Anglia, during the 11th century and the first half of the 12th, of some bye-names with the suffix -suna has already been noted.[18] Between the mid-12th century and the mid-13th no names of this type have been discovered in the region. Surnames or bye-names with the suffix -son begin to appear in Norfolk and Suffolk in the late 13th century. At that period there are very few, and more often they consist of an occupational term, with the suffix added (Revesone, or Prestessone, for example), than of a personal name and the suffix.[19] In the 14th century surnames with -son remain scarce; only 20 persons with names certainly in this category have been found in the Norfolk 1329-30 subsidy, and only 19 in the Suffolk 1327 subsidy.[20] Other occurrences of surnames with the suffix -son in the 14th century are relatively few, and do not suggest that names of the type were greatly increasing in numbers.[21] Occurrences in 15th-century sources are not much more numerous than those in the 14th century, and names in -son only form quite a small proportion of the whole body of East Anglian surnames in the early 16th century, by which time most people had settled hereditary surnames. During the 15th century, for example, four per cent of those admitted to the freedom of Norwich had surnames with the suffix -son, and amongst the freemen of both Lynn and Yarmouth the corresponding figure was three per cent for the same period.[22] In the 16th century the proportions are higher, 12 per cent at Norwich, nine per cent at Lynn, and six per cent at Yarmouth.[23] Outside the towns the surnames in this category were proportionally fewer in the early 16th century. In the Suffolk returns for the subsidy granted in 1523, only three per cent of those listed had surnames in -son.[24] The Norfolk returns for the same subsidy are incomplete, but in the extant subsidy rolls for some hundreds in the county rather less than three per cent of those listed had surnames in -son.[25] Surnames in this category were thus comparatively rare in East Anglia, at any period up to the early 16th century, though more common in the larger towns than elsewhere.

There is, however, the question of how far names given in the usual Latin formula, such as *Johannes filius Willelmi*, etc., are translations of vernacular surnames or bye-names ending in -son. During the 12th and 13th centuries the Latin formula is very common, and during the 14th century it is still often encountered in such sources as tax assessments, though less frequently than earlier. It seems unlikely that the Latin phrase can usually be a translation of vernacular names in -son, if only because in the 13th century the proportion of names in which the Latin formula is used in many sources is much greater than the proportion of surnames in -son that appear at later periods. There is also the point that many medieval sources, though written in Latin and giving most proper names in Latinised forms, do occasionally lapse into giving individual names in the vernacular. This is true, for instance, of the Pipe Rolls; under Richard I, for example, a Norfolk man appears as Richard *Tannator* in one Pipe Roll, and as Richard le Tanur in another, and similar inconsistencies in the treatment of occupational names are numerous.[26] If surnames or bye-names with the suffix -son were in use during *c.* 1150-1250, it is remarkable that no examples have been found. It cannot be supposed that all names of this type were consistently Latinised, even in sources which were quite inconsistent in the treatment of other proper names. The obvious conclusion is that there was a period, *c.* 1150-1250, when bye-names or surnames in -son were not used, and that during the second half of the 13th century a new growth of such names began.

This is not to say that the Latin formula with *filius* was never used to translate names in -son when after *c.* 1250 these do begin to appear. Many instances of surnames formed from a personal name and the suffix -son that occur in the late 13th or early 14th centuries are ones for which it might have been difficult to find a Latin translation. Such names occurring in the Norfolk 1329-30 subsidy, for example, include Gimesson, Madesson, Catessone, Dauwessone, Levessone, Batissone, and Jopyssone, and the Suffolk 1327 subsidy includes Bassisson, Jackessone, Maggessone, and Hendissone.[27] It may be suspected that occasionally names of the type, when easily translated, were rendered into Latin with the *filius* formula. However, this does not invalidate the argument that in *c.* 1150-1250 the Latin phrase is unlikely to have been used with complete consistency to render names with the -son suffix.

Surnames or bye-names formed from a personal name with a genitive -s added, or more rarely from a term denoting occupation or status with a genitive -s added, occur in East Anglia in the late 12th century.[28] During the 13th century such names are uncommon, but do occur with sufficient frequency in both Norfolk and Suffolk to show that the habit of forming surnames or bye-names in this way was well established.[29] In the early 14th century names of this type, though not common, were more numerous than those with the -son suffix. In the Norfolk 1329-30 subsidy returns, for example, there are 107 persons with names formed from a personal name with a genitival -s added. There are also a few names of the type le Persones, le Clerkes, etc.[30] In the Suffolk 1327 subsidy there are only 31 certain cases of surnames or bye-names formed from a personal name with -s.[31] During the 14th and 15th centuries such names continue to occur frequently,[32] but they only form an insignificant proportion of the total body of surnames in use. Amongst those admitted to the freedom both at Lynn and at Norwich during the period 1301 to 1500, persons with surnames formed of a personal name and a genitival -s made up rather less than one per cent of the total. At Yarmouth, where the record of admissions to the freedom does not begin until 1429, the proportion among those admitted up to 1500 was higher, over two per cent. In the 16th century the proportions are noticeably greater, two and a half per cent at Lynn, five per cent at Norwich, and four per cent at Yarmouth.[33] Figures for Norfolk as a whole were probably not very different from these in the 16th century. In the returns for certain rural hundreds for the subsidy granted in 1523, five per cent of all surnames were of the type.[34]

Certain characteristics of surnames or bye-names formed from a personal name with -s may be noted. In early instances (before *c.* 1350) a high proportion were the names of women. For example out of the 107 names of the type in the Norfolk 1329-30 subsidy, 38 were women, though women were only an insignificant proportion of those listed.[35] The explanation is probably to be found in Dr. Reaney's observation that women with such surnames in the 14th century were often widows, with surnames derived from their husbands' personal names, or in some cases husbands' occupations. Thus, in the Norfolk subsidy rolls just mentioned Alice Thomys was presumably the widow, or less probably the wife, of a man called Thomas, Katherine Wilkyns the widow (or wife) of one Wilkyn, and so forth.[36] If this explanation is correct, the acquisition by women of names belonging to this type must be reckoned a principal origin of such surnames.

Another characteristic is that such surnames are very frequently evolved from diminutive or pet forms of personal names. Gibbs, Robbs, Daukins, Jackes, Magges, Dix and so forth are common amongst names in the category during the 13th and 14th centuries. In the Norfolk subsidy of 1329-30, for example, in the case of 71 out of the 107 persons with surnames or bye-names formed from a personal name with an added genitive -s, the surnames or bye-names are from diminutive or pet forms.[37] This situation probably owes something to the difficulty that the translation of such diminutive and pet forms into Latin equivalents presented to clerks drawing up subsidy rolls. By the 16th century the predominance of pet and diminutive forms in names of this type has disappeared.

Some surnames with a genitive -s were really toponymics. Sometimes the presence of a preposition makes this clear, as in the case of William atte Personnes, listed in Suffolk in 1327.[38] In other cases it may be suspected that such names were topographic. Alice Prioures, for example, was listed at Thornham, Norfolk, in the 1329-30 subsidy, and the Prior of Norwich was also listed as holding property in the same parish.[39] Alice was probably dwelling on the Prior's land, perhaps as a tenant. In many cases, however, where names such as le Clerkes, le Persones, Smythys and so forth are concerned, it is difficult to know if the surnames originated with children of the clerk, parson, smith, etc., with a servant of these personages, or with persons living at or near the parsonage (or glebe farm), smithy, and so forth.

During the Middle Ages some East Anglian families had surnames that fluctuated, sometimes occurring with a genitive -s, sometimes without it, and there was a tendency for surnames to acquire an -s that had previously lacked it. At Fincham in Norfolk, for example, a family called Rykke occurs in the late 14th century. Early in the 15th century, however, some members of the family occur with the surname in the form of Rykkys, the first case that has been noted occurring in 1403. During the 15th century the name varies between the two forms. For instance, in 1441 Thomas and Edward Rykkys occur, and in 1443 Thomas, Edward, and Simon Rykkys, but in 1427-9 Edward and Thomas Rykke occur, and in 1452 Thomas, Edward, and Simon Rikke.[40] Other examples, at Fincham and elsewhere, could be quoted of families whose surnames fluctuated in the same way. It is probably this process which accounts for the increased proportion of surnames with a genitive -s in the 16th century.

Surnames composed of personal names without any suffix can already be found in the 11th century. One case of this, that of the Bainard family, has been discussed above.[41] This family was Norman, but surnames or bye-names of the type can be found among the peasant population in the late 11th century. The tenants on Bury Abbey's Suffolk lands at that period, for example, included Alduine Aelfuine, Lemmer Brihtmer, Goduuine Hachelard, Ordric Wihgar, and others with similar names.[42] In the 12th and 13th centuries names in this category were borne by large numbers of persons, and were derived from very many different personal names, some of them rare. Surnames formed from a personal name without addition were much more numerous than those formed from a personal name with an added -son or genitive -s. In the Suffolk 1327 subsidy roll, for example, 28 per cent of all surnames or bye-names listed were formed from personal names without -son or -s, and in the Suffolk 1524 subsidy the proportion was 23 per cent. Among the freemen of towns and cities the proportion was less, probably because of the very numerous locative surnames to be found. At Norwich, for example, 13 per cent of the freemen admitted from 1317 to 1400 had such surnames or bye-names.[44] Similar figures could be quoted for other sources which list surnames in large numbers. Since there are inevitably some surnames of which the origins remain doubtful, figures such as those just given cannot claim to be mathematically accurate. The doubtful cases are, however, too few to make much difference.

Since surnames ending either with a genitival -s, or the suffix -son, were still fairly rare as late as the beginning of Edward III's reign, those personal names which had become very uncommon, or totally disused, by that date were unlikely to give rise to surnames with either of these terminations. In fact there were numerous personal names that gave rise to surnames, some of which were fairly common, without the addition of either a genitival -s or of -son, but which noticeably failed to give rise to surnames with either of these additions. Most such names were those which became rare or wholly disused by *c.* 1350 at the latest, whereas those personal names which gave rise to surnames ending in a genitival -s or -son were mostly those that remained in use throughout the Middle Ages. This is evident if lists are made of those personal names which gave rise to the surnames in use in East Anglia in the early 16th century, by which time virtually the whole population had acquired hereditary surnames. The total number of personal names that have given rise to surnames is very large, and consequently in the lists set out below only those personal names that have given rise to at least moderately common surnames are mentioned. The figures given in the following lists for Suffolk are drawn from the Suffolk returns for the subsidy granted in 1523.[45] The Norfolk returns for the same subsidy are incomplete, and accordingly the figures given for Norfolk are based partly on the surviving returns for the subsidy granted in 1523, and, for the hundreds where the subsidy returns are unavailable, on the returns for the 'Military Survey', of 1522.[46]

I. Personal Names giving rise to surnames without addition of -s or -son

The number of occurrences of surnames in the sources for each county (as described above) is given in brackets after each name. Personal names giving rise to rare surnames only have been omitted. Cases in which surnames have more than one possible origin have also been excluded. Spelling variants have been consolidated under the most usual form of each name.

Norfolk		*Suffolk*	
Aencell (19)	Martin (49)	Aencell (5)	Martin (28)
Albon (16)	Matthew (17)	Albon (1)	Matthew (9)
Algar (19)	Michael (27)	Algar (6)	Michael (10)
Austin (18)	Neel (37)	Austin (14)	Neel (9)
Baldwin (17)	Osbern (25)	Baldwin (13)	Osbern (12)
Bernard (21)	Payn (45)	Bernard (22)	Payn (20)
Colman (22)	Randolf (26)	Colman (14)	Randolf (7)
Downing (25)	Rayner (17)	Downing (10)	Rayner (5)
Ellis (15)	Reynold (25)	Ellis (18)	Reynold (24)
Everard (22)	Salman (24)	Everard (23)	Salman (9)
Gerard (56)	Sewall (30)	Gerard (17)	Sewall (13)
Godfrey (20)	Thurkill (20)	Godfrey (13)	Thurkill (2)
Goodwin (37)	Toly (18)	Goodwin (21)	Toly (4)
Hamon (27)	Vincent (22)	Hamon (23)	Vincent (9)
Harman (38)	Wace (21)	Harman (14)	Wace (10)

Hervey (44)   Wulsey (15)   Hervey (21)   Wulsey (3)
Hobard (28)   Hobard (20)

In comparing the figures for the two counties it must be remembered that the total number of individuals in the sources for Norfolk (about 18,500) is rather greater than that in the sources for Suffolk (about 17,000).[47]

The great majority of names in the preceding lists are ones that were obsolete, or very rare, by the mid-14th century. It would be possible to add to the list a large number of personal names, all rare or disused by *c.* 1350, that gave rise to less common surnames without the addition of a genitival -s or of -son, but there would be little point in citing further examples. The personal names in the preceding list may be contrasted with those in the list that follows, and that contains personal names which gave rise to surnames including those ending with a genitival -s or -son.

II. Personal Names giving rise to surnames, including some with the addition of -s or -son.

The names in this list are derived from the same sources as those in List I above. Surnames that might be derived either from a personal name, or from some other source, have been omitted.

		Norfolk	*Suffolk*
Adam		(1)	(6)
	Adams	(10)	(4)
	Adamson	(5)	(0)
	Adye	(1)	(1)
	Atkin	(6)	(3)
	Atkins	(2)	(0)
	Atkinson	(6)	(5)
Alen		(91)	(27)
	Alkin	(1)	(0)
	Alens	(13)	(0)
[Alice]		(0)	(0)
	Alison	(10)	(1)
Alexander		(27)	(5)
	Saunder	(14)	(5)
	Saunders	(3)	(0)
	Saunderson	(8)	(3)
Amis		(15)	(4)
	Amison	(1)	(1)

	Norfolk	Suffolk
Andrew	(9)	(17)
Andrews	(36)	(5)
Andrewson	(1)	(2)
Anderson	(8)	(3)
Betts	(49)	(16)
Clement	(18)	(10)
Clements	(10)	(0)
Davy	(68)	(16)
Davys	(0)	(1)
Davison	(4)	(4)
Gilbert	(21)	(13)
Gybbe	(0)	(1)
Gibbs	(10)	(6)
Gibson	(13)	(4)
Gilson	(12)	(0)
Henry	(2)	(1)
Henrice	(1)	(0)
Hendry	(17)	(0)
Harry	(0)	(1)
Harris[48]	(12)	(9)
Harrison[49]	(33)	(14)
Hugh, Hewe	(2)	(2)
Hewse	(1)	(3)
Hewson	(9)	(0)
Hewlet	(1)	(0)
Hewling	(1)	(0)
Hewet	(9)	(5)
Hewetson	(0)	(1)
John	(3)	(2)
Johns	(5)	(5)
Johnson	(86)	(43)
Johnsons	(2)	(0)
Lawrance	(18)	(9)
Lawes	(41)	(2)
Lawson	(3)	(4)
Peter	(1)	(4)
Peterson	(4)	(2)
Peers	(21)	(9)
Person	(39)	(7)
Richard	(0)	(4)
Richards	(2)	(4)
Richardson	(15)	(14)

	Norfolk	Suffolk
Rickett	(1)	(0)
Dix	(22)	(4)
Dickson	(17)	(7)
Hicks	(5)	(2)
Hickson	(6)	(0)
Higgs	(2)	(0)
Higson	(1)	(0)
Robert	(2)	(4)
Roberts	(16)	(5)
Robertson	(0)	(9)
Robson	(5)	(6)
Robbs	(6)	(0)
Robins	(21)	(0)
Robinson	(19)	(8)
Dobb	(1)	(0)
Dobbs	(15)	(5)
Dobson	(3)	(4)
Roger	(12)	(12)
Rogers	(18)	(4)
Rogerson	(2)	(3)
Hodges	(5)	(1)
Hodgson	(2)	(0)
Hodgkin	(2)	(1)
Hodgkins	(3)	(0)
Hodgkinson	(1)	(0)
Hopson	(2)	(0)
Hopkins	(1)	(0)
Hopkinson	(1)	(0)
Hobb	(1)	(0)
Hobbs	(4)	(1)
Hobson	(8)	(3)
Stephen	(7)	(8)
Stephens	(4)	(1)
Stephenson	(20)	(8)
Stebins	(1)	(0)
Stebinson	(1)	(0)
Simon	(8)	(23)
Syme	(0)	(1)
Simmonds	(20)	(2)
Sims	(6)	(1)
Simpson	(13)	(8)
Thomas	(3)	(3)
Thompson[50]	(90)	(24)

	Norfolk	Suffolk
Tommys	(0)	(2)
Thomlinson	(2)	(1)
Tamson	(1)	(0)
Walter	(18)	(10)
Watte	(1)	(0)
Watts	(38)	(3)
Watson	(32)	(13)
Water	(2)	(8)
Waters	(0)	(2)
Waterson	(1)	(0)
William	(1)	(5)
Williams	(10)	(7)
Williamson	(20)	(6)
Wilson	(28)	(19)
Willinson	(7)	(0)
Wilcock	(1)	(1)
Wilkin	(14)	(4)
Wilkins	(15)	(1)
Wilkinson	(13)	(6)

The two lists given above include only the more common surnames, and if all the surnames derived from personal names, with
or without additions, were added in the appropriate places, the
lists would obviously be inordinately long. It does, however, seem
clear from the two lists just set out that surnames consisting of a
personal name with the addition of a genitival -s or of -son were
formed from personal names that continued to be common after
about 1350, and not from personal names that had become rare,
or totally disused, by that time, although many such personal
names (disused or rare by *c.* 1350) had given rise to surnames without
additions. This situation tells strongly against the view that surnames ending with a genitival -s or -son were widely used in the
13th and early 14th centuries, but that their existence is concealed
because the original sources are nearly all in Latin.

References
[1]McKinley, *op. cit.*, pp. 34-5; *see* also Reaney, *Origin of English
Surnames*, p. 22
[2]Reaney, *op. cit.*, pp. 101-107; F. M. Stenton, *Free Peasantry of the
Northern Danelaw* (1969), pp. 17, 18
[3]*Suffolk in 1327*, pp. 308-10
[4]Norfolk and Norwich R.O., N.R.S. 18476, mm. 5-8

⁵P.R.O. E179/149/7, mm. 12, 21, 51, 53, 61, 62, 64, 65
⁶Ipswich and East Suffolk R.O. HA/12/C2/11, m. 1; HA/12/C2/14, m. 2
⁷Reaney, *Dictionary of British Surnames*, p. 107
⁸P.R.O. E179/149/7, mm. 36, 37
⁹Norfolk and Norwich R.O., Norwich Old Free Book, f. 31
¹⁰P.R.O. E179/149/7, mm. 47, 66
¹¹*Suffolk in 1327*, p. 75; Hervey, ed., *Pinchbeck Register*, vol. i, pp. 139, 145
¹²P.R.O. E179/149/7, m. 53
¹³*Suffolk in 1327*, pp. 100, 188
¹⁴P.R.O. E179/149/7, m. 54
¹⁵Powell, *A Suffolk Hundred in 1283*, Table 16; *Suffolk in 1327*, pp. 173, 174, 195; Hervey, ed., *Pinchbeck Register*, vol. i, pp. 98, 107, 143
¹⁶Powell, *A Suffolk Hundred in 1283*, table 14; *Suffolk in 1327*, p. 187; *Rotuli Hundredorum*, vol. ii, p. 158
¹⁷Reaney, *Origins of English Surnames*, pp. 86-90; C. M. Matthews, *English Surnames* (1966), pp. 203-6
¹⁸*See* above, p. 3
¹⁹*See* e.g. Phillimore, *Placita Coram Rege*, pp. 34, 93, 116; Rye, *Cal. Norf. Fines*, vol. i, p. 128; Powell, *A Suffolk Hundred in 1283*, table 14
²⁰*Suffolk in 1327*, *passim*; P.R.O. E179/149/7, *passim*. These figures include surnames composed of an occupational term with the suffix -son added
²¹*See* e.g., *Index of Placito de Banco, 1327-8* (P.R.O. Lists and Indexes, xxxii), part i, pp. 379, 384, 400, 439; part ii, pp. 628, 613; Hervey, ed., *Pinchbeck Register*, vol. i, pp. 132, 144; Rye, *Cal. Norf. Fines*, vol. ii, pp. 236, 253, 286, 301, 320-21, 325, 331, 352, 354, 357, 367; *Feudal Aids* (1904), vol. iii, p. 444; P.R.O. E179/149/9, m. 71; L'Estrange, *op. cit.*, pp. 29, 80
²²L'Estrange, *op. cit.*, *passim*; Anon., *Calendar of the Freemen of Lynn, 1292-1836*, pp. 29-73; Anon., *Calendar of the Freemen of Great Yarmouth, 1429-1800*, pp. 1-17
²³L'Estrange, *op. cit.*, *passim*; Anon., *Calendar of the Freemen of Lynn, 1292-1836*, pp. 73-129; Anon., *Calendar of the Freemen of Great Yarmouth, 1429-1800*, pp. 17-51
²⁴*Suffolk in 1524, passim*
²⁵P.R.O. E179/150/206, 222, 247, 262, 281
²⁶D. M. Stenton, ed., *Great Roll of the Pipe for the Third and Fourth Years of Richard I* (Pipe Roll Society, New Series, vol. ii) (1926), pp. 48, 191; D. M. Stenton, ed., *Great Roll of the Pipe for the Fifth Year of Richard I* (Pipe Roll Society, New Series, vol. iii), p. 22

[27]P.R.O. E179/149/7, mm. 16, 25, 26, 36, 47, 48, 65; *Suffolk in 1327*, pp. 20, 63, 117, 200

[28]Davis ed., *Kalendar of Abbot Samson*, p. 7 (Segarus Aileues), pp. 51, 52 (Edrich Keteles). Aeluric Doddes, who occurs in the late 11th century, is perhaps an earlier case: Douglas, *Feudal Documents from the Abbey of Bury St. Edmunds*, p. 39

[29]*See*, e.g. Powell, *A Suffolk Hundred in 1283*, p. 28; tables 19, 24; Hudson, *Leet Jurisdiction in Norwich*, pp. 7, 17; Rye, *Cal. Norf. Fines*, vol. i, pp. 71, 100, 129, 130, 132

[30]P.R.O. E179/149/7, *passim*. A few doubtful cases have been excluded.

[31]*Suffolk in 1327*, *passim*

[32]*See* e.g. Rye, *Cal. Norf. Fines*, vol. ii, pp. 350, 352, 359, 361, 363, and *passim*; *Index to Placita de Banco, 1327-8* (P.R.O. Lists and Indexes, xxxii), part i, pp. 394, 402, 405, 433; Hudson, *op. cit.*, pp. 64, 65, 69, 70, 75

[33]L'Estrange, *op. cit.*, *passim*; Anon., *Calendar of the Freemen of Lynn, 1292-1836*, pp. 4-129; Anon., *Calendar of the Freemen of Great Yarmouth, 1429-1800*, pp. 1-51

[34]*See* sources cited in note 25 above

[35]P.R.O. E179/149/7, *passim*

[36]*Ibid.*, mm. 33, 38; Reaney, *Origin of English Surnames*, p. 92

[37]P.R.O. E179/149/7, *passim*

[38]*Suffolk in 1327*, p. 201

[39]P.R.O. E179/149/7, m. 65

[40]P.R.O. SC2/192/76; SC2/192/80; Norfolk and Norwich R.O., Ms. 7237

[41]*See* above, p. 3

[42]Douglas, *Feudal Documents from the Abbey of Bury St. Edmunds*, pp. 28, 29, 30, 32

[43]*Suffolk in 1327*, *passim*; *Suffolk in 1524*, *passim*

[44]L'Estrange, *op. cit.*, *passim*

[45]Printed in Anon, *Suffolk in 1524*. In a few cases there is some uncertainty about the precise numbers for Suffolk, as some individuals appear to be listed more than once in the Suffolk subsidy rolls, but the numbers involved are too small to affect the general picture. The Suffolk figures include aliens

[46]On these sources for Norfolk, *see* above pp. 89-90

[47]Anon., *Suffolk in 1524*, p. xvii; McKinley, *op. cit.*, p. 34

[48]Including Herries

[49]Including Herrison

[50]Some instances of this surname were probably derived from the village of Thompson (Norf.). Names spelt Thompston, and similar forms, have been excluded from the figures given here

CHAPTER 6

SOCIAL CLASS AND ITS INFLUENCE ON SURNAMES

An examination of the bye-names and surnames occurring in 12th- and 13th-century sources reveals a connection between the social class to which people belong, and the types of bye-names or surnames that they bear. Two points in particular emerge, that a high proportion of aristocratic or landed families tend to have locative bye-names or surnames, and that the peasant population, free and unfree, tend, when they have bye-names or surnames at all, to have ones that are either nicknames, or are derived from personal names. In the 12th-century Pipe Rolls, which mention many royal officials and persons holding directly from the king, the large proportion of locative bye-names or surnames is striking. Occasionally, however, the Pipe Rolls provide fairly long lists of persons in much humbler positions, as for instance when numerous tithings are amerced for allowing the escape of fugitives, and the names of both tithingmen and fugitives are given.[1] One such list for Richard I's reign gives the names of 72 persons, all either tithingmen or fugitives (some without any bye-names or surnames), and only seven out of these have surnames or bye-names that can certainly be classified as locative names. In general the character of the surnames or bye-names in this and similar lists is very different from that of the names that occur elsewhere in the Pipe Rolls, with about a fifth of the bye-names or surnames in it being derived from nicknames, and a slightly smaller proportion from personal names.[2] That the Pipe Rolls are not misleading in giving the impression that many persons of knightly or baronial status had locative surnames or bye-names can be seen from various sources that list large numbers of such persons more systematically than do the Pipe Rolls. The Norfolk section of the 'Cartae' of 1166 lists many holders of knights' fees, or fractions of fees, and out of these, 58 per cent have locative surnames or bye-names, and a further four per cent have surnames or bye-names derived from topographical features. The remaining 38 per cent includes some persons with no surnames or bye-names. In Suffolk, the 'Cartae' of 1166 similarly list holders of knights' fees, or fractions, and of these 54 per cent have locative surnames or bye-names and five per cent surnames or bye-names derived from topographical features.[3] Other lists of military tenants produce similar evidence. Out of the tenants-in-chief and military sub-tenants listed in a Norfolk return of 1242-43, 70 per cent had locative surnames or bye-names, and three per cent had bye-names or surnames that were toponymics.[4] In the return of holders of knights' fees in Norfolk who were charged with the feudal aid of 1302, 59 per cent had locative surnames or bye-names, and 10 per cent had topographical surnames or bye-names.[5]

The sources just mentioned deal with holders of knights' fees, but similar evidence can be obtained from the subsidy rolls. If the largest taxpayer in each township as shown on a subsidy roll is noted, the proportion of locative surnames amongst them will be found to be much higher than it is amongst the whole number of persons in the roll. This is admittedly a rough and ready method, for the largest taxpayers in each township are a group varying a good deal in wealth and status; some townships contain several large taxpayers, others contain none. Nevertheless the process does give a general view of how surnames of any given category were distributed among the wealthier section of the community. In the 1283 subsidy roll for Blackbourne Hundred, Suffolk, 12 per cent of all the taxpayers listed had locative surnames or bye-names, and nine per cent had surnames or bye-names that were toponymics, but of the largest taxpayers in each township, 43 per cent had locative surnames or bye-names, and 12 per cent had surnames or bye-names that were toponymics.[6] In the 1327 subsidy roll for the whole of Suffolk, 13 per cent of all taxpayers have locative surnames or bye-names, and a further 11 per cent have topographical ones, but if the largest taxpayers in each township are taken, then 54 per cent of them have locative names, though only six per cent have topographical ones.[7] In the Norfolk subsidy for 1329-30, 10 per cent of all the taxpayers listed have locative surnames or bye-names, and seven per cent have surnames or bye-names that are topographical, but of the largest taxpayers in each township 45 per cent have locative names, and 12 per cent topographical ones.[8] In the case of the 12th- and 13th-century sources it might be argued that many of those listed did not have hereditary surnames, and that the high proportion of locative names was due merely to the administrative practices of the officials who drew up the lists. By the time of the 14th-century subsidy rolls just mentioned, however, many landed families already had hereditary surnames, and it is possible to make a direct comparison between the names of large taxpayers, and those of the fairly numerous body of taxpayers as a whole, which shows that the wealthier classes had a much higher proportion of locative names than the average, and a rather higher proportion of topographical names.

At the period of the two 14th-century subsidy rolls just mentioned, most families of knightly or higher rank seem already to have acquired hereditary surnames but in most cases their surnames had only been hereditary for two or three generations, and there had hardly been sufficient time for the effects of social mobility to become manifest. Before the late 13th century it is very unusual to find a person of any wealth or standing with a surname or bye-name derived from a manual occupation, but from that period onwards cases of military tenants, owners of manors and advowsons, etc., having occupational surnames gradually increase. In late 13th-century Norfolk, for example, Parmenter, Harpyn, Parker, le Wafre, and le Keu all occur as the surnames or bye-names of men who appear to be landowners of some substance. Among the military tenants in Norfolk in 1302 were Nicolas le Pottere, Edmund le Leche, Simon le Ropere, Ralph *Mercator*, David *Mercator*, Roger le Sutere, and Simon le Cotere, all of them holding fractions of knights' fees only, but plainly representing the infiltration of occupational surnames into the knightly class.[9] Surnames derived from occupation can usually be assigned with some confidence to a given social class, though there are exceptions in names, such as Butler or Chamberlain, for instance, which may originate from feudal offices, but surnames in other categories cannot usually be assigned to origins in any one social stratum. Such surnames as for example Giffard or Peche, borne by aristocratic families, appear to have been originally nicknames of a humorous if not derisive character, and it is easy to find noble or knightly families with patronymic surnames. It is consequently not easy to trace the stages by which the surnames of the noble and knightly class ceased to have any characteristics differentiating them from those of the population at large. In the early 16th-century subsidy rolls for both Norfolk and Suffolk it is not possible to discern anything about the surnames of large taxpayers to distinguish them from the names of others listed for the subsidies. By that period the high proportion of locative surnames formerly characteristic of the wealthier classes had vanished.

It has, of course, been pointed out before that some locative surnames were those of landed families which derived their names from places where they had estates, and indeed this is one main source of locative surnames, but nevertheless the high proportion of surnames or bye-names in that category to be found amongst the knightly class in the 12th and 13th centuries seems surprising.

There is one other social group which has a high proportion of locative surnames, at least during the 13th century. This is the important but obscure class of minor functionaries, royal and seignurial, such persons as bailiffs of hundreds and manors, cacherells who were minor peace officers, clerks of sheriffs and coroners, sergeants errant, and so forth. It is much more difficult to find sources which record such persons in any number than it is to find sources listing tenants by knight service, but some evidence can be found in the Hundred Rolls, which frequently mention officials and their misdeeds. The Norfolk Hundred Rolls list just over 200 royal officials of this class whose surnames or bye-names are given, excluding those for whom no surnames are given, and excluding too such officers as sheriffs, escheators, or coroners, who were usually of higher status. Out of these more than 200 officials, 58 per cent have locative surnames or bye-names, the majority derived from places in Norfolk, and seven per cent have surnames or bye-names that are toponymics. The same source lists about 90 seign-urial officials of the same class, whose surnames are given, and of these 57 per cent have locative surnames or bye-names, and seven per cent topographical ones. In this respect there was little difference between royal and seignurial officials, and indeed it is clear from the Hundred Rolls that officials moved freely between the king's service, and that of other lords. An analysis of the names of royal and seignurial officials in the Suffolk Hundred Rolls produces similar results.[10] Officials of this class were no doubt mobile geographically, and must usually have moved away from their native villages to take service with the king, or some land-owner, and this may well explain why so many had locative sur-names derived presumably from the places where they originated, but no longer lived. Possibly the fact that as a class they were mobile socially may have led to their tending to use names that would at least not emphasise their usually obscure origins.

To turn to the other end of the social scale, the surnames of serfs present some interesting features. One of these is the presence of bondmen with occupational surnames or bye-names derived from trades that a serf would not be expected to practise. It is not surprising to find serfs with names derived from purely agricultural occupations, such as Shepherd, or from manorial offices such as Greve, Heyward, or Reve,[11] and it is understandable if bondmen appear with surnames or bye-names such as Carter, Redere, or Bucher, for these are occupations in which it is easy to imagine serfs spending at any rate part of their time.[12] It is, however, more surprising to find serfs with surnames or bye-names derived from skilled trades unconnected with agriculture. In about 1200 serfs at Tasborough, Norfolk, included Lefricus *Faber* (Smith), Ricardus

Carpentarius (Carpenter), and Radulfus *Textor* (Weaver), while at
Staverton, Suffolk, serfs at the same period included Johannes le
Macun (Mason) and Levricus le Pottere.[13] At this early period
the names were probably not hereditary, but later examples can
be found of serfs with such surnames or bye-names as le Blekestere
(Bleacher), Carpenter, *Cissor* (Taylor), Cupar, *Faber*, Fishere,
Ropere, Saltere, le Sayere (possibly Sawyer), *Sutor*, or le Wodebite
(Woad-beater).[14] There are also some bondmen with names
derived from trading or retailing. Early in the 13th century three
serfs at Burnham, Norfolk, were said to be the sons of the merchant
(*mercator*) of Burnham Deepdale, and later examples can be found
of serfs with surnames or bye-names such as Chapman or *Mercator*.[15]
In some instances these occupational names, particularly those
connected with trading, may possibly be nicknames, for bondmen
with names such as le Richeman or Prudhumme do occur, and these
were obviously nicknames in origin, probably ironical ones.[16] It
seems unlikely, however, that any large proportion of the occupational names borne by serfs can be accounted for in this way, and
in most cases the names must be from trades actually pursued by
serfs. If this is true, it cannot have been unusual for serfs to have
skilled occupations that were not agricultural.

Another surprising feature of serfs' names is that some have
surnames or bye-names derived from places outside, and sometimes remote from, the manors on which they dwelt. Examples of
this can be found from the early 13th century onwards. Robert
Salle, for example, a bondman at Burnham in north Norfolk in
1209, derived his name from a village about 20 miles from Burnham.[17] Kelyng, a name derived from a village in northern Norfolk,
appears about 1300 as the name of serfs in two Suffolk villages that
adjoin each other, Ashfield and Elmswell.[18] In the 15th century a
family of bond tenants in the manor of Forncett, Norfolk, were
called Lincoln.[19] John son of Robert le Scot and of Christiana atte
Hallegate, who acknowledged in 1290 that he was a serf of Lewes
Priory at Heacham, Norfolk, and that his mother had been a
serf, had a name suggesting a still more distant origin, but his
father's status is uncertain. Scot is further found as the surname of
a villein at Ixworth, Suffolk, in 1299, and in 1290 Thomas of
Rockland was adjudged to be a villein at Gressenhall, a village
about 10 miles from the nearest of the several places in Norfolk
called Rockland.[20]

It is conceivable that Scot might have been a nickname in origin,
but it is difficult to see how that could be true of the other locative
surnames just mentioned, and it must be considered likely that the
bondmen who bore such names, or their ancestors, came from the

places from which their names were derived. This must mean either that serfs were moved from one manor to another, or that persons coming into manors from the outside accepted or were reduced to servile status. How this might happen is suggested by the case of Geoffrey of Warwick, a tenant of St. Benet's Abbey, Holme, in Norfolk, *c.* 1200. Geoffrey was granted 20 acres at Wood Bastwick by a sealed charter, which leaves little doubt that at this stage of the proceedings he was a free man. Later, however, after the succession of a new abbot at St. Benet's, the 20 acres were regranted to him, without a charter, to hold in villeinage. How Geoffrey was induced to surrender his original charter does not appear.[21] It is not clear whether Geoffrey was in fact reduced to the position of a villein, since a tenant could hold land in villeinage while remaining personally free, but the specific statement that Geoffrey was regranted the land to hold without a charter does seem to imply that he was considered at this stage to be personally unfree. It is unlikely that his surname was hereditary, at so early a period, and it is probable that this is a case of a man moving from Warwick (a borough, and therefore a place whose inhabitants would be free) to East Norfolk, and there being reduced to the status of a villein. Some at least of the cases where bondmen are found with locative surnames derived from places well away from the manors on which they live may have resulted from similar processes.

One further piece of evidence that points in the same direction is the occurrence in the late 12th and the 13th centuries of Newman as a surname or bye-name of serfs.[22] The name Newman means a newcomer, and serfs who bore it were presumably either new arrivals in the manor or, less probably at an early period, the descendants of such new arrivals.[23] The rare name of Newbond must also signify either someone who had newly become a serf, or just possibly a bondman who had been moved from one manor to another.[24] There is little evidence from the 12th century about the movement of serfs from one manor to another, and little to show how far it was possible for freemen to be reduced to serfdom, but the surnames borne by serfs at a later period suggest that one or perhaps both of these processes may have occurred fairly frequently.

The names of the smaller free tenants are very varied in type, and it cannot be said that any one category predominates. Their surnames or bye-names are not noticeably of different types from those of unfree tenants, and indeed on manors where it is possible to obtain adequate lists of both free and unfree tenants from sources such as extents, it is not unusual to find that many surnames or bye-names occur among both the free and the unfree tenants. In an extent of the manor of Banham, Norfolk, taken in 1281-2, out of the 27 surnames or bye-names that occur amongst the customary tenants, 11 occur also amongst the free tenants.[25] In an extent of 1299 of a manor at Ashfield, Suffolk, out of 51 surnames occurring amongst the free tenants, 15 also occur amongst the villeins on the same manor.[26] And examples could be given of similar situations on other manors.

The surnames or bye-names of the peasantry, free and unfree, in the 13th century, include only a moderate proportion of locative names, but they do include many surnames or bye-names derived from personal names, which are in fact the most numerous category of peasant names, and they also include substantial proportions of surnames or bye-names derived from occupations, and from nicknames, two categories which are much rarer in the names of the knightly class. Amongst the free and unfree tenants of Bradcar Manor, at Shropham in Norfolk, listed in an extent of 1298-99, 26 per cent had surnames or bye-names that were locative, another 26 per cent ones that were derived from personal names, 15 per cent had occupational names, and 14 per cent had surnames or bye-names derived from nicknames.[27] An extent of another Norfolk manor, at Banham, made in 1281-82, lists numerous free and customary tenants, and taking both classes together, only eight per cent had locative surnames or bye-names, while 32 per cent had ones derived from personal names, 19 per cent had occupational surnames or bye-names, and 22 per cent had surnames or bye-names derived from nicknames.[28] In Suffolk, the surnames or bye-names of the free and unfree tenants listed in 1299 on manors at Ousden, Ixworth, and Ashfield belonging to the de Kriketot family show a similar pattern. Taking all three manors together, 19 per cent had locative surnames or bye-names, 22 per cent ones derived from personal names, 22 per cent had occupational names, and 12 per cent had surnames or nicknames derived from bye-names.[29] It is not surprising if the figures vary between one manor and another, for the total number of tenants on a single manor is not large, and presence of a single family, with three or four members all with the same name, can materially affect the statistics for an individual manor. It is also true that the free tenants of a manor included people of very varying status, a few of them persons who were large landowners elsewhere, so that the free and unfree tenants, taken together, cannot be considered as altogether representative of the peasant class alone. Despite these reservations, however, the evidence does suggest that, at a period when hereditary surnames were just beginning to become widespread, amongst the peasant population occupational surnames or bye-names and those derived

F

from personal names and nicknames were proportionately more common than among the wealthier classes, and that locative surnames or bye-names were proportionately less numerous, though not by any means rare.

Any consideration of a possible connection between categories of surnames, and the different social classes in towns, is made difficult by the lack of information about the poorer sections of the town community during the Middle Ages. If the lists of persons admitted to the freedom of towns or cities is examined, the most obvious feature is the high proportion of locative surnames in the period before 1400. At Lynn, for example, 56 per cent of the small number of recorded admissions to the freedom up to 1300 have locative surnames or bye-names, in 1301-50, 64 per cent, and in 1351-1400, 49 per cent.[30] At Norwich, where the record of admissions does not start until 1317, 49 per cent of freemen admitted up to 1350 had locative surnames or bye-names, and for the whole of the 14th century, 38 per cent of Norwich freemen admitted had locative names.[31] It is difficult to say how accurately such figures represent the position among the town populations as a whole. If the names of the parties to a large number of deeds made in 1285-1306 concerning property in Norwich are examined, 66 per cent of them are found to have locative surnames or bye-names. The parties concerned included not only inhabitants of Norwich, freemen and others, but also an unknown proportion who lived outside the city. Nevertheless this piece of evidence perhaps suggests that the high proportion of locative surnames or bye-names found amongst the city's freemen may not have been very different from that for the city's whole population. At Bury St. Edmunds, 55 per cent of the taxpayers listed in the 1327 subsidy roll had locative surnames or bye-names, but at Ipswich, only 26 per cent of taxpayers in the same subsidy had such names.[32] This evidence, too, does not cover all the inhabitants of the two towns, but it does indicate that in the East Anglian towns during the 14th century the proportion of locative surnames or bye-names amongst the population tended to be high.

After *c.* 1400 the proportion of locative surnames borne by freemen of towns is much lower. At Norwich, only 17 per cent of those admitted to the freedom during the 15th century had locative surnames, at Lynn only 26 per cent, and at Great Yarmouth, 18 per cent.[33]

The significance of the varying proportions of locative surnames among town freemen, the places from which such names originated, and so forth, is discussed elsewhere in this paper. It is only intended to point out here that there was in the earlier Middle Ages a clear difference between the extent to which locative surnames or bye-names were in use in towns, and the extent to which such names were in use for the bulk of the population in the countryside as listed, for example, in the subsidy rolls.

References

[1]For examples of such lists for Norfolk and Suffolk, *see* D. M. Stenton, ed., *Great Roll of the Pipe for the 9th Year of Richard I* (Pipe Roll Society, New Series, vol. viii) (1931), pp. 245-6; D. M. Stenton, ed., *Great Roll of the Pipe for the 10th Year of Richard I* (Pipe Roll Society, New Series, vol. ix) (1932), pp. 86-8; D. M. Stenton, ed., *Great Roll of the Pipe for the 1st Year of John* (Pipe Roll Society, New Series, vol. x) (1933), pp. 275-88

[2]D. M. Stenton, ed., *Great Roll of the Pipe for the 10th Year of Richard I*, pp. 86-7. Those with no surnames or bye-names, and those only described as the son of some other person, have been ignored when calculating ratios

[3]H. Hall, *Red Book of the Exchequer* (Rolls Series) (1896), part i, pp. 391-412. Earls and heads of religious houses have been excluded from these figures

[4]*Book of Fees* (1923), part ii, pp. 902 *seq.* Earls and heads of religious houses have been excluded

[5]*Feudal Aids* (1904), vol. iii, pp. 389-448. Dukes, earls, and heads of religious houses have been excluded

[6]Powell, *A Suffolk Hundred in 1283*, tables 1-38

[7]*Suffolk in 1327*, *passim*

[8]P.R.O. E179/149/7, *passim*

[9]*Rotuli Hundredorum*, vol. i, pp. 500, 515; Rye, *Cal. Norf. Fines*, vol. i, pp. 109, 114, 115; *Feudal Aids* (1904) vol. iii, pp. 397, 417, 423, 430, 440, 442

[10]*Rotuli Hundredorum*, vol. i, pp. 434-543; vol. ii, pp. 142-200

[11]Bedingfeld, *Cartulary of Creake Abbey*, pp. 24, 28, 117; Powell, *A Suffolk Hundred in 1283*, p. 89; W. Hudson, 'Three Manorial Extents', *Norfolk Archaeology* (1901), vol. xiv, p. 49

[12]Powell, *A Suffolk Hundred in 1283*, p. 72; P.R.O. C133/89/8

[13]B. Dodwell, *Feet of Fines for the County of Norfolk, 1201-1215, and for the County of Suffolk, 1199-1214*, pp. 125, 144

[14]Powell, *A Suffolk Hundred in 1283*, pp. 79, 80, 89; Hudson, 'Three Manorial Extents', *Norfolk Archaeology*, vol. xiv, pp. 36, 49, 52, 53; P.R.O. C133/89/8

[15]Dodwell, *op. cit.*, p. 101; Powell, *A Suffolk Hundred in 1283*, pp. 72, 79, 82; P.R.O. C133/89/8

[16]Dodwell, *op. cit.*, p. 144; Powell, *A Suffolk Hundred in 1283*, p. 79; P.R.O. C133/89/8

[17]Dodwell, *op. cit.*, p. 101

[18]Powell, *A Suffolk Hundred in 1283*, p. 82; P.R.O. C133/89/8

[19]Cambridge University Library, Document 591, Courts held Monday after St. Peter ad Vincula, 34 Henry VI, and 12 Oct., 35 Henry VI

[20]Bullock, *op. cit.*, pp. 6-7; P.R.O. C133/89/8; *Abbrevatio Placitorum* (Record Commission) (1811), p. 221

[21]West, *St. Benet of Holme, 1020-1210*, vol. i, p. 118

[22]Dodwell, *op. cit.*, pp. 103, 144, 147; Powell, *A Suffolk Hundred in 1283*, p. 79

[23]Reaney, *Dictionary of British Surnames*, p. 229

[24]Rye, *Cal. Suff. Fines*, vol. i, p. 86

[25]W. Hudson, 'Three Manorial Extents', *Norfolk Archaeology*, vol. xiv, pp. 32, *et seq.*

[26]P.R.O. C133/89/8

[27]W. Hudson, 'Three Manorial Extents,' *Norfolk Archaeology*, vol. xiv, pp. 23-32

[28]*Ibid.*, pp. 32-38

[29]P.R.O. C133/89/8

[30]Anon., *Calendar of the Freemen of Lynn, 1292-1836*, pp. 1-30

[31]L'Estrange, ed., *op. cit., passim*

[32]*Suffolk in 1327*, pp. 215-20

[33]L'Estrange, ed., *op. cit., passim*; Anon., *Calendar of the Freemen of Lynn, 1292-1836*, pp. 30-73; Anon., *Calendar of the Freemen of Great Yarmouth* (1910), pp. 1-18. The figures for Great Yarmouth are based on admissions to the freedom beginning in 1429

CONCLUSION

Very many individual surnames to be found in East Anglia during the Middle Ages have inevitably not been touched upon in this paper. Even of those surnames which were more common in East Anglia than elsewhere it has been only possible to mention a small proportion. There are even whole categories of names that have not been treated. There are surnames derived from the degrees of relationship, such as Brothers, Cousins, Neve, and so forth. There are surnames derived from nicknames, present in East Anglia in great variety, and including some bizarre examples. Space of course does not permit every individual surname to be treated, and the categories of surnames that have been omitted are those which it might not be fruitful to deal with regionally. Such surnames or bye-names originating from nicknames as Al for drunken, Caldelovered, Crepunderhuitel, Bindedevel, Cheseanbred, Milkandbred, Ryghtup, Fayreandgood, Chykenmouth, Brodballoke, and many others may attract attention by their picturesque nature, and by the flavour of robust humour which some have.[1] It is however in many cases little use conjecturing what characteristics or what incidents may have given rise to these soubriquets, and it is also true that many such designations fell out of use during the Middle Ages, and did not survive to become a permanent part of the general stock of hereditary English surnames.

Some types of surname, therefore, have been left on one side, and not separately discussed. From the investigation of East Anglian surnames from all categories to be found during the Middle Ages certain general impressions can be gained, impressions that could be supported by citing very many examples for which there has not been space. One impression is that many surnames in the region originated with a single family. This is, from the limitations of the medieval evidence, very difficult to prove in any individual case, as has been stated in discussing some examples.[2] Despite this difficulty, both the way in which many less common surnames were distributed, and the links that can sometimes be established between persons bearing the same surname, suggest that many surnames did spring from a single origin, and then in some cases ramified. Naturally there are surnames to which this would not apply. Some occupational names, for example, were very widespread as early as the 13th century. But in general the impression left by the study of East Anglian surnames is that many names, more perhaps than has usually been allowed, go back to a single origin.

The evidence for this should be considered together with the evidence that surnames provide for geographical mobility, and perhaps for social mobility too. Locative surnames seem to reveal a population given to frequent moves over limited distances, and one for which longer migrations were quite common.[3] The sharp changes that occurred in the distribution of some surnames between the 14th and the 16th centuries point to the same conclusion, which agrees with certain other types of evidence on the same subject.[4] The disappearance by the 16th century of the differences observable earlier in the types of surname used by the various social classes also suggests a measure of social mobility, at any rate over the period between the mid-14th and early 16th centuries.[5]

It is very exceptional at any time during the Middle Ages to find any Norfolk or Suffolk village dominated by a single surname, or two or three names. Such sources as tax assessments or manor court rolls usually show that each township or manor contains a great variety of surnames. This is consistent with a situation in which the population was fairly mobile, and in which many surnames originated with one family, and subsequently dispersed.

One other impression that results from a study of East Anglian surnames is that the early incidence of some toponymics and some occupational surnames was confined to certain restricted areas. In the case of toponymics this no doubt was often due to the nature of the medieval landscape, with its local variations. Where occupational names were concerned, this must have usually been caused by some occupational terms being employed only in limited areas within the region. The evidence suggests that some occupational words were very restricted locally in usage, and this may have been true of some topographic terms as well. The relative scarcity of Middle English texts that can be confidently related to any one region makes it difficult to trace variations in the use of occupational or topographic terms locally, and the evidence that can be obtained from surnames may accordingly be all the more valuable.

References

[1]Douglas, *Feudal Documents from the Abbey of Bury St. Edmunds*, pp. 26, 30; Hervey, ed., *Pinchbeck Register*, vol. i, pp. 98, 103; *Rotuli Hundredorum*, vol. i, p. 487; Rye, *Cal. Norf. Fines*, vol. ii, pp. 346, 427, 429; D. M. Stenton, ed., *Great Roll of the Pipe for the 3rd and 4th Years of Richard I*, p. 46; P.R.O. E179/149/7, m. 34

[2]*See*, e.g. the discussions above of Underburgh (p. 108) and Enginour (p. 48)

[3]*See* above, pp. 76-82, 90-5

[4]*See*, e.g. the discussions of Thatcher, above, p. 52; And for a discussion of other evidence on the subject, *see* J. A. Raftis, *Tenure and Mobility* (1964), pp. 129-182

[5]*See* above, pp. 141-43

Index

Lawes, surname of: 136
Lawrance, personal name of: 136
Lawson, surname of: 136
Laxfield, Edric of: 22
Lea (or Legh), surname of: 115
Leadbeater, surname of: 47
Leadsmith, surname of: 47
Lead working, names from: 47
Leche, Edmund le: 143
Ledbettere, Matilda le: 27
Legh, *see* Lea
Leicester, borough of: 85, 88
Leicester (or Leycestr'), surname of: 85, 88
Leicestershire, locative surnames from: 81, 84, 85, 88, 96
Leicestershire, surnames in: p. xi
L'Engynur. Robt., *see* Jenour
Lenham (Kent): p. xii
Lenham, de, surname of: 79
Lepmaker, surname of: 52
Lesbury (Nthmb.): 82
Leveday, personal name of, 127
Leveday, surname of: 20
Levessone, surname of: 131
Lewes, priory of (Suss.): 81, 145
Lewes, de, surname of: 79
Leycestr', *see* Leicester, surname of
Leyker, surname of: 52
Lincoln, city of: 80, 96
Lincoln, family named: 145
Lincolnshire, locative surnames from: 42, 78, 80, 83, 84, 86, 89, 96
Lincolnshire, surnames in: 43, 53
Lindraper (or Lyndraper), surname of: 44, 50
Lindsey (or Linseye), surname of: 106
Lindsey, parts of (Lincs.), locative surnames from: 96
Lindsey (Suff.): 106
Lingate (Norf.): 118
Lingwood, Ric. de: 14
  See Sartryn, Roger del
Linseye, *see* Lindsey, surname of
Linter, surname of: 43
Lister, surname of: 42
Litester, surname of: 42
Litleker, grove called: 110
Lock-making, names from: 47
Lockman, surname of: 47
Locksmith, surname of: 47
Loddon (Norf.): 9
Lokyer, surname of: 47

Lolimer, surname of: 47
London, Wm. de: 27
  His father, *see* Staninges, Reginald de
London, Inhabitants of: 50, 85
London, de, surname of: 79
London, surnames in: 54, 77
Long Melford, *see* Melford, Long
Lord, surname of: 20, 38
Lorimer, trade of: 47
Lothingland, Hundred of (Suff.): 9, 10, 11
Lothingland, manor of (Suff.): 11
Lound (Suff.): 26
Louth (Lincs.): 80
Lowestoft (Suff.): 26
Luminur, Jn. le: 28
  His widow, Alfreda: 28
  His son, *see* Peyntur, Robt. le
Lund, Ranulf de: 11
Lund, Robt. de: 11
Lyndraper, surname of, *see* Lindraper
Lyngate (Norf.): 118
Lynn, Bishop's, *see* Lynn, King's
Lynn, King's (Norf.): 21, 32, 38, 47, 48, 50, 82, 83, 84, 100, 109, 110, 116, 130, 131, 148

Macun, Jn. le: 145
Madder: 42
Mader (or Madour), surname of: 43
Maderman, surname of: 43
Madermanger, surname of: 43
Madesson, surname of: 130
Madour, *see* Mader
Madster, surname of: 43
Magges, surname of: 132
Maggessone, surname of: 131
Maltmilnere, surname of: 49
Maltster, surname of: 49
Manby (Lincs.): 96
Mannekin, Robt.: 10
  See Boyton, Mannekinus de
Mareis, surname of: 111
Mareschal, Agnes: 27
Mareschal, Peter le: 16
Mareschal, Wm.: 16
Market Street (Norf.): 118
Market Weston, *see* Weston, Market
Marlesuein (of Ringstead and Holme by the Sea): 8
Marlswein, Guibertus: 8
Marsh, surname of: 110, 111

Marshall, surname of: 32, 46
See Mareschal
Marsham (Norf.): 105
Martin, personal name of: 134
Mason, Simon le: 28
His father, *see* Harple, Bonet de
Mason, surname of: 51
See Macun, Mazoun
Massingham, Great (Norf.): 105
Massingham, Little (Norf.): 105
Matthew, personal name of: 134
Mattishall (Norf.): 14, 60
May, Robt. (?*c.* 1200): 6
May, Wm. (early 12th cent.): 6
May, Wm. (1212): 6
Mayster, Matilda le: 27
Mazoun, Margery le: 27
Medemaker, surname of: 49
Medeman, surname of: 49
Medewe, Hen. atte: 27
His son, *see* Dilham, Roger de
Medwe, atte (or in the Medwe, or *de Prato*), surname of: 115
See Medewe
Melford, Long (Suff.): 60
Meller, surname of: 48, 49
Melman, surname of: 51
Melner, surname of: 48, 49
Mercator, Ralph: 143
Mercator, David: 143
Mercator (Merchant), surname of: 31, 145
Mercer, Jn. le, Dean of Norwich: 28
Mercer, surname of: 50
Merchant (*Mercator*), surname of: 31, 50
Messor, surname of: 33
See Heyward
Metronymics: 13
Michael, personal name of: 134
Midlands, East, locative surnames in: 78
Midlands, East, locative surnames from: 83, 96
Midlands, South East, locative surnames from: 80, 84
Midlands, West, locative surnames from: 81, 97
Mikleker, de, surname of: 110
Mildenhall (Suff.): 60, 105
Mileham (Norf.): 28
Milkandbred, surname of: 151
Miller (*Molendinarius*), surname of: 20, 31, 48, 49

Milner, surname of: 48, 49
Milward, surname of: 49
Mitenmaker, surname of: 44, 56
Mitford, hundred of (Norf.): 110, 112
Molendinarius (Miller), surname of: 31
Moliner, surname of: 49
Moor, surname of: 110
Moorman, surname of: 119
Mortimer, Ric., his son Hirdman: 61
Moses, *see* Moyse
Motonn, surname of: 20
Mower, surname of: 35
Moyse, surname of: 129
Moyse (or Moses), personal name of: 129
Muchelker, grove called: 110
Mundy, family of: 25
Muner, surname of: 48
Muntchesney, family of: 23
Musician, occupation of: 52
Mustarder, surname of: 49
Mustardman, surname of: 49
Mustardor, Jn. le: 16
Mylyur, surname of: 48

Nab, the, at Burgh St. Margaret (Norf.): 125
Nab, *see* Nabb
Nabb (or atte Nab), surname of: 117
Nailer, trade of: 47
Narford (Norf.), vicar of: 11
Nayn, Clement: 14
His son, *see* Pryce, Wm.
Neathird, surname of: 34
Neatishead (Norf.): 34
Needler, surname of: 47, 48
Needle-maker, trade of: 47
Neel, personal name of: 134
Nes, Gilbert de: 11
Nes, Wm. de: 11
Ness (Suff.): 11
Neteshird, Jn. de: 61
Neteshirde, Stephen de: 61
Nethergate, Gundewynus de: 11
Nethergate, de, surname of: 118
Netherhous, Wm. atte: 108
Netherhouse, surname of: 108
Neuton, Benedict de: 11
Neve, surname of: 151
Newbiggin, surname of: 82
Newbiggin, place name of: 82
Newbond, surname of: 37, 146
Newehosebonde, le, surname of: 37